Best of BC
LAKE FISHING

Karl Bruhn

Frank Amato Publications
Portland, Oregon

Edited by Elaine Jones

Cover photograph by Doug Leighton
Interior drawings by Ian Forbes
Interior maps courtesy of Ministry of Environment
Interior and cover design by Carolyn Deby

Typography by CompuType, Vancouver, B.C.
Printed and bound in Canada by Friesen Printers, Altona, Manitoba

Includes index.
ISBN 1-878175-28-9

Published by
Frank Amato Publications
P.O. Box 82112
Portland, Oregon 97282
(503) 653-8108

Disclaimer

Driving and Fishing British Columbia

British Columbia has much of the finest lake fishing for trout in the world. But there is a catch. Lakes can vary from year-to-year depending on such factors as access, fingerling plants, winter-kill, kill or no kill regulations, etc. For this reason *call ahead* to the regional fisheries biologist for the best information and also contact a reputable fly or tackle shop in addition to contacting lodges or resorts on the lake. Many of the best lakes are obviously very popular. So reserve cabins or camping space early.

Road travel in B.C. varies from wonderful to very difficult. In many cases you really need four wheel drive, plus two extra spares, because you might be 50 miles on a difficult road with no services. B.C is the place for a fishing adventure of a lifetime, but you must be prepared! I am sure you will love the province as I do.

Frank Amato

Contents

Skeena
8

Omineca-Peace
9

Chilcotin
5

Cariboo
6

Thompson
3
Nicola

2
Lower
Mainland

7
Kootenay

Vancouver Island
1

4
Okanagan

Introduction

Pull out a map of British Columbia and the eye is immediately drawn to the amoeba-shaped blue spaces which impart life and colour to the otherwise dull sheet of paper. The province is literally pock-marked with lakes. From the large blue ribbons of the mountain-trough lakes to the pot-hole lakes of the plateaus and the glittering tarns of the alpine high country, B.C. offers lakes in infinite variety. Choosing among them can seem a fool's game, especially for the angler. Each individual lake is special; each is unique in its own way. Yet choose we must and this book is designed to provide a starting point. Tucked into the pages which follow are pinpoint descriptions of some of British Columbia's finest angling lakes.

The project, involving months of research and years of rod-in-hand travel across the province, was not undertaken lightly. Included in the discussion of lakes are many waters which have long been personal favourites. Giving away such "secrets" is not without its qualms. The hope, of course, is that those who follow the trails blazed here will bring with them an understanding of angling traditions and a deep-seated spirit of conservation. British Columbia offers some of the finest lake fishing in the world, not just in terms of fish sizes and numbers, but also in the incredible diversity of the landscapes which ring the lakes. All this is threatened as we speed pell-mell into the next century. Anglers can and should play a lead role in protecting both quality angling waters and the province's remaining unscarred landscapes. Only by banding together and sharing their secrets will anglers be able to protect the province's best lakes from the various forms of "development" which threaten on all sides.

With minor variations here and there, the book is divided into chapters which follow provincial Fisheries Branch management regions. Each chapter contains a listing of the region's best angling waters, an overview of the region and one or more topics of particular interest to the area. These topics tend to be eclectic, covering everything from snatches of early history to the minutiae of aquatic insects and their life cycles, but the guiding principle was to increase awareness and understanding of the aquatic environment. Anglers who understand their sport in these terms quickly become dedicated conservationists with the knowledge needed to help make crucial decisions. It is my hope that this book will help anglers reach a deeper understanding of the aquatic environment and its essential fragility. Much of the true pleasure to be had from angling lies in understanding the often complex, interrelated factors at work under a lake's surface. And, of course, anglers with a basic grasp of how the underwater world functions will catch more and better fish than their fellows.

Finding one's way to the lakes discussed, especially the more remote waters, is not simple. The network of backroads which criss-cross the province is constantly changing. Old roads are closed, new roads are built, once-familiar access roads are washed out in wet years and never rebuilt. Where possible I have tried to provide information on the condition of individual roads, but of course these conditions vary with the time of year and the amount of industrial traffic using the roads. In general terms, backroading B.C.-style requires at least high-clearance vehicles and often four-wheel drive. Those inexperienced with the intricacies of backroad travel had best venture in the company of more experienced friends. Serious trouble awaits those who venture lightly onto unknown backroads.

Many of the backroads in the province are logging roads, and meeting a fully-loaded logging truck on a tight bend is the stuff of nightmares: always seek out local logging company offices before using their roads. This really cannot be stressed enough, especially for those new to travel in areas of active logging. Most companies have free maps of their road networks which can only be obtained locally. This is just as well, as it forces anglers to stop at local company offices, often the only source of information on the latest new roads, roads which have washed out, and so on.

The directions provided with each lake listed are aids to general location, not definitive directions. Care was taken to ensure that all the lakes listed could be pinpointed by using the directions, but actual travel to the lakes can only be planned with the use of one or more maps. Aside from very general locator maps, this book does not contain maps. Collecting and fine-tuning maps is part and parcel of lake angling in British Columbia.

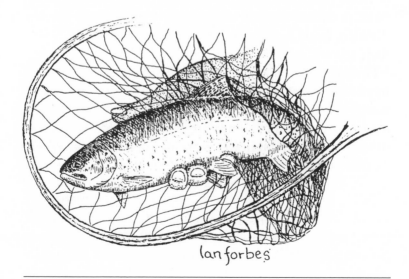

Ian forbes

One of the most comprehensive guides to the province's lakes is the *B.C. Fishing Directory and Atlas* published by Art Belhumeur. The maps in this guide locate more B.C. waters than any other guide I've seen, but even these maps will fall short from time to time, mainly due to the ever-changing nature of the province's backroads. The *British Columbia Recreational Atlas* is useful in a general way, but is not geared to anglers seeking very small waters. It is, however, a useful addition to any angler's map collection and should not be overlooked. Some of the best local maps are produced by the B.C. Forest Service. These maps provide the best guide to backroads, but are available only from local Forest Service offices or, sometimes, from regional tourist information centres. Some local anglers' clubs have also produced maps to the lakes of their regions, but again, these are only available locally. In some regions private individuals have produced guides to the region's lakes and these can be invaluable. The message, I think, is fairly clear. Anglers seeking new waters for the first time should seek local advice and track down the most up-to-date maps of the region.

Information on lodges and campgrounds is not provided in the book. The best source of this information is the *B.C. Accommodations Guide*, available free from Tourism British Columbia, Parliament Buildings, Victoria, B.C. V8V 1X4. This government branch produces a number of other publications of general interest to anglers, including a province-wide guide to freshwater fishing which is geared to tourists, not anglers. User-maintained Forest Service campsites are found on many remote lakes, but are pinpointed only on locally-available Forest Service maps.

This underscores the need to consult all available sources of information. Actively seek local tackle shops, lodges, Forest Service and logging company offices and, most important of all, regional Fisheries Branch offices (addresses are supplied at the end of each chapter). Fisheries staff will not only help anglers find specific lakes, they will take the time to explain the reasons behind angling regulations and thus help anglers reach a better understanding of provincial fisheries management goals.

And that brings up the subject of angling regulations. Like the backroads, regulations constantly change and are therefore not included with the lakes listed in this book. It is the responsibility of each individual angler to become familiar with the regulations specific to the waters being fished. B.C.'s fishing regulations represent a real triumph of careful, concerned management. Not long ago regulations specific to individual waters were seen as an unattainable goal. Now that this dream has become a reality, anglers complain that the rules governing their sport have become too complex. I would argue that complex rules which allow specific regulation of individual waters are in the best interests of all anglers. This kind of regulation allows anglers to bring their concerns to local fisheries managers with the knowledge that specific regulation is not only possible but easily achieved. Given that managers are thinly spread across the province—a situation that is unlikely to change in the foreseeable future—anglers must help fill the gap, and the regulations permit this type of angler involvement. When a local lake in my own home region was threatened by overfishing during critical trout spawning seasons, local anglers called for and got regulations which closed the lake during spawning times.

When it comes to angling, I remain a firm optimist, and this is reflected in the fish sizes given with each lake listed. Providing such information is a gamble at best, even with intimate local knowledge. Lakes are living entities, constantly changing and rearranging themselves in response to a host of factors which are themselves always evolving. So saying that Fish Lake holds rainbow trout to 10 pounds and better may be true for the spring of 1991, but entirely false by the spring of 1992. Generally, unless something drastic happens, a lake which is capable of producing exceptional fish will recover and again produce good fish in a few years' time. The fish sizes provided with each lake should be seen as an indication of the lake's potential rather than a hard and fast statement of fact. Also, despite the advent of metric measures, I have opted to stay with angling tradition and give fish sizes in pounds and inches. This is accepted practice in angling circles and I'll not break with the tradition.

Finally, some acknowledgements are necessary. Every source I could lay hands on was used to cross-check the information contained in the lakes listings and the book in general. A number of Fisheries biologists and technicians provided much-needed information and patient, careful explanations. I would like to thank them all for their help with this project and help provided in the past for magazine stories I was researching. Without their assistance, this book would not have been possible. Art Belhumeur's *B.C. Fishing Directory and Atlas* was often consulted and regularly provided location of waters not found anywhere else. Pacific Rim Publication's four guides to freshwater fishing lakes, produced by Bob and Alison Griffith in conjunction with the Ministry of Environment, provided important information for lakes in the Lower Mainland, Vancouver Island, the Okanagan and the Thompson-Nicola regions. These guides are invaluable to anglers and are free for the asking from regional Fisheries Branch offices. Well-known angling writer Dave Stewart, editor of a number of fishing guides produced by B.C. Outdoors magazine, also deserves special mention. Dave and I worked together on two guides produced by the magazine, spending days at a time locked in a small room papered from end to end with maps. Dave knows more B.C. waters than anyone else I know, and this book would have been the poorer were it not for those weeks spent with him poring over maps and talking fishing non-stop. My thanks, Dave, for blazing so many trails for us to follow.

CHAPTER ONE

Vancouver Island

*I*t is perhaps just as well that Vancouver Island's lakes have remained something of a secret. This is not to say the island's wealth of lakes has lingered in obscurity. Anglers who call Vancouver Island home have long since discovered its many fine lakes, and there is a regular contingent of visiting anglers who come to fish for wild cutthroat and rainbow trout in lakes nestled in mountain folds. In the main, however, it is saltwater salmon fishing and river fishing for steelhead which draws anglers to the island. Travelling B.C. lake fishers have traditionally concentrated their efforts on such destinations as the Thompson-Nicola and the Cariboo. This makes lake fishing on the island rather special. Once north of the more heavily populated southern portions of the island, anglers can expect uncrowded conditions and fine angling, especially those who take the time to sleuth out the countless small, hidden lakes once-removed from the main roads which provide primary access.

Many of the lakes discussed in this chapter, as elsewhere in the book, are precisely this type of lake. In the main they are small lakes requiring perseverance to locate. This reflects my own prejudices. I like small, secluded lakes. Mostly one has these waters to oneself, a privilege which is becoming increasingly rare even in B.C. where such angling was once taken as a matter of course. Those days may be behind us now, but it is still possible to find enclaves of solitude where the only sounds an angler might hear during the course of a day's fishing are the call of a loon or the rush of wind over an eagle's wings. These are special moments and the island's small secret lakes provide one of the best remaining chances to store such memories. With the privilege come certain responsibilities.

Vancouver Island anglers are among the most spirited conservationists in the province. I recall speaking to a provincial Fisheries Branch biologist working on rebuilding east-coast island sea-run cutthroat trout populations. He had recently returned from a speaking tour aimed at raising awareness of the plight of these fish. Anticipating hard opposition to the conservation measures he was about to introduce, the biologist was surprised to discover that the anglers who packed his meetings not only approved of the proposed measures, but were ready to help in any way they could. In some cases they called for even harsher conservation measures than those the government was proposing. Island anglers, he later told me, are the most ethical and concerned group of fishers he had ever encountered. They know they have something special in their home waters and are ready to do what it takes to ensure those special qualities are not further eroded. Given this spirit, visiting anglers must tread with caution. Those not personally motivated to minimize their impact and reduce their take of fish should not be surprised if they are taken to task by local anglers. This is now an established angling tradition on the island. Unlike elsewhere in the province where fellow anglers might be reluctant to use the Observe, Record and Report program to turn in those who violate fish and game laws, island anglers will not hesitate.

The reasons for their protectionist attitudes soon become clear to the rod-in-hand visitor. Vancouver Island lakes offer good fishing for such traditional B.C. species as rainbow and cutthroat trout, as well as unique opportunities to fish for brown trout and smallmouth bass. The large, relatively isolated lakes of the north and central parts of the island pro-

vide cutthroat fishing for large wild fish. The following section of this chapter attempts to explain these special fish and
the harsh aquatic environment in which they grow. From
the angler's perspective, the key fact to bear in mind is that
these are extremely slow-growing wild fish. A 20-inch trophy
will have taken eight years or more to grow and it is doubtful whether hatchery fish will ever replace such fish. At the
time of writing, angling regulations allow anglers to keep
one lake-caught fish greater than 20 inches (50 centimetres)
in fork length. While this may seem unduly harsh to many
anglers, in my view keeping even one such fish requires a
good deal of soul-searching. The time of B.C.'s wilderness
of plenty is gone for good. Each large, wild, lake-resident
cutthroat represents a triumph over harsh natural conditions.
Concerned anglers will release all such fish. I urge all others
to read the next section in this chapter and carefully consider the consequences of keeping large wild fish. Given
the ever-mounting pressures on our remaining stocks of wild
fish it is sheer folly to continue the "harvest."

Once an angler comes to an intimate understanding of a
given lake, the question of keeping or releasing large fish
takes on an altogether different complexion. The angler lucky
enough to find a lightly fished lake holding good numbers
of large, older fish might reasonably be excused taking the
odd one for the table. Reaching such an understanding of
a lake requires time and considerable effort and here the island lake fisher is fortunate. Most island lakes remain ice-
free through the year. This means the dedicated angler can
fish all year and can more easily come to an appreciation
of the dynamics at work in a given lake. Cutthroat fishing
in particular is often best in late fall and early winter. This
is one of the special joys of lake fishing on the island. I have
taken many fine cutthroat trout in late October and through
November. December and January fishing is generally slower, but a spate of warmer weather in February can often
produce good fishing. By March the spring season begins

in earnest. So it is only during the peak of summer heat and for about two winter months that island lake fishing is really slow. Even this can be avoided by fishing high-elevation lakes in summer and low-lying lakes during the coldest months.

Many of the island's lakes hold both rainbow and cutthroat trout. This is not, strictly speaking, unique to Vancouver Island, but the island does provide one of the best chances in the province to fish for both species within the same lake. In some cases this is an entirely natural mix; in others the mix is the result of stocking programs. The section on lake-resident cutthroat in this chapter provides some insights into what happens when cutthroat and rainbow trout occupy the same lake. For many anglers it will be enough to know both may be caught in the same lake, and I'll only add here that such waters are definitely worth searching out.

How to fish island lakes is an entirely personal matter. I prefer the fly above all other methods mainly because fly fishing requires the angler have at least a nodding acquaintance with the aquatic environment. I find it a more pleasurable way to fish as well, but other methods certainly work and I have no trouble with them provided the main object remains something more than merely putting fish in the boat. However, the emphasis throughout this book is on fly fishing and I offer no excuses for this prejudice. Large island lakes are most effectively fished with the various trolling lures, but fly fishers who take the time to pick their spots will also do well on such waters, as will the spin-fishers. The key lies in finding the right spots. The section on reading lakes in chapter four will help anglers discover the most likely places.

Finally, the list of lakes at the end of this chapter should not be taken as a complete listing of the island's best fishing lakes. Quite aside from the fact that no one could possibly claim to know them all, there is a great deal of pleasure to be had in exploring and finding special lakes that are not listed or discussed in any book. Inevitably, the best things in life are the things we discover for ourselves.

Closeup: The Mystery of Large Lake-Resident Cutthroat Trout

*A*s the sun slips behind the hills, a solitary angler anchored in the bay below is cast in sudden shadow. Taking his cue, he reaches for the heavy rod and quick-sinking line tucked alongside the boat's wooden gunnels. Until now his light rod and dry flies had served him well. Through the early afternoon he had hooked and released countless small cutthroat trout—the bright, colourful fish of 12 to 14 inches typical of Vancouver Island's coastal lakes. These fish came to the fly so willingly that choice of pattern was unimportant, just so the long, fine leader lay nicely on the water. But the mountain shadows stealing across the bay signal a change. The leader tied to the sinking line is short and heavy, allowing the large weighted fly to turn over easily at the end of each long cast. The quarry now is larger and heavier too, but the angler's movements remain calm and deliberate: he knows the biggest and best fish of the coastal lakes will come neither easily nor willingly.

Below the bobbing boat there is a more subtle shift of activity, also triggered by the waning light. From the cover of

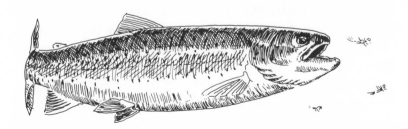

pondweeds ranged on either side of a nearby creek, small silvery sticklebacks suddenly come to feed on microorganisms, a risk they dared not run in bright daylight. On the sandy bottom beneath the boat, camouflaged by virtue of their mottled coloration, lethargic sculpins stir their large-headed bodies and steal from cover, always hugging the protective bottom. Closer to shore, black undulating leeches uncurl their snake-like bodies from beneath small rocks and begin their own dark, secretive rounds. And deep in the pondweed thickets a host of aquatic insects, everything from large predatory dragonfly nymphs to the immature forms of mayflies and damselflies, sense the failing light and quicken their darting, scrambling dance.

Of all this the angler is well aware; in his mind's eye he sees it clearly and in that sense he too is part of the hidden world beneath the surface of the lake. While he cannot see his deeply sunken fly, an imitation of the skulking bullheads, he imagines its movements and matches the actions of the line in his hands to those of the sculpins below. For a time the big muddler minnow fly rests peacefully against the sand, then darts forward several centimetres, stirring a little sand and leaving a small cloud to settle slowly behind. Now it inches along in small even pulls, just as the naturals often seem to browse aimlessly along the bottom. Ever so slowly the line is retrieved and the arm begins anew the gentle rhythm of casting. Cast, count down to bottom, begin the long contemplative retrieve and cast again. The angler remains as rapt in concentration as the Eastern monk in his transcendental meditations.

Two other elements are now added to the underwater drama unfolding below the angler. From the depths of the lake where they have remained hidden through the day comes a large mass of small silvery fish. These are the fry of sockeye salmon, hatched out of the gravel of tributary streams earlier in the spring and destined to spend two years in their freshwater nursery before taking to the sea. Their movement is vertical, from the dark protective depths safe from predatory trout, up towards the surface where they find the tiny life forms they require. They have reason to avoid the lake margin where deep water meets shallow and where the angler has set his anchor. This edge, where the last slick of spilling water from the creek gives way to still water, is the haunt of the lake's largest fish. Here the cutthroats roam, flashing shoreward when some food item is spotted, darting deep when shadow of osprey or eagle is cast from above.

These fish are an enigma, their existence but dimly understood even now. The waters in which they are found are generally poor in the vital nutrients which are the building blocks of the aquatic food chain. Biologists specializing in the study of fish and their environment have devised a method for measuring a lake's ability to nurture life. By analyzing the water's chemical and biological makeup, they determine the amount of total dissolved solids in the water. The greater the number of these solids a given unit of water holds, the greater its ability to nurture life. So while the nutrient-rich waters of B.C.'s southern interior typically yield counts of between 200 and 300 for total dissolved solids, average coastal lakes will yield counts of only 20 to 30 for the same measure of water. Hence a southern interior lake is capable of producing or supporting about 10 times as much life per volume of water as a typical coastal lake. Not surprisingly, scientists describe coastal lakes as nutrient-deficient and interior lakes as nutrient-rich.

Biologists have been heard to quip that the waters of coastal lakes are like battery acid, incredibly clear and pure but incapable of supporting life. In reality, coastal lakes are far from barren, but the analogy does point up the importance of water chemistry to lake productivity, a question of no small interest to anglers. Lakes can be acidic, neutral or alkaline. A scale called "pH" has been devised to measure the degree of acidity or alkalinity. The scale ranges from 0 to 14 with 0 representing the greatest acidity and 14 the greatest alkalinity. Seven represents the point of balance, but an increase of one in either direction represents a 10-fold increase. Hence a lake with a pH of six is 10 times more acidic than a lake with a neutral pH of seven.

Large, fast-growing trout are most often found in hard, alkaline waters; small, slow-growing trout are often products of soft, acidic waters. Similarly, nutrient-poor lakes are most often acidic while nutrient-rich waters are most often alkaline. These are not hard and fast rules; exceptions exist. Generally speaking, though, alkaline waters produce exceptional fishing while acidic waters yield poor angling. Most coastal lakes are acidic. Common pH values in coastal lakes might range between six and 6.5. In rich Kamloops trout waters common pH values range between 8.4 and 8.6. Generally speaking then, a typical coastal lake is about 100 times more acidic/less alkaline than a typical Kamloops trout lake. Even the best coastal lakes, often found close to some natural deposit of limestone, are still far more acidic than average interior lakes. Common pH values of such lakes might range between seven and 7.5, about 10 times more acidic/less alkaline than hard interior water.

The angler casting for large trout in the dark bay with its spilling creek knows little or nothing of water chemistry and the mysteries of total dissolved solids. Nor does he particularly care. He does know that once the mountains cast their shadows over his chosen piece of water, large fish regularly come within reach of his sinking line. The proof is lying at his feet in the form of a deep-bodied, superbly conditioned cutthroat some 18 inches in total silver-sided length. But the quarry he seeks is larger yet. He has taken fish to 28 inches in this same spot and he hopes to equal or better that record at any moment. He knows the chances of taking a larger fish are good. Experience has taught him that large cutthroat tend to hunt the shallows in small schools and it is only minutes since he boated the fish now nestled against the wooden ribs of his boat.

Again the line snakes out over the water; the longer the cast the better, since more water is covered and the fly is available to the fish for longer periods. Again the wait while the fly sinks. Only a few years ago fishing a fly this deep would have been difficult if not impossible, but the advent of quick-sinking, high-density lines has broadened the fly fisher's scope dramatically. Finally he begins again the manipulation of line and fly which so cunningly imitates the sculpin's movements. No other method of fishing does this so well; even the experienced ultra-light spinning enthusiast with his arsenal of baitfish imitations cannot match the fly fisher's convincing portrayal of this small fish.

Suddenly a solid bump is felt against the line. The angler lifts the rod smartly and feels the hook drive home. A heavy boil of water erupts out from the boat, but the fish does not show. Only a small portion of its big back breaks water. Then it powers for deep water, the line coiled at the angler's feet leaping up and through the guides and out over the lake. Suddenly the reel is singing, its ratchet madly whirring. Just as suddenly it stops. The fish has found deep water and here the tussle begins in earnest: the angler straining arm and line as far as breaking strength will permit, the fish head down in the depths, its broad, powerful tail keeping it in position. From time to time it will shake its big head vigorously, or arch its body and thump the line with its tail. The angler hangs on. So things will remain until the line breaks, the hook slips free or the fish finally comes to the boat.

How then do we account for such fish in water the scientists tell us will barely support life? Fishing during a cutthroat trout broodstock derby (for hatchery purposes) in typically nutrient-poor, acidic coastal water, I witnessed the collection of 10 fish by rod and reel. The smallest weighed eight pounds while the largest was a massive trophy-sized fish of 14 pounds so deep it would have put many a salmon to shame. This impressive catch, with an average weight of almost 10 pounds for each fish, was achieved by eight rods over three days. Even if we disregard the fact these were reasonably skilled anglers who knew where and when to target their quarry, here is evidence writ large that such exceptional trout can and do exist in nutrient-poor coastal waters.

Unfortunately the scale samples taken from these fish went astray. Age and annual growth rates, all clearly visible to the trained eye studying such samples, would have provided invaluable information. All was not lost, however, since Fisheries Branch researchers conducted two three-day net surveys of the same lake. Scale samples taken from fish captured in these nets indicated cutthroat trout grow an average of about one inch a year between their second and seventh years in acidic water. The difference between rich interior and poor coastal waters could hardly be seen more clearly. A seven-year-old coastal-lake cutthroat trout proved barely 16 inches long! Only then, between years seven and eight, does the growth rate suddenly leap forward. In its eighth year the coastal-lake cutthroat becomes the sort of fish anglers prize. Typical size of these fish captured by net was about 21 inches fork length, indicating a growth rate of five inches in a single year.

Anglers who know these fish will have seen the evidence for themselves. Fish of smaller size show all the signs of a hard-won existence: long, thin bodies and too-large heads. The relatively low aquatic insect populations of the poorer coastal lakes is sufficient to sustain small fish; the smaller cutthroat, those to about 14 inches, are often wonderful fish, bright in colour and nicely proportioned. It is when the fish attain lengths of between 14 and 17 inches that life is hardest. While there is some evidence to suggest certain strains of the cutthroat learn the business of hunting forage fish early in life, most, it seems, do not become adept predators until they reach about 16 inches in length, normally in their seventh year. Then they grow considerably faster, as the net survey results indicate, and by the time they reach a length of 18 inches, they are a really good fish. Even so, the cutthroat remains a strange fish.

Having learned the intricacies of hunting and swallowing fish smaller than itself, the cutthroat makes a strange adaptation. It concentrates its new-found skills on only a few select species. The prickly three-spined stickleback and the spiny sculpin become the main items of its virtually unvarying diet. Even when juvenile salmon are available in good numbers, the cutthroat displays little or no inclination to harvest this bounty. Dr. Kim Hyatt, a research scientist with the Pacific Biological Station's salmon production section, has long studied coastal lake productivity and its effects on juvenile salmon, notably sockeye. He has found there is virtually no cutthroat predation on juvenile salmon. Sockeye do, as we have seen, take the precaution of staying deep during the day, but even under cover of darkness when they are readily available on the surface, the cutthroat makes no attempt to hunt these silvery masses. This is startling, all the more so given the predatory response of rainbow trout to the presence of sockeye juveniles (see the section on Babine Lake in chapter eight).

The largest cutthroat, it seems, are content to stay with what they know. They stalk the near-shore areas from the edges of drop-offs, big, powerful fish easily capable of chasing down small kokanee or young salmon, but concentrating instead on hapless sticklebacks or sculpins. This lackadaisical approach to the all-important business of survival remains an inexplicable cutthroat trait, part of the strange mystique which surrounds this fish. There is, however, an important exception to this rather general rule, one which has particular significance on the lakes of Vancouver Island. Many island lakes hold both cutthroat and rainbow trout. Sometimes this is a natural mix, but often it is a result of provincial Fisheries Branch stocking programs which are extensive here as elsewhere in the province. In such lakes the cutthroat becomes an entirely different fish.

The reason for this is not known, although a study of 27 coastal lakes by Nils-Arvid Nilsson and Thomas Northcote (1981) provides some fascinating insights. Food, size and growth of cutthroat and rainbow trout were studied. Some of the lakes held only cutthroat trout, some only rainbow trout and some held mixed populations. The study's major finding surprised even its authors. The cutthroat which lived separately showed typical slow growth rates. This was true whether small fish such as stickleback and sculpins were present or not. Rainbow trout on their own grew faster and larger than the cutthroat. The real surprise, however, came when lakes with mixed populations were studied.

Suddenly, the picture was reversed. In lakes with mixed populations, it was the cutthroat which grew larger—and substantially larger. They grew faster as well. Not only did they grow faster than cutthroats in lakes without rainbow trout, they grew faster and larger than even the fast-growing trout from the rainbow-only lakes. This despite the fact that rainbow trout have clearly been shown the more aggressive of the two. From a fish which feeds placidly, haphazardly picking what it can, the cutthroat aggressively assumes the role of top predator, displacing the rainbow trout from productive nearshore areas and claiming all for its own. Suddenly all small fish are potential targets, although the evidence indicates they stop short at eating other trout. Even cutthroats as small as eight inches were found to eat other fish, but only in waters where rainbow trout were also present.

The angler who has had good success taking larger cutthroats with small surface-film patterns will take exception, as will those who have had success with any number of aquatic insect imitations fished on the wetline. The explanation is simple. Cutthroat trout continue to take aquatic and wind-blown insects all their lives. The preference may well be for sticklebacks and sculpins, but let a strong hatch develop, as in a good rise of early-season chironomids, and even the largest cutthroats in the lake will come to the surface to sip as daintily as the fabled brown trout. Careful observation of bulging surface rises during a good hatch will reveal that many of the small, spreading dimples creasing the lake are made by very large fish. The cutthroats share this trait with all trout; even the large piscivorous rainbow trout of B.C.'s north country will stop to take advantage of a strong hatch of insects.

It is a mistake to underestimate the trout's addiction to aquatic insects, or any insect for that matter. The reaction of cutthroat trout to an emergence of carpenter ants is a striking example, but the same holds true for any insect. They need only appear in sufficient numbers to trigger a response from the fish. Then baitfish imitations can be cast until the arm grows weary and still be ignored, even when placed amid the frenzied fish flashing beneath the surface. Coastal cutthroating demands good nymphing skills, even if it is the tinsel-bodied patterns which account for the majority of larger fish.

Which leaves only our mythical angler, still straining line and leader in the shadowy bay far up the lake. We'll let him have his fish: it finally comes to the boat in grudging cutthroat fashion, with violent head shakes which yet threaten to throw the hook firmly fixed in the corner of the powerful jaw. Spent beside the boat, the large gill plates with their purple sheen gaping wide, the fish reveals the deep silvery flanks which mark the largest cutthroats, a fish of 10, perhaps 12 years. The angler reaches down with long-nosed pliers and plucks the hook free. Reviving the fish is the work of a moment in experienced hands. With a powerful flick of tail, it returns to its lake: a mystery briefly touched, a memory stored.

Discovering the Carpenter Ant

*W*hen a wind-blown insect falls upon the water it is the ordinary child and the exceptional angler who take note. All the best anglers share with children this curious sense of wonder for the intricacies of nature. What is this strange creature? Where did it come from? Where is it going and what is it doing? Children are endlessly fascinated by nature; they desperately want to know about this secretive

Carpenter ant

world. So it should be with anglers too, for it is in knowing the small secrets that we come to a better understanding of the whole. Seen in this light, angling is not so much about catching fish as it is about exploring the natural world around us. Anglers who approach the sport in this spirit slowly acquire a treasury of small secrets, bits and pieces of nature's larger puzzle. This knowledge makes them exceptional anglers. Not only do they catch the most fish, they regularly take the largest fish—and just as regularly release them back to the water.

To consistently catch large trout means the angler must regularly fool the oldest and canniest of fish. Despite all talk of "wise old fish," the truth is that fish do not acquire wisdom. They do, however, learn through conditioning, as anyone who has watched aquarium fish knows. A young fish will attack virtually anything it can swallow; even small sticks and other debris may be tested. But the older fish, having experienced the passing of several seasons, soon learns there is a regular pattern to this business of feeding, and it quickly comes to recognize the various food items which will form the staples of its diet. As the seasons pass it becomes ever more circumspect in its feeding behaviour and grows increasingly suspicious of anything which deviates from the norm, however tempting the unusual morsel may at first appear. Only at certain specific times will these larger fish again feed with the abandon of youth, normally triggered by the emergence of an aquatic insect or some other dietary staple it has come to know. The angler who is attuned to these special times in the season of the trout will catch more and better fish than those who are not, but a deeper sense of satisfaction lies in the knowledge gained, in having unravelled one of nature's small mysteries.

Such journeys of discovery are not limited to the aquatic environment. To discover the secrets behind what is beyond doubt the most intense feeding spree of the year in B.C.'s coastal lakes, one must travel far from water to the deepest recesses of the ancient coastal rainforest. Here we find one of the coast's most fascinating insects, *Camponotus herculeanus*, that giant of the ant kingdom known as the carpenter ant. These hard, shiny black creatures, reaching lengths of five centimetres, live out their secretive lives deep in the heart of the forest. Replanted second-growth forests provide little of the habitat they require and while it is unlikely the rapid cutting of remaining coastal old-growth forests will doom the carpenter ant (the ant is, after all, one of nature's great survivors), one can only assume their numbers will be reduced as their preferred habitat continues to shrink. That this will also affect the coast's trout populations is a striking example of nature's intricate web and one which the angler can readily appreciate. It is doubtful whether the handful of "habitat ecologists" now in the employ of various forest companies will see the connection between a forest-dwelling ant and the lake nestled in the fold of mountains far below.

Worse yet for *Camponotus herculeanus* is the ever-growing demand for cedar as a roofing material in the large urban centres of both Canada and the United States. This demand seems entirely unreasonable given the wealth of alternative materials available, but cedar shake and shingle roofs are considered chic in some circles, with the result that dead standing cedar snags in the forests of the B.C. coast are now valuable enough to be logged by helicopter. These dead standing trees are, of course, valuable to wildlife as well, the colourful wood duck and the pileated woodpecker chief among those which have immediate public appeal, but the lowly carpenter ant also requires such trees. This ant lives in recesses within the dry wood of these dead trees, but the ant cares little whether the trees are standing or lying on the forest floor as either suits its purposes equally well. Here they feel safe and begin the work from which they take their somewhat fanciful name. In reality they are excavators rather than carpenters, hollowing out vast areas deep within the logs to provide a relatively secure home for the large colonies they eventually form. Only the bear, the woodpecker and man can reach them in the complex, multilayered homes they build for themselves in the soft wood of the cedar.

Inevitably, as the colony grows and its intricate tunnel networks become ever longer, the point is reached where even the massive length and girth of an old-growth cedar tree is saturated with ants. Either because there is no more room or simply because the time for expansion is right, a new colony will be formed, and the providential ants have long since made provision against such a day. Deep within the log's most secret and best-protected passages lies a small cadre of elite winged breeders, born and reared for the sole purpose of establishing new colonies. In the spring of the year, when the skies clear and the sun's warmth can penetrate to slowly bake the trees which hold such colonies, activity in the dark tunnels reaches fever pitch. Soon a long, black line of breeders makes its way to the escape hatches provided them. Suddenly, usually sometime in May, but perhaps as early as April or as late as June, the coastal skies swarm with flying ants. This mass exodus consists of both males and females and mating takes place in mid-air, an awkward coupling, as even with two sets of wings each, the ant is an ungainly flyer. They are at the mercy of even the slightest breeze; given a real wind, the ants are dispersed far and wide.

This last seemingly insignificant fact, the ants' basic unsuitability for flight, makes all the difference for the coast's cutthroat and rainbow trout. Unable to control their flight paths, and perhaps not recognizing water for the hazard it is, many thousands of ants are swept into lakes and tidewater each spring. Once on the water they are trapped. Their heavy exoskeletons and long, dangling legs break through the water's surface tension; even their double sets of wings are not enough to pull them free. So there they lie, struggling, with beating wings. The wings are designed to break off once the fertilized female reaches the ground (males die soon after mating) so wings soon litter the water, ending any last desperate chance the ant might have had to break free.

The trout respond to this sudden wealth with unabashed gluttony. Fluttering, struggling insects on the water's surface always elicit an immediate and normally savage response from trout, but nowhere more so than on the coast. The usually cool, hesitant arrival of spring on the coast slows the emergence of aquatic insects to a virtual standstill. By contrast, the southern interior's sudden rush of sun and hot weather promotes short but intense hatches of insects and the fish respond accordingly. A hatch of midges or chironomids which might build, peak and end within the period of a week in the interior will require a month or more to go through the same evolution on the coast. So while there may well be a weak hatch in progress over a period of several weeks, there is little to trigger a gangbusters-style feeding spree—until the splashy, all-in-a-rush arrival of *Camponotus herculeanus*.

Anglers who have not witnessed the response of coastal trout to the arrival of the carpenter ant will be hard-pressed to believe the bacchanal which ensues. Even the largest cutthroat trout, long supposed by many to feed exclusively on forage fish, race to the surface. In the large lakes of the coast, and even in some not-so-large lakes, cutthroat trout can grow to exceptional sizes; I have seen cutthroat as heavy as 14 pounds and many in the 10-pound class. This makes for an astonishing sight, all the more so because coastal lakes are notoriously moody, with only rare signs of surface activity. Suddenly, and quite inexplicably for those who fail to notice the struggling black bodies, the entire surface of the lake comes alive with fish. For rainbow trout this is not uncommon behaviour, but for cutthroat trout, especially the larger, older fish, such behaviour is virtually unknown. Only the struggling carpenter ants will bring them up from the depths to feed so carelessly upon the surface. On many coastal lakes it is the only time during the year when such fish are within reach of a dry line. Unfortunately for the angler, this incredible frenzy is quickly over, usually lasting for only a period of several days, often less.

The emergence of the carpenter ant may extend for a period of some weeks, although normally a week or so is all it takes for this sexual migration to begin, peak and end. The corpses of dead ants will litter the water for a considerable period following the final emergence, but the trout will pay little heed. Why this should be remains something of a mystery, although I favour the theory which holds that ants are difficult to digest and the fish, once stuffed to near bursting following the initial gluttony, retreat to some safe refuge and slowly digest their windfall. Whatever the explanation, it is true that the worst fishing of the coastal season follows the emergence of the carpenter ant. It will be some weeks following its arrival before the fishing returns to anything approaching normal.

To know this ant is to know the secret behind the most ferocious feeding frenzy the cutthroat and rainbow trout of the coast will display all year; to miss it by so much as one day is to experience coastal lake fishing at its lowest ebb.

The curious, watchful eye of the child may see it first, but the angler attuned to the secret seasons of the trout will not be far behind. Few can say as much.

Vancouver Island Lakes

*T*he island has been divided into three sections: North, Central and South. North island lakes are listed first as these waters receive the least angling pressure. As conditions on easily reached waters become ever more crowded, it becomes increasingly important that anglers spread themselves out. Crowds and quality angling rarely go hand-in-hand. It is for this reason that some of the island's most popular waters, lakes such as Elk and Beaver, for instance, have not been included.

North Vancouver Island

Logging roads are the primary access to the lakes of this region. Most major logging companies provide free maps of their various road networks as well as essential information on safe travel, road restrictions and best travel times. Pick up these maps either directly from the companies' local offices or at travel information centres. In the main, camping facilities are limited; a few lakes have no developed sites, but nearby campsites are never hard to find. The public campsites established by the logging companies always have the best view or vantage, and the road network maps pin them down beyond doubt. North Vancouver Island as defined here extends from the north tip of the island south as far as Hwy 28, the Campbell River to Gold River road.

» NAHWITTI, KAINS AND GEORGIE LAKES—These are typical coastal cutthroat lakes; no rainbow trout and soft, acidic waters. Relatively light angling pressure (by southern standards) makes for a mixed population of fish with representation from various year-classes, including some larger fish for canny anglers. These are wild fish, so catch-and-release fishing merits consideration. Some of the best cutthroat fishing in the northernmost area of the island is found in these lakes. Kains and Nahwitti are both on the road from Port Hardy to Holberg and are definitely worthy of a longish stop by those headed to Cape Scott Park. It's a toss-up as to which provides the better angling, but Nahwitti is the favourite. Georgie Lake is reached by taking a secondary road off the Holberg road about seven kilometres west of Port Hardy. It lies due north of Kains Lake. There are whispered (unconfirmed) rumours this lake holds rainbow trout as well as cutts.

» KLAKLAKAMA, LITTLE KLAKLAKAMA AND SCHOEN LAKES—The late 1980s planting of yearling cutthroat trout into Klaklakama Lake is exciting, but it is the opportunity to fish in Schoen Lake Park as well which makes this group special. Schoen Lake Park is one of the island's three wilderness parks, making the lake one of a small select group which has never seen logging. It holds a mixed population of rainbow and cutthroat trout, with good fishing except during hot weather. Fly fishers would do well to search the estuary areas of the three creeks feeding the lake, two at the far end and Schoen Creek on the south shore. Rudimentary trails lead to smaller lakes and large natural meadows. Camping is good both here and at Klaklakama. To get to the Klaklakamas take the Nimpkish Main (Woss) road off the Island Hwy about 70 kilometres south of Port McNeill; the first side road crossing the Nimpkish River passes both lakes. The same road network also connects with the Schoen (Davie) road, but all three lakes are better reached by leaving the highway at the Davie/Schoen Main crossing; the first left-hand fork goes to Schoen, the next left goes to the Klaklakamas. The highway exit is difficult to anticipate.

» ALICE AND VICTORIA LAKES—Natural limestone deposits in the Marble River drainage work magic on the water chemistry of nearby lakes, and these two large mountain-trough lakes, both part of the Marble River basin, are prime candidates (see the section on lake-resident cutthroat in this chapter for an explanation of how this works). Both these lakes hold large rainbow and cutthroat trout as well as Dolly Varden char and kokanee; bring heavier-than-normal leader material and take extra precautions when tying knots. Some sleuthing may be required to find suitable fly fishing water, but trolling with baitfish imitations (lures or fly patterns) should produce results, especially in the prime fishing months: April to June and again in September/October, although the fishing is said to hold through the hot-weather months as well. The paved road from Port McNeill to Port Alice passes the west side of Alice Lake and access to Victoria Lake is on good logging road from Port Alice. Nearby Benson Lake, reached via the Keogh Main logging road, is said to provide similar angling.

» WOLFE, ATLUCK AND ANUTZ LAKES—All three drain into the southern end of Nimpkish Lake. Nimpkish is home to some very large rainbow and cutthroat trout, but the lake acts as a wind funnel and is dangerous, especially for small fishing boats. Anutz has been stocked with rainbow trout and has a nice campsite. Atluck and Wolfe both contain rainbow and cutthroat trout as well as Dolly Varden char. Wolfe reportedly grows the largest fish; try the outlet with soft-hackled wet fly or baitfish imitations. To reach these lakes leave the Island Hwy 16 kilometres north of Woss to hit the T-junction at the Zeballos Main road (past the first junction which is River Main). Turn south (left) on Zeballos Main; Wolfe Lake is about eight kilometres in on the right; the road to the west (right), just before Wolfe, goes to Atluck. Anutz is closest to Nimpkish; turn north (right) on to River Main after leaving the highway.

» CLAUD ELLIOT LAKE—There are only sketchy reports on this small and little-known fly-only lake which holds both cutthroat and rainbow trout and drains into the Tsitika River via two smaller lakes and Claud Elliot Creek. To get there leave the Island Highway at the Woss Camp turnoff, but turn north rather than south to Woss. Follow this road to the first branch road north; this goes directly to the lake.

» MUCHALAT AND UPANA LAKES—Muchalat holds both rainbow and cutthroat trout as well as Dolly Varden char and kokanee. Expect fast fishing for smallish rainbows and cutts, mostly taken trolling or spinning, but there are reports of strong hatches when the fly will do well on this relatively large lake. It holds occasional large fish, but is mainly a good pan-fry lake for family fishing. Smaller Upana holds small rainbow trout but is an intriguing lake with a signed route leading to the nearby Upana Caves. Both lakes can be reached from the Woss-Gold River road; the Muchalat turnoff is about 20 kilometres north of Gold River, while the Upana cutoff is about 15 kilometres north, with stretches of rough washboard.

» DONNER AND KUNLIN LAKES—These two small lakes within Strathcona Park hold only small fish—bright, beautifully coloured cutthroat trout in good numbers. Smaller Kunlin Lake is lower in elevation (259 m) than subalpine Donner (564 m) but both are best fished in July and August, with Kunlin also providing good fishing during June. The access road to both lakes is easily missed, as there are three roads branching south off Hwy 28 in the same general vicinity. Take the middle (Ucona) road south about 12 kilometres east of Gold River. Four-wheel drive may be required to reach Donner Lake, five kilometres beyond Kunlin, but the road in any case stops short of the lake and a short walk is required. Definitely worth the effort.

» THE SAYWARD FOREST LAKES—The area bounded on the south

by Campbell Lake, Discovery Passage to the east, the Salmon River to the west and Johnstone Strait to the north contains dozens of small lakes, many of which have been stocked annually since the mid-1980s. Collectively they are known as the Sayward Lakes, or Sayward Forest Lakes. The provincial Fisheries Branch is researching a lake fertilization program for seven lakes in this region, with 1993 as a target date for initial fertilization. If all goes well, angling for larger trout might be expected by 1995-96. Meanwhile, there are a number of lakes which hold better-than-average fish. Try Grace, Spirit and Farewell lakes, between 40 and 55 kilometres northwest of Campbell River via the Menzies and Long Lake mainlines to the Blackwater Lake road, for sizable cutthroat and rainbow trout. Spring and fall are the best times for most of the lakes in this region; the proximity of one lake to the next makes for varied angling and interesting exploration.

Central Vancouver Island

This area is bounded in the north by Hwy 28, the Campbell River-Gold River road. Hwy 4, the Parksville to Port Alberni road, defines the southern boundary. Lakes west of Alberni Inlet are included in this section, while lakes east of the inlet are included under the lakes listing for southern Vancouver Island.

» QUINSAM LAKES—All three provide good fishing for larger trout, both rainbows and cutthroats. Upper Quinsam reportedly holds the largest fish, with rainbows and cutthroats to four pounds as well as Dolly Varden char. Middle Quinsam and Quinsam were stocked with steelhead fry in 1982 and 1983; Middle Quinsam reportedly has the larger fish, but Quinsam also holds kokanee as well as rainbows and some large cutts. All are within 35 kilometres of Campbell River, south of Campbell Lake and west towards Strathcona Park. To get to the Upper and

Middle lakes, take Hwy 28 (Gold River road) to the Argonaut Main turnoff. Upper Quinsam Lake is directly off this road; branch to Middle Quinsam Lake. For Quinsam Lake take the Duncan Bay Main logging road.

» WOWO LAKE—A small fly-only lake stocked with rainbow trout which reportedly grow to good sizes; it could be a real gem. Reached over the Oyster River road system, about 14 kilometres of gravel; less than 30 kilometres from Campbell River.

» BUTTLE LAKE—This lake holds small fish, but it has one of the island's most scenic mountain views and was made famous through the writing of Roderick Haig-Brown. Best times to fish are April to June and September-October, but is generally said to hold through the summer for cutthroat and rainbow trout. There are nice walking trails to small nearby lakes from the south end. The lake is in Strathcona Park; access is off Hwy 28 from south arm of Upper Campbell Lake.

» FORBIDDEN PLATEAU LAKES—Among the real gems of the island, these 10 stocked alpine tarns produce surprisingly large rainbow trout. Fish sizes range from moderate to large; the average is about 14 inches. Their alpine setting and superb views make them special. Lake size ranges from 93-hectare Moat Lake to two-hectare Kwai (average about 10 hectares); elevation ranges from 930-metre-high McKenzie to 1,173-metres for Lady Lake. All are in Strathcona Park and reached by signed hiking trails from Mt. Washington/Forbidden Plateau ski areas. Best fishing is in August and through the autumn months.

» WILLEMAR LAKE—One of the more productive cutthroat lakes due to a "rain-shadow" effect: lower annual rainfall prevents quick flushing of lake nutrients. Good fishing with some larger cutts (stocked). This relatively small lake also holds rainbow trout, Dolly Varden char and kokanee. Nearby Forbush Lake also provides good angling. Take the Comox Lake Main logging road past Comox Lake; it goes directly to Willemar, about 30 kilometres from Courtenay.

» CAMERON LAKE—This large, often wind-swept lake (caution: sudden, strong winds) on Hwy 4 is of note due to the presence of brown trout. These are among the most difficult of trout to fool and offer a good challenge for technical fly fishers. Stocked with rainbow and cutthroat trout; also holds kokanee. Located about 20 kilometres from Parksville.

» LOWRY LAKE—A small, secret lake holding large rainbow trout located just outside the southeastern boundary of Strathcona Park. Expect fish to four pounds; a good fly lake. Low elevation (137 meters) makes spring (April/May) and fall the most likely fishing months. To get there, take the Great Central Lake road off Hwy 4 past Port Alberni, then the Ash River Main to the Thunder Mountain branch; good roads all the way.

» OSHINOW LAKE—A five-kilometre-long alpine lake in Strathcona Park known for its exceptional rainbow and cutthroat trout. Stunning mountain scenery and trout reported to eight pounds make this lake a must-see. Also known as Deep Lake, it lies about 60 kilometres northwest of Port Alberni and is reached via Hwy 4 and the Ash River Main (see above) past Elsie Lake on good roads.

» NIMNIM, TOY AND JUNIOR LAKES—All three lakes produce exceptional fish and are admirably suited to fly fishing; Toy is limited to fly-only fishing. Lake size varies from 50 hectares for Nimnim, the largest, to less than five hectares for Junior, the smallest. Nimnim grows the largest fish, with cutthroat of four pounds and better, as well as stocked rainbow trout. Toy and Junior have been stocked with cutthroat trout and hold rainbow trout as well. To reach Nimnim, about 50 kilometres north and west of Port Alberni, take Hwy 4 to the Great Central Lake road, the Ash Main to Dickson Lake, then the Long Lake road to a branch road north from Elsie Lake. All are good-surface roads. Toy and Junior are nearby to the west on the same branch road.

» DORAN LAKE—Draining into Great Central Lake from the alpine country between Great Central and Sproat lakes, this small, stocked lake produces large rainbow trout. This is a go-for-the-experience lake; catch-and-release fishing is strongly advised. To get there take a small, easily missed logging branch road to the north off Hwy 4 just past the west end of Sproat Lake. Look for the Taylor River cut-throat spawning view area on the opposite side of the highway. Best fishing months are September/October.

» GRACIE LAKE—Reputed to hold exceptional rainbow trout, this small lake lies above Nahmint Lake. Until recently a long hike was required, but logging road access is now possible and hillsides around the lake show logging scars. It was stocked with rainbow trout for the first time in 1989. To get there take the Sterling Arm Main immediately after crossing the Somass River bridge at Port Alberni, then go south on Nahmint road (junction near Sproat Lake's Two Rivers Arm).

» NAHMINT LAKE—In the late 1970s this lake was said to produce the largest rainbow trout on the island. It is still reported to hold very large fish, but one suspects these are steelhead, the sea-going strain of rainbow trout. Either way, they must be released, as angling regulations stipulate mandatory release of all large rainbow trout from this lake. Nahmint is a long, mountain-trough-style lake and is best fished by trolling, but there is a bar where the Nahmint River flows in—a likely spot for casting tinsel-bodied flies. Also holds cutthroat trout. Directions are as for Gracie Lake; Nahmint lies just beyond Gracie.

» KENNEDY LAKE—This is another nutrient-poor coastal lake, but with a large population of three-spined stickleback. Cutthroat trout in this lake feed almost exclusively on these small, prickly fish. Look for extensive pondweed beds, which are ideal stickleback cover. Suitable fly imitations will bring some very large cutthroat, but patience is required. Clayoquot Arm provides the nicest setting and good remote (boat access) camping places. Best access is from Clayoquot Main road off Hwy 4 shortly before the Tofino-Ucluelet junction. Take this road to the Kennedy River bridge. Nearby Muriel Lake provides much the same fishing but is considerably smaller, so there is less water to search.

» MEGIN LAKE—There is air access only to this remote lake off Shelter Inlet. It holds cutthroat trout, with some large fish, but they are not easy to catch. Rainbow trout are likely also present. Shoreline trolling and casting off the river mouth where Megin River enters the lake are probably the best bets. Lovely remote lake in stunning old-growth spruce forest setting; cabin and canoes available with permission from Tofino Air. The lower river provides excellent steelhead fishing in season. Contact Tofino Air in Tofino for details on this and other remote fly-in lakes in Clayoquot Sound area.

» SPIDER LAKE—A relatively small lake with many bays, Spider is an interesting lake to fish, with intriguing spots to anchor and cast for cutthroat trout and good-sized smallmouth bass. Nearby Horne Lake provides good fishing for rainbow and cutthroat trout to about two pounds with some larger fish. To get there, take the Horne Lake road off the Island Highway north of Qualicum Beach.

South Vancouver Island

This area includes all waters from the south tip of the island north to Hwy 4. Many of the lakes in the southern areas of the island, notably those on the east coast, are more productive than the lakes in the north and central portions. There are many and varied reasons to explain this, but generally lower annual rainfall provides a ready explanation. In areas of heavy rainfall, lake nutrients are quickly flushed through the system, leaving behind soft, acidic waters which are virtually sterile when compared to coastal lakes in areas of more moderate annual precipitation. Here is yet another example of the aquatic environment's fragility: a few centimetres difference in total annual rainfall can drastically alter the chemical and biological balances within a given lake. Rainfall is not, however, the sole factor behind the generally higher productivity of these lakes. Nearby mineral deposits can also have a dramatic influence, especially if the mineral happens to be limestone.

» FATHER AND SON LAKE—A small, walk-in alpine lake holding exceptional rainbow trout. Stocked occasionally, the lake produces fish to five pounds and better. Nearby Limestone Mountain provides a good clue as to why: limestone-enriched waters grow large fish quickly. Scuds (small freshwater crustaceans: see the section on scuds in chapter five) are likely present. Catch-and-release is recommended for larger fish. The snow is usually gone by June; should provide good fishing through to October. To get there take the Bamfield road from Port Alberni to the Thistle Mine road (be careful not to veer off on the Museum Creek road). Parking space is provided; the walk is short, about one kilometre. A path circles the lake.

» LABOUR DAY LAKE—Another visually striking high-country lake with larger fish yet than found at Father and Son Lake. Good anglers can expect rainbow trout to eight pounds-plus. Can be reached from the Bamfield road (turn north at the junction with Franklin Main), but the Cameron Main logging road off Hwy 4 is quicker. Look for Cameron Main near the summit of Hwy 4 and turn south, carry on to the (often rough) Lake road which ends at the parking spot for this lake. Walking distance is about the same as for Father and Son Lake and a path also circles this somewhat larger lake. Indian Lake, a small alpine tarn holding numerous rainbow trout, can be reached by hiking south from this lake; topographical maps are required.

» HENRY AND KAMMAT LAKES—These two subalpine tarns are off the Cameron Main road and provide an interesting side trip during fishing excursions to Labour Day Lake. Both have been stocked with steelhead fry and provide fast action on the fly amid lovely settings. Take Cameron Main as for Labour Day Lake, but head south on the Cop road after passing the turn for the Y.C. Main road; requires logging road map (T.F.L. 44 East Map) for final approach. Nice camping.

» FREDERICK AND PACHENA LAKES—Both are typically nutrient-poor coastal lakes, but with minimal pressure so there should be some larger fish, both cutthroat and rainbow trout. The lakes are included here due to their close proximity to the superb and relatively little-known ocean-front camping at Pachena Bay. Early September is suggested as the best time for both lake fishing and uncrowded beach camping. To reach these lakes take the Bamfield road from Port Alberni, then the Franklin, Sarita and Pachena roads (all good surface).

» ROWBOTHAM, HIDDEN AND FISHTAIL LAKES—Three alpine gems requiring short walks (.5- to 2.5-kilometre trails) from Arrowsmith Lake. All three are stocked with rainbow trout. Topographical maps are required to pinpoint these lakes. To get to Arrowsmith, take the Englishman River logging road south of Parksville to a branch road crossing the river. This goes directly to Arrowsmith, also a good rainbow trout lake.

» BRANNEN LAKE—This well-stocked suburban Nanaimo lake grows large rainbow and cutthroat trout. A good, easy-to-get-to lake for anglers visiting Nanaimo, it provides a ready opportunity to try for larger trout.

» LONG LAKE—Vancouver Island's smallmouth bass lakes are little known outside the island, although a contingent of dedicated island bass anglers now fishes hard for these quality game fish. Long Lake holds some very large smallmouth as well as good rainbow and cutthroat trout. Fly fishers will want to try for these scrappy fish which take a fly willingly. The lake is just north of Nanaimo beside Hwy 1 on the water (east) side.

» NANAIMO LAKES—This chain of four lakes in the Nanaimo River drainage holds rainbow and cutthroat trout to four pounds and better. Fourth and Third lakes are smaller than the others and better suited to fly fishers who enjoy intimate waters. Access is on paved road (as far as First Lake) from Hwy 1 south of Nanaimo on Nanaimo Lakes Road.

» PANTHER (HEALY) LAKE—A small, fly-only lake reputed to hold larger rainbow trout, its high elevation ensures good fishing all summer. Reached from the Nanaimo Lakes Road on a branch road north from Second Lake.

» RHEINHART AND SILVER LAKES—Two small, shallow, high-elevation lakes admirably suited to fly fishing. Rheinhart holds both rainbow and (stocked) cutthroat trout; Silver has only cutts. Rheinhart is lower in elevation; good fishing starts in May and holds through June, then in September/October. Silver, at 850 metres elevation, is best from June on. To get there, take the Chemainus River road west from the town; Silver is about 32 kilometres in, Rheinhart about 42 kilometres.

» FULLER LAKE—This is a very productive lake reached on paved logging road from Chemainus; it lies in Fuller Lake

Park (picnic areas, boat launch). Stocked with "catchables" but grows rainbow trout to four pounds and better, with reports of fish to six pounds.

» QUAMICHAN AND SOMENOS LAKES—These two popular lakes lie east of Duncan off the paved roads to Maple Bay. Cutthroat and stocked rainbow trout grow to large sizes (five pounds) in Quamichan. Somenos holds wild and stocked cutthroats as well as stocked rainbow and brown trout. The lake is a wildlife reserve for wintering waterfowl.

» NITINAT LAKE—A large tidal lake with a narrow inlet (Nitinat Narrows) from Juan de Fuca Strait, Nitinat provides anglers with an opportunity to catch large chinook salmon in fresh water as well as lake-resident and sea-run cutthroat. Try the mouth of the river where it flows into the lake for resident cutthroat trout, as well as the river itself upstream (check regulations). Nitinat Narrows (the outlet) provides good sea-run cutthroat fishing in April/May and September/October near the lake. Good logging road all the way from the village of Lake Cowichan via Youbou. A branch road before the Nitinat River crossing goes to the Carmanah and Walbran forests.

» TUCK LAKE—Rainbow and cutthroat trout to about two pounds in this small stocked lake off the west end of Lake Cowichan. Low elevation makes spring and fall the best fishing times. Best approach is from Lake Cowichan as for Nitinat, but watch for a branch road north off Franklin Main shortly after Lake Cowichan.

» WILD DEER LAKE—Another small, productive lake suited to fly fishing, it grows large rainbow trout, with fish to four pounds-plus reported. Take a good paved logging road 25 kilometres west from the Island Highway at Cowichan River bridge.

» LANGFORD LAKE—This fair-sized urban lake just west of Victoria is included here for its smallmouth bass fishery.

Holds some very large bass as well as rainbow and cut-throat trout.

» PROSPECT LAKE—This good smallmouth bass lake, with fish to four pounds reported, also holds rainbow and cutthroat trout. Paved West Saanich and Prospect Lake Roads north of Victoria lead to this popular lake.

» SPECTACLE LAKE—Located within Spectacle Lake Provincial Park north of Victoria, this small lake is the only brook trout lake on the island. These colourful members of the char family take on an even more brilliant coloration during the fall spawning season, at which time they become aggressive and are easily caught. They are much more difficult to fool at other times (see the section on brook trout in chapter six). Spectacle Lake brookies do not reach large sizes.

» FAIRY AND JUNE LAKES—These two small cutthroat trout lakes near Port Renfrew hold both lake-resident and sea-run strains. Fairy Lake has a trout-release restriction during the October to April spawning season, when only flies may be used. Fly-only June Lake requires a hike of about eight kilometres on the West Coast Trail. To reach June Lake take the paved road from Port Renfrew to popular Fairy Lake, then the Gorden Creek logging road to the start of the West Coast Trail.

» SALTSPRING ISLAND LAKES—The lakes of this island, reached by ferry from Swartz Bay, are special by any standard. Both cutthroat and rainbow trout grow to trophy sizes. Smallmouth bass were introduced in the 1930s and have done remarkably well. The provincial Fisheries Branch has helped these fish by building artificial tire reefs to provide the structure they require for their lurk-and-ambush style of feeding. Bass grow to about eight pounds in St. Mary's Lake, making heavy leaders a must, as bass traditionally break for cover when hooked. The lake also holds large cutthroat and rainbow trout, mostly taken by trolling, but there is a strong spring chironomid hatch and good action for skilled wet-line fishers all year. Stowell and Cusheon lakes also provide good fishing for cutts and bass, but sizes are generally smaller. Weston is a good fast-action rainbow lake ideal for introducing youngsters to the fly.

For more information contact:

Fisheries Branch
2569 Kenworth Road
Nanaimo, B.C.
V9T 4P7

Vancouver Island Tourist Association
302-45 Bastion Square
Victoria, B.C.
V8W 1J1

CHAPTER TWO

The Lower Mainland

Only a few short years ago, going "up country" meant a tortuous drive and long hours behind the wheel. Time and dedication were required to slip the city. Now we glide effortlessly on superhighways. The angler taking his breakfast in a downtown apartment is assured of fishing the afternoon rise of mayflies on a lake nestled in wooded hills of sweet-scented interior pine. Never mind that several hundred others are headed in the same direction, or that hidden in the mountains clearly visible from the apartment window lie a score of lonely high-country lakes where rainbow trout are rising even as the dishes are cleared and the angler prepares to drive several hundred kilometres west.

Such Lower Mainland waters are no myth. Small, uncrowded alpine and subalpine tarns abound in nearby mountains. Secret low-lying lakes await those adventurous enough to take a second look at their own backyards. The four-wheel-drive vehicles now ubiquitous on city streets make short work of the roads to such lakes, but even two-wheel drive is adequate for those prepared to stretch their legs over the final few rough kilometres characteristic of the Lower Mainland's small hidden lakes. While much effort has gone into improving angling conditions, little or nothing has been done to improve road conditions of the final spurs which provide access to the shores of these quiet little lakes. This is deliberate and the reasons are plain: these are angling waters intended for peace and solitude far from the madding crowds. The beery revellers and their music boxes have lakes aplenty more suited to their needs. If a short hike or walk of a few kilometres will keep them at bay, the price seems little enough.

Anglers, as always, will be concerned with the sizes of fish likely to be encountered. These lakes are not rich in the way of good interior lakes. A 16-inch trout may well prove the trophy of the day; some will never grow fish much longer than 10 or 12 inches. Cousins to the lakes of Vancouver Island, their typically acidic, nutrient-poor waters tend to grow small fish. Skilled anglers know there are often very large fish as well, but a 21-inch coastal trout typically requires eight years to grow and represents enough of a triumph over its harsh environment to be carefully released. There are exceptions, the handful of productive lakes which grow 21-inch trout in half the time or less. Anglers tuned to the indicators which mark such water will discover them readily enough (see the section on reading lakes in chapter four). Some of the most productive lakes are described in the listing at the end of this chapter, but it is a sad mistake to concentrate solely on lakes which produce large fish.

This argument is best made in specific terms. A low-lying lake in the Pemberton area is renowned for the size of its fish. The setting is nice, but there are countless lakes more visually striking; only the remarkable size of its rainbow trout makes it noteworthy—so special are these fish that regulations stipulate they must be released. Less than 50 kilometres away, off the southern end of Lillooet Lake, lies another small angling lake. Rainbow trout here typically measure 10 inches, the bright, lovely little fish of the Lower Mainland's high country. Catching enough for a frying-pan feast should present few difficulties even for the neophyte. And it is fine angling, this working of light rods and dry flies on a pristine lake in an alpine valley where the fishing will hold all summer. To dismiss such fine sport in high-country settings simply because the fish do not grow to bragging size is foolishness.

Fishing only for larger fish, and only larger trout at that, is a notion which seems to have taken hold of a good many otherwise sensible anglers. Targeting large trout is a noble endeavour only so long as it does not become an obsession. The same might well be said of fishing only for trout. The angler who turns down the chance to fish for arctic grayling or bass or brook trout out of some conviction that only trout are a worthy species is misguided at best. Much of the true pleasure to be found in angling lies in the diversity of species available, each requiring different skills and tactics and each providing its own unique window on the aquatic environment. Far from avoiding the challenge these fish offer, the well-rounded angler actively seeks them out, if for no other reason than to discover whether the lessons learned on trout waters will take these fish as well. And in the case of at least two non-salmonid species available in the Lower Mainland, trout tactics will prove woefully inadequate.

Some of the best angling available in the Lower Mainland each year goes unnoticed by the vast majority of anglers. A trout of 20 inches taken in a far-flung lake is seen as a trophy by anglers who are unaware that fish of 20 pounds and better may be found within city limits. They are not trout, these large wily fellows who patrol the Lower Mainland's shorelines after the fashion of the tarpon cruising saltwater flats, but they will rise to the dry fly and fight like demons once hooked. What is this wonderful tackle-straining fish? The lowly carp, the largest member of the minnow family. Carp are believed to attain weights in excess of 20 pounds in the Lower Mainland; I believe they may go to 30 pounds and perhaps more. Unlike the trout, which sinks out of sight when the hot weather arrives, carp continue to feed through the hottest months, thus providing sport within minutes of the city through the summer—provided, of course, the angler can fool them. This is by no means certain; carp are an extremely wily opponent and can be many times more difficult to fool than the much-vaunted trout.

Dedicated trout fishers will shudder at this heresy. The carp is not officially considered a game fish, yet I recall carp-fishing trips where rainbow trout were fooled but the carp leisurely swimming by the same offering remained maddeningly unconvinced. Entire schools finned their way disdainfully past my carefully placed bait while the rainbow trout which followed took without hesitation. Fishing for carp will humble even the canniest of trout fishers. The angler who can consistently take carp of over 20 pounds need fear nothing from any game fish.

My advice to those who would take carp on the fly is to start again at the beginning. Start with bait, slim bobbers and fairly stout rods of the type designed for steelhead fishing. A hooked carp will immediately break for cover, usually dense weed growth. A long, stout rod provides leverage for the heavy side-arm pressure required to arrest this headlong rush, but there will be times when even this is not sufficient. Later, eight-weight-and-better fly rods can be tested against the carp's bulldoggish determination, but one must first learn its habits and the bait rod is the place to start. Evening is the time to try; after work on a hot summer's day is ideal. Steal down to some quiet lakeside spot where carp are known to dwell, carefully bait a hook small enough to go undetected in the carp's extremely sensitive mouth, hide nearby or stay low and wait for the bubbles which mark the passing of a school of carp. The bait must rest against the bottom and the line must be allowed to run free—only after the carp has taken the bait and is swimming away with line spooling from the reel is the hook set. This is vital. If the carp feels even the slightest resistance, it will immediately expel the bait. At all costs resist the overpowering urge to strike the moment the line begins to jiggle. Carp are suspicious creatures and will not "hit" as do predatory fish.

They are also inordinately adept at expelling offending objects from their mouths. It is part and parcel of the way they feed, plucking a mouthful of matter off the bottom, then expelling it and picking the choicest morsels thus uprooted. This accounts for the surface bubbles which mark the passing of a school. They are omnivorous but feed mainly on small crustaceans, nymphs and benthic creatures such as snails. During the summer months, usually starting in July, they will pluck insects from the surface and this is when the dry fly has its greatest chance of success. Bottom-fishing for carp with a fly is possible, but even taking them on bait seems difficult enough.

There are a few bait-fishing tricks which help immensely. If a weight is used, it should be one which allows the line to pass through freely, a pyramid-style weight or a shot-ledger made of several split-shots pinched to a separate piece of line and threaded to the mainline are both suitable, but avoid weights if at all possible. Carp have a good sense of smell and taste, excellent vision and seem to recognize danger all too readily. Extreme caution is required, even going so far as to wash hands before handling bait or hooks. A piece of warm, sticky fresh bread about the size of a small egg and balled around the hook makes a good quick bait, but adding something sweet is often more effective. Try boiling a half cup of juice from canned corn, add a quarter cup of canned, crushed corn and enough cornmeal to get the mass solid but moist. Remove from heat and add flour to

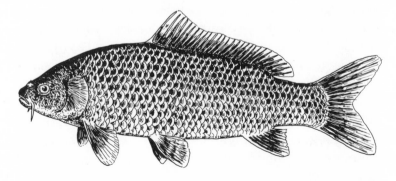

Carp

get the right consistency. No weight is needed with either of these baits.

Locating them is the other trick and here the carp are, for once, very obliging. Carp gather in large near-shore schools during their spring spawning time, cavorting about on the surface, splashing noisily and generally creating a ruckus. They cannot be caught at this time as they do not feed during spawning, but it is the time to spy out their waters and assess the sizes and numbers of fish available. Hatzic Slough, Como Lake, the Sumas and Pitt rivers and Popkum Creek are likely places to try. Even Burnaby Lake holds good carp, but do not be limited to these locations. The exploring involved in finding good, handy carp waters is in itself rewarding and there is satisfaction in ferreting out one's own secret spot.

Carp tend to feed in regular lanes or travel paths, circulating freely about the lake's near-shore area but generally following the same beat. The angler can use this habit to advantage. Take note of the path travelled by roving carp and cast the bait to this area. The next school to come along will be covering much the same beat. It is almost impossible to cast directly to a school of feeding carp. A cast will scatter the lot, but their movements are fairly predictable and this is especially important when the time for the dryline arrives. By determining the likely travel path, a dry fly can be left quietly on the surface in a prime spot. If a school passes close and the fly fails to attract notice, try twitching it enticingly. I think a fairly hefty fly should be used as the carp has a large mouth and likes to engulf something substantial. A fighting butt is also worth considering. Once on, a strong wrist is needed to match the carp. After its initial quick run, the carp becomes determined and can keep this up for a good long time. An evening of half a dozen such fish will tire even the strongest wrists.

A large carp is among the most difficult of all fishes to hook and land. They are imposing adversaries for any angler and those who can claim to regularly take them on the fly have earned the right to boast. It may be hard for dyed-in-the-wool trout fishers to accept that this minnow is a more wily opponent, but the truth is that carp are many times more difficult to fool. While carp make a wonderful fish for the table, provided the skin and underlying layer of fat is removed, dubious water quality in many Lower Mainland carp waters makes them suspect. A clean Okanagan lake is the place to try for carp for the table.

A good case can also be made for another Lower Mainland fish generally shunned by anglers, the black crappie. Nicknamed "papermouth" for its soft, paper-thin mouth, the crappie is a large sunfish, attaining weights up to about one pound in the Lower Mainland, although it grows much larger elsewhere in Canada and the U.S. Anglers should not be deceived by its small size; it is a fiery fighter, twisting and turning wildly, often beating the water to a froth. These fighting qualities coupled with its thin mouth make the crappie a challenge for even the most experienced angler.

The fiery, slab-sided crappie prefers clear weedy lakes and streams. They seek shelter and are often found around

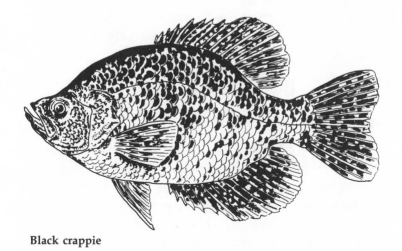

Black crappie

sunken trees or weed beds close to deep water. Crappies are willing takers of almost all baits, small spinners, tiny jigs or a carefully plied nymph. The lighter the tackle the better. They are a school fish, so catching one usually means a bonanza. When a fish is felt, accepted practice is to tighten the line gently but firmly. Under no circumstances should the hook be solidly set. This will tear the crappies' thin, sensitive mouths and the fish will be lost. There is a knack to hooking and landing crappies. Very light hands are needed, not unlike the soft touch required to hook trout feeding on chironomids. Look for crappies in Burnaby, Trout and Deer lakes, Sumas River, Dewdney, Nicomen and Sturgeon sloughs, Pitt Lake, Allouette and Stave rivers and Whonnock Lake.

There are also sound conservation and environmental reasons for pursuing these fish. Both are found in the environmentally sensitive sloughs of the Fraser River. These sloughs represent important habitat for wildlife as well as fish. Increased recreational use of the sloughs lends weight to arguments for their preservation and protection. There is very little evidence to suggest either species displace trout and salmon from limited habitat. In the Fraser Valley the habitat occupied by carp and crappies is for the most part unsuited to trout and salmon. They fill their own ecological niche, surviving in water too low in oxygen or too hot in summer to support salmonids and thus provide fine fishing where none would exist otherwise.

Closeup: Wild Waters of the Lower Mainland

Wild waters and remote wilderness sound out of character for the densely populated Lower Mainland region, but a closer look reveals many pockets of wilderness on the fringes of the urbanized belt. The region's official boundaries stretch north up the mainland coast as far as remote Bute Inlet where wild rivers penetrate the Coast

Mountains to within a hair's breadth of the Chilcotin. Between here and Vancouver lie countless lakes and streams which rarely see an angler over the course of a year. The Sunshine Coast encompasses the still-lightly-fished cutthroat trout lakes of the Powell Forest as well as the rich, unknown ponds of Texada Island. North of Squamish and scattered throughout the region's hidden high country lie secret alpine tarns, many previously barren and recently stocked by a provincial Fisheries Branch concerned with the growing demand for remote angling opportunities in wilderness settings.

So while the Lower Mainland has its meccas of urban fishing where anglers stand shoulder-to-shoulder, it has its wild, secret places too. Directing anglers to such wilderness gems is not without its qualms: the solitude which makes them special is as delicate as the morning mists swirling above a lake. But there is a strength in numbers too; only by banding together and acting in concert will anglers save the precious places from the various forms of development which threaten on all sides. It is a sad contradiction all too typical of the times that only by press of numbers will the wild places retain a vestige of what makes them remarkable.

Many of the small secret lakes of the Lower Mainland proper, mostly lying to north and south of the Fraser's broad valley and stocked by Fisheries Branch staff, are briefly described in the listing at the end of this chapter. These lakes are exceptional in their own right, but the waters which concern us here are wilder and generally more difficult of access. I have tried, in the thumbnail sketches which follow, to impart a little of each remote lake's unique character in the hope that those who follow will catch the spirit required to keep them what they are: wild lakes with wild fish in wild settings. Long may they abide.

Unwin Lake

"Jim, this is nice," I says. "I wouldn't want to be nowhere else but here. Pass me along another hunk of fish and some hot corn-bread."

We catched fish and talked, and we took a swim now
and then to keep off sleepiness.
—*The Adventures of Huckleberry Finn*, by Mark Twain

There are two basic philosophical approaches to fishing for
trout, the lazily content approach adopted by Huck Finn and
his pal Jim and the dyed-in-the-wool, dead-earnest approach
epitomized by hard-boiled fly fishers with bulging vests, natty
waders and hand-crafted landing nets. The one goes fishin';
the other angles. One is given to large shady hats, tin bait
cans and gaudy red and white bobbers; the other to dainty
dry flies, spider-web thin leaders and big words for small
bugs. It happens that my good friend and sometimes fishing partner, Dennis Gustafson, has a decided Huck Finn turn
towards trout fishing. On the half-dozen or so occasions each
year when we pursue the trout together, each in his own way
shows remarkable forbearance in accommodating the other's
peccadillos. I bring expensive, exquisitely tied flies; he packs
worms. Rarely does the basic philosophical schism come between us, but every once in a long while we come danger-
ously close.

Unwin Lake in early June is as if made to order for those
who tend towards the angler end of the philosophical scale.
There are a half dozen exciting shoals begging for the careful working of a nymph in the half-light of early morning
or late evening. There are steeply shelving drop-offs patrolled
by wise, old yellow-bellied cutthroat who take skilfully
manipulated sub-surface flies just often enough to keep the
pulse racing. It is a lake to challenge and intrigue; always there
is the promise of big fish for the dedicated angler.

For the motley crew of Huck Finn worm danglers who
aspire to such waters, Unwin in early June can be a wonderfully mellow sort of lake. There are open places to camp with
thick layers of dry moss just made for the whiling away of
an afternoon. There are comfortable shoreside places to sit
where one need not expend even what energy and thought

it takes to deliver a cast; the fish are right under your nose. There is a second lake to explore only a short hike away and, for the true Huck Finn devotee, even an island to hide out on. There is no trick to catching enough small fish for a meal most anytime. Bring your own corn-bread.

As with so many worthwhile things, getting there is not easy. The lake itself is about one kilometre from the beach over a good trail, but to reach that particular stretch of beach within the protecting arms of Tenedos Bay means penetrating the waters of Desolation Sound Marine Park. Typical jumping-off points are the village of Lund or the government wharf at Okeover Arm from where the long run (or paddle) around Sarah Point is avoided. There are no roads and no way of getting a boat on the lake without portaging over the trail. The payoff is in having an entire lake to oneself, a lake that is fished only rarely. Limiting out on good-sized fish is the rule rather than the exception.

As things turned out, our June trip was one of the exceptions, at least for me. We established camp on a lovely, flat, moss-covered rock where the lake narrows to river size. This narrows divides Unwin into two distinct parts, almost as if it were two separate lakes. The entrance to the narrows is shallow, but the water under our small bluff was deep, the deepest hole in the narrows and as good a spot as any for a few casts on a hot spring day.

The first cast whispered the line to the water with only the faintest of ripples to signal its arrival on the mirror-calm surface. A slow count of 25 allowed the fly to sink before starting its oh-so-careful creep to shore. A dedicated angler can on occasion sense an impending strike. It was one of those occasions. Meanwhile, partner Dennis was jangling a glittering array of spankingly silver baubles to which he'd affixed a murderous-looking hook and an earthworm as big around as my thumb. "Ford Fender," he explained when he saw the look on my face. Ker-klatter, ker-klatter, KA-WHOMP and the whole mess hit the water as if someone had pitched a bushel of fist-sized boulders into the water. "Nice," I said, but my concentration was broken and the nymph twitched to the surface troutless.

Then, "Hey, lookee here. Got one!" My head whipped around in time to see the respectable bend in his rod and the silly Huckleberry grin on his face. This was too much for my reserve. "Managed to fool one, did you?" I inquired. "One?" he yelped. "One? Look at this. Look! There must be half a dozen of 'em following it in. Son-of-a-gun, look at 'em all." I sauntered over, fast. And, sure enough, there they were. Four, maybe five nice coastal cutts excitedly darting around the one he had hooked. The fly failed to take a fish through the afternoon and the flyrod was soon discreetly laid aside. It was the worm which fetched our fish-fry dinner for the campfire that night and I left off any further attempts at serious angling for the duration of our stay. Sure, I wet a line now again, but mostly, "We catched fish and talked, and we took a swim now and then to keep off sleepiness." Much the best approach at Unwin Lake on a mellow day in June.

Goat Lake

At the turn of the century a determined man of the woods named Tom Ogburn poled his way upstream to the shores of Goat Lake. Before him spread a majestic mountain-ringed wilderness lake and Tom knew he had found his special place. From that day on Goat Lake was home; he was not to leave until the day he died in 1932.

Much has changed at Goat Lake since Ogburn's time: The river he poled to reach the lake is now virtually a still-water channel due to the MacBlo dam at Powell River; the hillsides towering above the lake's eastern shore have been logged, as has the Eldred River watershed at the head of the lake, and a logging road now provides access (travel is restricted; inquire locally). The time of pole and paddle may be gone forever, but it is easy to see why an itinerant roamer like Ogburn, a free spirit who had spent much of his earlier life trapping and prospecting the wild country of both Canada and the U.S., should finally put down roots at Goat Lake. Even now the feel and flavour of wilderness remain strong, and for those who share a spiritual kinship with men of Ogburn's ilk, the big mountain-trench lake will still cast a powerful spell. Ogburn operated a fishing and hunting retreat geared to the wealthy timber barons then emerging in coastal B.C. and the western U.S. These hard-headed tycoons returned to Goat Lake and Ogburn's rustic lodge year after year, lured, one suspects, more by the prospects of fine sport than any fanciful notions of wilderness. Double-digit trout cast a powerful spell in their own right. Somehow, in the mysterious way of the trout, these coho-sized cutthroats have survived. A 1986 study of the Powell-Goat drainage by provincial Fisheries Branch staff found both lakes to be at or near carrying capacity. Large, older fish form a significant part of the population. All this makes the shallow-water sand flats fronting the mouth of the Eldred River a place to be fished with something approaching reverence. This still visually striking stream of clear water, navigable a good distance upstream, flows in at the head of the lake over a broad estuary which, in Ogburn's day, would have been covered in impressive stands of first-growth cedar, hemlock and fir. Today only stumps remain, but with its backdrop of soaring peaks and the promise of large trout, Goat Lake remains among the most special fishing spots of the Lower Mainland region.

Part of the explanation behind the survival of these huge cutthroats lies with the rainbow trout which were introduced to the system in the 1930s. Between 1926 and 1937, 520,000 rainbow trout eggs were used to stock the Powell/Goat drainage. These fish too have survived, and while never attaining any great size (average weight is between one and 1.5 pounds), they do provide fine sport. More important, perhaps, is their relationship with cutthroat trout: when in mixed populations with rainbow trout, the cutthroat becomes a different fish, growing faster and larger than when left on its own. This strange dynamic is described in the section on cutthroat trout in chapter one.

The seasonal movements of the rainbow trout in Goat Lake are of interest to anglers. For much of the year these fish circulate freely about the lake, but always clear of the productive shoreline zones which are the exclusive preserve of the cutts. This makes them damnably difficult to catch, but some time in April and continuing through much of May, Goat Lake rainbows school along the Eldred flats in preparation for their spawning run up the river. This is the only time I know when these fish are concentrated in large numbers in a given area. They provide excellent sport despite their relatively small sizes, constantly reminding one that these are now wild fish, even if originally stocked. A novice fly fisher could expect to hook and release between 25 and 50 of these fish on a given spring day.

Which brings us to the most important point of all concerning Goat Lake. It takes a minimum of eight years for a Goat lake cutthroat to approach what most B.C. anglers would term a large trout. Growth is slow, making every large cutthroat something of a triumph. If ever there was a lake requiring catch-and-release angling, this is it. While much of the original magic which captured Ogburn's heart yet remains, the future does not augur well for Goat Lake. Let it not be said that anglers too must shoulder blame when the final cards are played.

The Ponds of Texada

The pond-like lakes of Texada Island are anomalies. More akin to the nutrient-rich lakes of the interior than the softwater lakes of the coast, they abound in aquatic riches all too rare on the coast. The entire island is itself an anomaly, with an unusually high degree of mineralization. Gold, copper and iron mining started as early as 1883; nearby Powell River and Courtenay/Comox were still covered by forest when The Rock, as it is locally known, boasted three saloons and the only opera house north of San Francisco. Today Texada is known principally for its limestone deposits, the largest and richest in the Pacific Northwest, and this should rivet the angler's attention, even if the gold and wooden-floored opera house of a bygone era do not.

Limestone does wonderful things for trout water. A lake of poor weed growth and relatively few aquatic insects will be transformed by its presence (see the section on cutthroat trout in chapter one). Healthy weed growth and large aquatic insect populations are associated with quality angling and Texada has all three. Good numbers of three to five-pound cutthroat trout are found in Emily, Paxton and Priest lakes, despite the fact they have never been enhanced in any way. The island's many smaller lakes tend to over-populate, as angling pressure is minimal to non-existent. The fish of such waters are incredibly numerous, brightly coloured and superbly conditioned, but small in size. Always ready to come to the dry fly, these wonderful fish of the small ponds make ideal quarry for youngsters ready to try manipulation of rod, fly and line.

This brings us to the crux of the dilemma now facing Texada's ponds. The uniqueness of the island's limestone-enriched waters has not gone unnoticed by anglers living nearby. Many would like to see rainbow trout introduced to the island, but initial reaction from the Fisheries Branch has been cool. Things have changed drastically since the '20s and '30s and fisheries biologists, along with many others, now see value in preserving those places which thus far have escaped the hand of man.

The ponds of Texada are among the last remaining enclaves of wilderness in a generally highly developed region. In the past, stocking was often willy-nilly, with very little thought to wild-stock management. Today, with major environmental changes looming, the Fisheries Branch has recognized wild-stock preservation as the cornerstone of its management philosophy. Some form of management for Texada's ponds

seems inevitable. Whether such management strives to
preserve what exists or whether it attempts to improve on
nature's design is surely one of the larger questions facing
us as we speed pell-mell towards the twenty-first century.
Will there be a place for Texada's small, brilliantly coloured
fish in that new world?

Clowhom Lake

Clowhom is known by name to many, but few have seen
its mountainous shores and still fewer tested its waters with
rod and reel. Difficult access bars all but the adventuresome.
A seaworthy boat is required to reach the lake's lower end
at the head of Salmon Inlet on the backside of the Sechelt
Peninsula. A second boat, one capable of handling a
16-kilometre long coastal lake, crew and camping gear is also
required (a good canoe suits the purpose). Two approaches
are possible: from the public boat ramp in Sechelt or from
the private ramp in Egmont. Leaving from Egmont should
be avoided by those inexperienced with the intricacies of running heavy tidal rapids. The powerful Skookumchuck, a coast
Indian word for turbulent water or rapid torrent, stands guard
over the entrance to Sechelt Inlet.

My partner was at home in these waters and we made our
approach from the north, through the shifting saltwater
rapids. The Skookumchuck's boils and crashing currents
made for a white-knuckle run, if not for my stalwart friend,
certainly for me. Then the long run to the head of Salmon
Inlet and the logging camp and B.C. Hydro dam at the outlet of Clowhom. Our map showed the dam, but the warning did little to mitigate our regret on seeing a wall of cement
where a river should have tumbled to tidewater. Permission
to tie up at one of the docks was readily granted and arrangements made to trade a few hours work stacking various items
in return for a ride up the logging road to the head of the
lake, canoe, camping gear and all. Such accommodations are
readily made in country beyond the reach of roads.

Before the dust and rumble of the pickup had faded we were on the water and making for the headwaters river where our new-found friend had told us of a small private cabin. The owner, he assured us, would appreciate a status report, not having visited for some time. So the small tent remained in its pack and we lived the high life with armchair and dinner table. The wild country visible from the porch of our little home was as if designed to waylay wandering anglers. The Clowhom River itself is deep-channeled and forms a pond-like opening at the cabin's front door, then necks down to river size again immediately upstream. This clear, secret stream is ringed by towering peaks, snow-capped through the year. Taquat Creek carries meltwater off these peaks and slips them into the lake alongside the Clowhom River. Where the flow of the two streams intermingles lies a lip to deeper water almost certain to be patrolled by wild cutthroat trout and Dolly Varden char. The evening found us fishing here, but both trout and char remained elusive.

Long after the sun had set, over mugs of spiked tea, we found the cabin's logbook and discovered one of Clowhom's secrets. Besides notes written by the owners, passersby had added their comments. Reading by candlelight and searching carefully for any reference to fish and fishing, a pattern soon emerged. May, a few large fish taken; June, no fish; July, a few; August, a little better. Then September: "Took our limit before lunch. . . .Caught all we could eat for breakfast. . . . Fishing excellent, caught all we wanted. . . .Got our limit, enjoyed every minute." The secret was out, but this was May and we had only the next day to find where Clowhom hid its trout through the spring and summer.

It was a mystery we failed to solve. We fished up river and down through the morning. We tried the drop-off by the river mouths with a variety of flies and a box of spinning gear. We tried trolling, casting and even drifting a humble worm and got not so much as a half-hearted strike. Soon we were on our way down the lake, trolling slowly much of the way and stopping at every likely-looking spot to test the water with muddler minnow fly and spin-cast worm, but we reached the waiting boat without a fish to show. Some September day under Indian summer skies we'll explore anew the coast mountain lake waiting at the head of Salmon Inlet for the adventuresome few.

Lower Mainland Lakes

*E*levation plays a key role in determining the angling quality of Lower Mainland lakes. High lakes provide good angling during the hot-weather months while lakes of lower elevation are best fished in spring and fall. Also, high-country lakes most often provide uncrowded angling conditions. For this reason, many Lower Mainland waters are grouped by elevation. On the other hand, lakes lying north and south of the Fraser Valley are found under the Remote Urban Lakes heading, as no popular, easily reached Fraser Valley lakes are listed. Lakes of the Sunshine Coast are broken into two groupings: the waters of the Powell Forest and the lakes of the Sechelt Peninsula.

Squamish North High-Elevation Lakes

The lakes under this heading are alpine, subalpine or high-elevation waters where ice-off may not occur before July. These are the lakes to fish during high summer when the doldrums have set in on lakes of lower elevation. Such waters often provide excellent dry-fly fishing and most traditional B.C. patterns should do well, although the smaller patterns tend to out-perform the large, bushy-style flies. Those who have conquered the intricacies of chironomid fishing can expect fast fishing. Ultra-light spinning tackle will also do well, but only the finest lines should be used, as the fish in these lakes rarely grow large. It is their spectacular settings which makes these lakes special.

» MAMQUAM LAKE—A large hike-in lake in the scenic southwestern part of Garibaldi Park, reputed to hold rainbow trout to three pounds and better. Located in the Black Tusk Nature Conservancy Area, a tough 11-kilometre hike is required from Elfin Lakes, which are about another 11 kilometres from the parking area. There are no developed campsites at Mamquam, but tenting is possible; there is an overnight shelter with wood and propane at Elfin (fee charged). Total elevation gain is about 1,100 metres. To get there turn east off Hwy 99 onto the Mamquam Road, four kilometres north of Squamish, then on a good logging road to the parking lot just beyond the Mamquam River bridge.

» GARIBALDI AND LESSER GARIBALDI LAKES—These two alpine-meadow lakes reached over the Black Tusk trail are in the scenic heart of Garibaldi Park, with wildflowers, glaciers, spectacular mountains, and volcanic rock walls. The lake is normally iced over until July, then provides good fishing for smaller rainbow trout through the fall, with occasional larger fish (16-18 inches). Turn east off Hwy 99, 37 kilometres north of Squamish on the paved road to the Rubble Creek parking lot. Hike is about nine kilometres and climbs 810 metres on a well-graded trail. Watch for impressive stands of old-growth fir and cedar on the way. Nearby Lesser Garibaldi holds lower numbers of smaller fish.

» ANNE, LITTLE ANNE, BELKNAP, AND NORTON LAKES—This group of small and difficult-to-reach lakes lies north of Indian Arm in the Hixon Creek area. All have been stocked with rainbow trout to provide quality wilderness fishing, but Norton Lake has long had a reputation for producing fair-sized rainbow trout with some reports of heavy fish. Topographical maps should be used as both Annes require short hikes. South of Squamish, take the Stawamus Creek logging road west off Hwy 99, then the Indian River road to the Hixon Creek spur, about 50 rough kilometres from Squamish.

» ASHLU CREEK LAKES—Two alpine lakes in the headwaters of Ashlu Creek were stocked with rainbow trout in the late 1980s to provide high-country wilderness angling. Take the Squamish River road west off Hwy 99 and cross the river to the Ashlu Creek road; poor road conditions may mean a long hike is required.

» LIZZIE LAKE—This relatively large alpine lake off the east side of Lillooet Lake offers fast fishing for small rainbow trout. Little Lizzie Lake is nearby, over a rough road which is best walked. This same trail crosses into the headwaters of the Stein Valley. To get to Lizzie turn south off the Duffey Lake Road at Joffre Creek on the Lillooet Lake road; follow this as far as the third Forest Service campsite where the Lizzie Creek road branches off to the east and leads to the lake.

» JOFFRE LAKES—Three small high-country lakes in the Joffre Creek Recreation Area (established walk-in campsites) produce small rainbow trout in a wilderness setting. Unlike many of the other lakes under this heading, roads are good all the way, but all three lakes require short walks. The two most distant lakes, about two kilometres from the end of the road, are alpine lakes. Turn south off the Duffey Lake Road about 30 kilometres northeast of Pemberton onto the short access road to the parking area and trailhead for these lakes.

» LAKE LOVELY WATER—The 1,300-hectare hike-in-only provincial recreation area (parks status under review) takes its name from this high-country lake reputed to hold rainbow trout to about one pound. A boat is required to cross the Squamish River, then access is by trail for about five kilometres. Contact the Parks Branch for specific trail information or study relevant topographical maps.

» CHEAKAMUS LAKE—Again, it is the setting which makes the lake special more than its fish, although Cheakamus is believed to hold sizeable Dolly Varden char. Rainbow trout typically measure 10 inches. A pleasant 3.2-kilometre long trail through old-growth timber leads to the lake from the parking lot. Take a logging road east off Hwy 99, 48 kilometres north of Squamish (follows Cheakamus River). Mountains tower 1,600 metres above the thickly forested shores of this glacier-fed lake.

» JANE LAKES—These two small, walk-in lakes are reported to hold large, fussy rainbow trout. Jane is the larger of the two and holds the largest fish as well, notoriously difficult rainbows to four-pounds-plus. Nearby Crater Lake is tiny, but grows trout to about two pounds with good numbers of smaller fish. A gravel road branching east off Hwy 99 between the turnoffs for the Cheakamus River road (going east) and the Callaghan Creek road (going west) leads to these lakes. Expect to walk about three kilometres of this road unless equipped with four-wheel drive, but even then some walking will likely be required.

Squamish North Low-Elevation Lakes

These lakes are the other side of the coin from the lakes listed above. Generally, they are lakes of low to mid-elevation best fished in spring and again in the fall, although there are exceptions. A late-arriving spring means the fishing will hold longer than normal, just as a cool, dismal summer means better fishing in June and July. Late July through August is probably the worst time to fish the lakes under this heading. Fall fishing begins as soon as water temperatures cool. The fish found in these lakes tend to be considerably larger than those found in the high-country lakes.

» LUCILLE LAKE—Five-pound-plus rainbow trout and some eastern brook trout have been reported in this small lake. The lake foreshore is owned by Alpine Lodge, which provides access, boat rentals and facilities. The lake is near Hwy 99 and is reached by crossing the Cheakamus River just south of Garibaldi.

» STANLEY LAKE—Handy to nearby Lucille Lake, this tiny lake produces rainbow trout to about 16 inches and provides nice small-water angling. Stanley lies north of Lucille Lake, just off the south end of Daisy Lake on Hwy 99.

» STARVATION LAKE—There have been reports of larger rainbow trout (five-pounds-plus), but mainly fish in the two-pound range are found in this tiny lake tucked between Hwy 99 and the Cheakamus River. To get there take the Cheakamus River Road off Hwy 99 and stay on the east side of the river to the end of the road. A walk may be required for the final approach. Difficult shore fishing; boat recommended.

» BUTTERFLY LAKE—This lake was known to hold rainbow trout to four pounds and better and likely still yields some larger fish, although reports of good catches of 10-inch fish indicate a change. Still, unless the lake has been altered in some drastic way, it should again provide good fishing for larger trout at some time; it's a lake to watch. It drains into the Cheakamus River from the west side and is reached by taking a spur east off the Squamish River road shortly past Cheekye. Rough road conditions will likely mean a walk of several kilometres.

» HUT LAKE—This is one of a number of previously barren lakes stocked with rainbow trout. How large the planted trout will grow in such lakes is a function of the chemistry and biology of each individual lake. Anglers will have to test the waters until a body of lore is established. This makes for intriguing angling. Access is difficult and the setting is in wild country. Directions are as for Starvation Lake, but a rough road to the west is taken shortly after the first crossing of the Cheakamus River; expect some walking. Levette Lake is passed on the way.

» STUMP LAKE—This walk-in lake in popular Alice Lake Provincial Park, 13 kilometres north of Squamish, holds mainly smaller rainbow trout with occasional larger fish, but it is the planting of splake some years back which makes this lake unique. Splake are a cross between lake char and eastern brook trout, also a char (see chapter six). This fertile hybrid is popular in eastern Canada but virtually unknown in B.C. Survival and growth rates are unknown. Char become aggressive and are more easily caught in the fall months—a good time to probe for these fish. A hike of less than one kilometre on a trail from the north end of Alice Lake provides access.

» IVEY LAKE—This Pemberton area lake was officially designated a catch-and-release lake in the late 1980s, but anglers who earlier discovered its exceptional rainbow trout traditionally released their fish. Single barbless hooks make sense and are in any case mandatory. The rainbow trout grown in this smallish lake are huge, to eight pounds and perhaps better, so it is prudent to prepare for release of large, strong fish. Heavy leaders are a must to minimize fish stress. To get there, watch for a gravel B.C. Hydro road branching west off the paved road to D'Arcy immediately after leaving Pemberton.

Remote Urban Lakes

The term may seem contradictory, but there are, in fact, a number of lakes not far from urban or suburban areas which qualify as remote. Considerable effort is required to reach many of these waters, which seems only fitting. Most lakes were stocked under a Fisheries Branch program initiated in the mid-1980s to develop small-lake wilderness fishing opportunities, so there is no question there are fish to be caught. The fish tend to be small, but there are exceptions: some lakes hold rainbow trout to five pounds and perhaps more. Lakes with smaller fish most often provide fast angling; lakes holding larger fish are no different here from anywhere else in the province: fussy fish and slow an-

gling with exciting exceptions when the hatch is successfully matched during a feeding spree.

» WIDGEON LAKE—This is a tough lake to get to, first by canoe or other shallow-draft boat across Pitt Polder and up
Widgeon Creek, then a hike of between 10 and 12
kilometres over a Forest Service trail (old logging road).
It is a large lake; consider packing float-tubes on bicycles.
The lake does have a reputation for large rainbow trout,
so the effort involved should pay handsome rewards.
Nearby boat-access only Fossli Provincial Park (53 hectares)
with its short hiking trail (three kilometres) makes an interesting side trip. Contact the Forest Service for trail particulars.

» DENNETT AND MUNRO LAKES—These two small walk-in lakes
(Dennett is tiny) in Coquitlam's Burke Mountain Regional Park are worthy of a fall outing for the chance to catch
eastern brook trout at the peak of their spectacular fall
coloration. Hiking distance is the same for both, about
four kilometres, but reaching larger Munro involves a
tough, steep walk with faster fishing as a result. Fish in
both lakes are small. Access to the park is north off Hwy
7 on Coast Meridian Road; contact Fisheries Branch or
GVRD for trail particulars.

» MORGAN LAKE—One of a small group of lakes between
Alouette and Stave lakes. Access is restricted, but Morgan is a fly-only lake with mandatory release required,
normally an indication of quality angling. Nearby Cedar
(Sayers) Lake has a single-hook and bait-ban restriction
with a one-fish limit. Both hold eastern brook trout; Cedar also has rainbow trout, but there is no confirmation
of this species in Morgan. Ongoing logging road construction in the area between Stave and Alouette lakes makes
for changeable access (traditionally by way of Devil's
Lake); contact Lower Mainland Fisheries Branch office for
updates. Adventurers with topographical maps and a boat

suited to Alouette Lake can reach Morgan by a combination of boating and hiking.

» STACEY LAKE—This tiny lake on a good road in the high country south and west of Harrison Lake is stocked with rainbow trout, as is nearby, but more difficult to reach, Campbell Lake. Both are part of the small-lake wilderness angling program initiated by the Fisheries Branch in the mid-1980s. To get there, leave Hwy 7 east of Harrison Mills on the Woodside Mountain logging road.

» GRACE, WOLF AND FRANCIS LAKES—These three lakes are known for their abundant but small rainbow trout and wild settings. All are in the same general area northeast of Harrison Mills. Take the logging road south of Weaver Lake (a rainbow trout spawning view area in March/April) off the Morris Valley Road to Grace Lake; Wolf is immediately to the south, Francis is past Grace on a steep continuation of this road. Nearby Morris Lake is reputed to hold large cutthroat trout.

» MOSS LAKES—On the east side of Harrison Lake with access through Sasquatch Provincial Park (northeast of Harrison Hot Springs), this small group of walk-in lakes are known for good numbers of small rainbow trout and uncrowded angling conditions. It usually requires a hike over a rough road which is closed to vehicles, south near Deer Lake in the park.

» SLOLLICUM LAKE—In alpine country 1,700 metres above Harrison Lake, this walk-in lake has a persistent rumour concerning the size of its fish. The setting alone will make the walk worthwhile, with larger fish, if any, an added bonus. Look for a branch road forking east within five kilometres north of Sasquatch Park. Walk from where the road gets too rough to drive. Topographical maps will show the way to a second nearby lake.

» FLORA, GREENDROP AND LINDEMAN LAKES—This group of small lakes north of Chilliwack Lake are known favourites. There are large fish for skilled fly fishers, notably in Flora, which lies in an alpine valley separate from the others. Greendrop and Lindeman are drained by Post Creek in an adjacent valley. All have fair to good numbers of smaller fish, but provide a better-than-average chance of larger rainbow trout. Lindeman also offers cutthroat trout. Look for the rough 8-kilometre trail to Flora Lake's alpine country from near Chilliwack Lake Provincial Park (past the Post Creek campsite). Allow at least two days, preferably longer. Greendrop and Lindeman are reached over the Centennial Trail near the campsite at Post Creek. Lindeman is about three kilometres in and is suitable for family hiking; Greendrop is another three kilometres up the trail. All three are ideal fly-fishing lakes.

» HANGING LAKE—This alpine gem is known to anglers for its fair-to good-sized rainbow trout and picture-perfect setting. Reached by trail (about five kilometres) off the south end of Chilliwack Lake.

» MANNING PARK LAKES—Of the four lakes in the Lightning Lakes chain, Flash Lake is reputed to hold slightly larger rainbow trout than the others, but eight to 10-inch fish are typical in these high-country lakes. Conditions are somewhat more crowded than in the remote lakes previously outlined due to the park's popularity. The Heather Trail winds through more than 24 kilometres of subalpine meadows with the carpet of wild flowers extending on either side to a width of about five kilometres. Tiny Snowshoe Lake is about 13.5 kilometres in on this trail from the Blackwell Peak parking area and provides alpine fishing for small rainbow trout.

» GARRISON LAKE—Large rainbow trout are reported in this small hike-in lake reached over a poor trail from a logging road near Sunday Creek off Hwy 3. Access is difficult, with some searching involved, but reports of heavy rainbow trout will make the effort worthwhile for dedicated anglers.

Powell Forest Lakes

A canoe route links eight coastal lakes in the Powell Forest immediately north of Powell River on good logging roads. This chain of lakes provides fair-to-good angling for cutthroat trout, especially during spring and fall, and is highly recommended. The road to the start of the circuit at Lois Lake is unrestricted. From Lois it is possible to reach the other lakes by canoe with short portages averaging about 1.5 kilometres. By road, access to the Powell Forest lakes is restricted to nonworking hours. Contact the local Forest Service office in Powell River before travelling these roads, as travel times and road conditions vary considerably. All the lakes contain wild cutthroat trout and some hold kokanee as well. None have been stocked. A brief description of each follows.

» LOIS LAKE—This large lake (dammed) is the start of the Powell Forest canoe route, a good bet for anglers who enjoy paddling lake chains. It produces many good fish and has not been heavily fished in recent years. Concentrate on the areas around islands and back bays. Lois connects with Khartoum Lake, which is best fished at the outlet to Lois and where the creek flows in at the head of the lake. Both are best in spring and fall.

» HORSESHOE LAKE—The shoreline is strongly indented with narrow deep bays; concentrate on points and the channel connecting to Nanton Lake, especially near weed beds. There are some big fish and many smaller—a good trolling lake.

» NANTON LAKE—This small lake produces large fish in surprising numbers. A nice creek flows in from Ireland Lake where spawning kokanee can be seen in September/-

October. Concentrate on the channel from Horseshoe, the creek mouth and shallows to each side. This lake is known for its strong spring midge hatches which bring the larger cutthroat to the surface.

» IRELAND LAKE—A sure producer of small fish, with some larger. Concentrate on the creek inlet area from Dodd Lake and the outlet shallows to Nanton. Buggy nymphs on sinking lines work well.

» DODD LAKE—Once the chain's top producer of large fish, Dodd is now recovering from overfishing in the 1960s and 1970s. Some very large cutthroat are left, and are best taken trolling or fly casting/spin fishing in bays and shallows. Catch-and-release is advised; this lake needs to rebuild.

» WINDSOR LAKE—Higher in elevation than the others, it may be frozen in March; there are good midge hatches in April or shortly after ice-off. The fish tend to be small, but it is a lovely lake.

» POWELL AND GOAT LAKES—Powell is a large inlet-style lake difficult to fish without intimate local knowledge. Often wind-swept during afternoons, the lake is best suited to larger boats, although it is part of the canoe route (evenings or early mornings are best for small-boat crossings). It holds rainbow trout stocked in the 1930s and exceptional cutthroat. Goat is a mountain-trough-style lake and is described in the section on wild waters in this chapter.

Sechelt Peninsula Lakes

With a few exceptions, cutthroat trout fishing on Sechelt Peninsula lakes was poor until a major lake restocking program was initiated in the late 1970s. Since then many of the lakes have recovered and some are now overstocked. Generally, the fish will not be as large as those found further north in the harder-to-reach Powell Forest area.

» CROWSTON LAKE—This lake was barren until stocking in 1984. A small weedy lake in a wilderness setting, it now produces 14- to 16-inch fish. Look for the gravel access road off Hwy 101 just east of Trout Lake.

» WORMY LAKE—Not part of the stocking program, but it is said to produce many good fish and is rated as an excellent early-season lake. Northeast of Halfmoon Bay for about 10 kilometres by logging road to the lake.

» TROUT LAKE—A small lake located on Hwy 101 in the Halfmoon Bay area, Trout is overlooked by many anglers. Fish hard against the weed beds on the far side. This is a productive lake with cutthroats in the two- to 2.5-pound range. Contains sticklebacks, leeches, snails.

» KLEIN LAKE—A pretty lake in rugged country, this is a popular local lake. Overstocked, it should produce many smaller fish. Leave Hwy 101 at the Egmont road, then watch for a logging road at the west end of North Lake.

For more information contact:

Fisheries Branch
10334-152A Street
Surrey, B.C.
V3R 7P8

Southwestern B.C. Tourist Association
Box 48610, Bentall P.O.
Vancouver, B.C.
V7X 1A3

CHAPTER THREE

Thompson-Nicola

The Thompson-Nicola is British Columbia's trout-fishing mecca. Rod-in-hand travel to the rolling, lake-dotted plateau framed by the Fraser River in the west and the Okanagan system to the east is like undertaking a pilgrimage. Anglers have been venturing here since the early 1800s, lured by tales of a special breed of trout. They called them silver trout, these fish which dazzled the eye and grew to impossible sizes. Those who came with flies and fly rods brought back incredible tales, but the anglers who followed soon learned that the size, strength and raw power of this magnificent new fish matched in every way the wild settings in which they were found. Within the span of a few decades, the reputation of these waters was solidly established, but nowhere more so than in fly fishing circles. In the wilds of far-flung British Columbia, it was whispered, there lived a trout which readily took the fly and provided sport unlike any other.

What followed is unique in the history of angling. Rich barren waters in other parts of the globe have been stocked and produced excellent angling, but in every case I know of the fish were brought in from overseas. Tasmania's fabled brown trout fishery has a similar history, but the fish introduced to the barren lakes of the Central Plateau were brought in from England. The waters of Tasmania, New Zealand and South America all produce incredible fishing for large trout, but only the Thompson-Nicola came complete with its own strain of fish specially adapted to the waters in which it was found. Its range was not extensive, limited to Kamloops Lake and a handful of other large interior lakes, but this was soon remedied. The countless small barren lakes of the plateau were soon stocked with this unique strain of trout, both officially and otherwise, and even today the names of these lakes remain synonymous with some of the best small-lake angling in the world.

A unique set of circumstances conspired to make all this possible. When Fort Kamloops was established in 1812, the large, chrome-plated trout found in the waters of the big lake were simply called silver trout. When the science of the day was called upon to identify these fish, they were officially classed as a new species and given the name *Salmo kamloopsii* in honour of the lake. Today we know them as Kamloops trout and they are officially classed as *Salmo gairdneri*, the term used for all strains of the rainbow trout, be they the small fish of the alpine tarns or the large seagoing strains we call steelhead. The silver trout of Fort Kamloops, it turned out, was not a separate species, but yet another example of the rainbow trout's amazing ability to change shape, size and coloration as an adaptation to its environment. It took some time for this to become evident. Attempts to move the Kamloops to waters outside its British Columbia home met with almost universal failure. The fabled trout of the Kamloops country could not be moved because it was—and remains—a product of its unique environment.

There are various theories to explain the presence of these fish in the large lakes of the interior. The view now held by many is that they were originally seagoing fish. Some of these steelhead trout naturally adapted to life in the large lakes, while others were forced to make the adaptation when routes to the sea became blocked for one reason or another. So they were large rainbow trout right from the start, but experience has shown that steelhead stocked in lakes do not necessarily retain their size. Steelhead fry stocked in waters which produce small trout do not grow to large sizes. They adapt to the biological and chemical factors at work in the environment to which they are introduced. In the case of Thompson-Nicola waters, the majority of which are replete with all the elements required to grow superbly conditioned fish, the steelhead becomes the Kamloops trout, a bright silver fish renowned for its speed, strength, and endurance.

The Nutrient-Rich Lakes

Climate and the make-up of the soil surrounding the lakes of the southern Interior Plateau account for the exceptional condition and fast growth rates of the fish. We have already seen how the lakes of Vancouver Island and coastal British Columbia in general typically require between six and seven years to grow a trout measuring 16 or 17 inches. The rich lakes of the interior will produce fish of similar size in as little as two years. Where coastal lakes are acidic, the interior lakes are alkaline; while the coastal lakes are nutrient-poor, the interior lakes are nutrient-rich: it is the surrounding soil which makes the difference. The soil of the interior is highly mineralized. As rainwater seeps through the soil

on its way to the lakes, it dissolves and carries with it the minerals and nutrients required to produce fertile waters. Calcium, potassium and magnesium are carried into the lakes by underground springs, natural seepage, creeks and streams. The result is a potent brew which has all the requirements necessary to grow rich flora and fauna.

These small rich lakes of the plateau were originally barren of fish, but they teemed with aquatic insects. Mayflies, dragonflies, damselflies, caddisflies and a host of others lived in superabundance, with few predators to check their growth and spread, until man entered the picture and began the stocking process which continues to this day. When Kamloops trout were first introduced to such super-rich waters, they grew at rates which are inconceivable today. T. W. Lambert, in his 1907 *Fishing in British Columbia*, recounts the tale of a three-day fly fishing trip to Lac le Jeune during the summer of 1897. Lambert and a friend caught 1,500 fish over the three days. Cleaned and salted, the catch weighed an incredible 700 pounds. Another lake, unofficially stocked by anglers with nine trout, produced fish weighing in excess of 15 pounds only three years later. Fish of eight and 10 pounds were considered common fare.

Of the minerals which are ultimately responsible for the richness of these lakes, calcium is the most important. Usually it is picked up as the water seeps through the soil or when it passes over a natural deposit of limestone. Scuds, the small crustaceans which more than any other single factor account for the Kamloops' superb condition, require calcium to grow. It is calcium which neutralizes otherwise acidic water. Calcium also plays a key role in helping develop the marl bottoms which characterize many of the interior's best lakes. For all that, the presence of calcium and other vital minerals is not enough to account for the richness of these waters. Climate is the other key ingredient, and here again the difference between coast and interior could not be more dramatic, especially from the angler's perspective.

Relatively short winters and a long, hot, dry growing season mark the southern interior climate, but it is the low annual rainfall which is vital for both anglers and fish. Low rainfall and the regular-as-clockwork afternoon winds which are the bane of Kamloops waters combine to create extraordinary rates of evaporation. High annual rainfall on parts of Vancouver Island and the Lower Mainland flushes large volumes of water through the regions' lakes—valuable nutrients are washed away with the rain. In the dry, semi-arid interior this is not a problem, but even so, the mineral deposits added to the lakes through seepage would be in relatively low concentrations were it not for the combination of heat and wind which quickly evaporates lake water. Water is picked up and dispersed by evaporation, but the vital minerals and nutrients are left behind in far greater concentrations than before.

So it really is a fortuitous set of circumstances, a combination unique to the southern Interior Plateau, which has brought us the Kamloops trout. Deep blue along the back with a fine scattering of black spots, its sides are remarkably bright, flashing like chrome when the fish jumps or turns suddenly under water. In its third or fourth year, when it will spawn for the first time, it develops a rosy hue along the sides and cheek plates which grows darker and more pronounced as the May spawning time draws closer. But the younger fish remain uniformly bright with snowy white undersides and little or nothing of the coloration which gives the rainbow trout its name. At first they feed greedily, in the way of young fish, but they soon learn the seasonal cycles and the various food items each season brings. Very quickly they key to the staples of their diet, making them a difficult fish for the angler who knows little of their habits. For all the richness of its waters, the staples of the Kamloops' diet are relatively few and their various cycles easily learned.

The Seasons of the Fly

Through the winter months when the lakes remain sealed beneath their layer of ice, the Kamloops sustains itself on scuds. These small crustaceans and their role in the aquatic food chain are important enough to warrant a section of their own (see chapter five). Scuds are available to the fish through the year, but are most important in winter and fall when other aquatic creatures are at their lowest ebb. So under their roof of ice the trout browse on scuds and leeches, the stand-bys to which they always turn when the aquatic insects are inactive.

It is in the spring when the warming snow melts the slowly rotting ice from the surface of the lakes that the Kamloops again becomes an active hunter. Ice-off in May signals the start of the midge hatches. These tiny, worm-like creatures are found in every lake in the province but are incredibly abundant in the rich waters of the interior. The hatch typically peaks towards the end of the month and the fishing may then become poor with this superabundance of feed in the water. The fish become extraordinarily fussy, keying specifically on one type of midge to the exclusion of all others, or taking the midges only during one specific stage of their journey from lake bottom to surface. But early on, when the hatch is just starting, the Kamloops will take them all and the first rods on the water in spring can do remarkably well with suitable imitations.

Next come the mayflies. The much-celebrated mayfly is not as significant in Kamloops waters as it is elsewhere, but it is still an important element in the seasonal cycle and no angler should venture on Thompson-Nicola waters without a variety of patterns, including adults and nymphs. The mayfly hatch begins as the midges taper off, normally late in May and early June. If the traditional afternoon wind concentrates the emerging mayflies in one corner of the lake, there can be incredibly fast fishing as the Kamloops follow the wind-blown insects.

As spring warmth increases, terrestrials such as ants take to the air. Given the right conditions—a good wind during a peak emergence, for instance—these non-aquatic insects can become available to the fish in large numbers. A short but intense feeding spree follows, but it is the aquatic insects which draw the most attention. During the first two weeks of June, conditions are normally right for the emergence of damselflies. This aquatic insect leaves the safety of its weedy home and rises to within centimetres of the surface. There it levels off to begin an awkward shoreward swim in full view of the fish looking up from below. This triggers an immediate and often savage response and makes for some of the most exciting fishing of the year.

Almost at the same time and continuing for some period afterward, the large dragonfly nymphs begin their shoreward journey, creeping slowly along the bottom as if loath to follow the example of their close relative, the damselfly. This is less explosive angling: patterns must be fished deep on sinking lines or leaders long enough to get the fly to the bottom and keep it there for the longest time possible. It is nonetheless exciting angling, as a Kamloops which takes the hook on or near bottom will almost always burst to the surface, leaving the angler frantically stripping in line to recover the large U formed in the line by the fish's surface rush.

By the middle of June the first sedge, or caddisfly, hatches begin and anglers who know this hatch will long since have started eagerly scanning the water for the first signs of the large travelling sedges for which the Thompson-Nicola is famous. The caddis is one of the more fragile aquatic insects and entire populations have been wiped out by a variety of factors, but there are still many lakes which support good populations. This insect provides the most exciting, nerve-tingling angling of the year wherever populations are strong enough to produce a good hatch. The Kamloops preys on the caddis from the moment it leaves the safety of the home it has built for itself and heads for the surface. At the surface it has difficulty breaking free of its skin and, as an adult, getting airborne from the water's surface. The sight of these large insects struggling on the surface sends the fish into a frenzy unlike anything they display during the emergence of other insects. Anglers traditionally fish adult imitations on the dry line, skittering the fly across the surface after the fashion of the naturals. The explosive takes which follow are for many the high point of the Thompson-Nicola angling season.

After the first week or two of July the summer doldrums set in. Fishing in the lakes of higher elevation will remain good for several more weeks as the later-starting hatches catch up, but, inevitably, high water temperatures take their toll. The fast fishing of the spring and early summer winds down and a long period of slow fishing follows. The hatches are off and the fish seek the depths where cooler water makes life more comfortable. For the angler it can be a dreary time, searching the water with deeply sunken flies, such as scuds or leeches or various nymph patterns, in the hope of enticing a strike. When it does happen the reward seems greater for the hours put in, but it is slow fishing and many a veteran Thompson-Nicola trout fisher digs out the salmon gear and heads for the coast. Still, there are fish to be caught for those who would work for them and on the highest lakes the summer doldrum period can be relatively short.

In early September the flying ants make a second appearance. These late summer ants are more eagerly received than the spring emergence, almost as if the fish were as anxious to feed at the surface as are anglers to dig out their long-neglected dry lines. By contrast the fish greet the Indian summer hatch of beetle-like backswimmers and water boatmen with reluctance. They do take them, however, and suitable imitations will enjoy a brief but intense flurry before they are put back in their corner of the fly box for another year.

By the middle of the month any lingering hatches of midges, never as intense as the spring break-out to begin with, will have tapered off to nothing and the time will have come for the searching patterns, the scuds and leeches and dragonfly nymphs. This late-season fishing can be very good, even if there is little call for the dry line and the time of explosive surface takes is well past. As if they know the time of ice is fast approaching, the fish feed with a reckless-ness that is reminiscent of the spring. This is almost cer-tainly caused by lower water temperatures, but whatever the reasons, it is a fine time to be on the water. There is a snap-py crispness to the air, the aspens are a browny gold, shore-side bushes turn red and the fish fight with a special vigour.

For newcomers to the sport, spring and fall offer the best chances of success as the fish are more certain to respond, especially to scud and leech patterns. Many anglers seem reluctant to use leech patterns, but they are a good fly for searching any time and are especially effective near or after sunset and in spring and fall. They are also relatively easy to fish, as virtually any combination of retrieves will answer as long as they are slow. In any case, no fly box for Thomp-son-Nicola waters is really complete without a few good leech patterns, notably in the 2.5- to four-centimetre size range. The larger leech patterns are not taken as readily and are ungainly to cast as well.

At the height of the season, late May, June and early July, the fishing often becomes quite complex for all but ex-perienced hands. Choosing a fly pattern based on the colour of the lake bottom and its vegetation is always a good way to start, but the key, as always when fishing the fly, lies in experimentation and observation. This really cannot be

Leech

stressed enough. The successful anglers will always be those who are attuned to what is happening around them and who are ready to leave behind preconceived notions and risk experimentation.

Closeup: A Primer of Thompson-Nicola Aquatic Insects

*F*ussy rainbow trout in wonderfully rich, small, angling lakes are the hallmarks of the Thompson-Nicola. The region provides some of the best small-lake angling in the world. For the angler who ventures out unprepared, these waters can also provide some of the world's most frustrating angling. Large, well-fed trout in rich waters are rarely easy fish. The Kamloops trout in particular is notorious for keying to specific foods at specific times. With few exceptions these food items are aquatic insects. The angler who knows the seasonal patterns of these insects and has a working knowledge of their habits is well on the way to consistent success.

Fortunately, several generations of dedicated anglers have laid the groundwork for those who follow. The seasonal patterns of the Kamloops trout and its basic food items are well known. In recent years anglers have taken to very precise imitation of the various aquatic insects important in Thompson-Nicola lakes. Technical fishing is the term most often used for this style of angling. Newcomers to the sport should not be put off by such exacting standards. Entire generations of anglers managed handsomely fishing basic "buggy" fly patterns. These impressionistic patterns resemble real-life insects only vaguely; any one might be taken for a wide number of insects. Old standbys such as the Carey look like nothing that ever lived in a lake, but give the impression of just about everything.

If there is a knack to successfully fishing buggy-looking

flies it lies in the way they are moved. Creeping along the bottom, the Carey or any of its many equivalents is a dragonfly nymph; rising slowly from the bottom, it is an emerging caddisfly; fished just subsurface and sculling shoreward, it is an emerging damselfly, and so on. The impressionistic pattern, for all its blurred vagueness, should still be fished to represent something in particular. Whether the angler opts for exact replicas or vague impressions, a smattering of aquatic lore is required.

Coming to a basic understanding of the handful of aquatic insects which are the mainstays of Thompson-Nicola waters is not difficult. It is out on the water that things become complex. Keen observation is required to solve the riddle of the day. Turning over shoreside rocks, searching among the reeds for signs of emerging insects, or scooping a newly hatched insect from the surface to make the necessary identification are all part of the day's work.

The aquatic world is a fascinating place, full of wonder and mystery. A tiny creature creeping about its weedy underwater home will suddenly leave its safe refuge to struggle to the surface. In the nether zone of the surface film, a place neither entirely water nor entirely air, the insect tears itself out of its skin and transforms into an airborne thing of grace and beauty. Knowledge and experience of this strange, secretive realm is one of the bonuses of angling.

Brief sketches of the major aquatic insects are provided below, along with their most likely times of emergence. The specific classifications given are always for the dominant species. Matching patterns are not provided. There is an ulterior motive behind this omission. The sketches which follow are bare-bones basics; it is hoped they will lead to further reading. Matching fly patterns can be found in a number of excellent books specifically focused on aquatic insects. Some of the best titles are listed in the Bibliography at the back of this book.

Midges

Order: Diptera **Family:** Chironomidae

**Chironomid
(midge) larva**

» **IDENTIFYING FEATURES**

Larvae: The body looks like a segmented tube, almost like a thin worm. Important colours include shades of red, green and brown.

Pupae: The head, thorax and wing pads are closely clumped together; the thorax is much larger than during the pupal stage (it contains the wings of the adult). White tufts (breathing filaments) are visible at the head and the tip of the abdomen. The body remains segmented with no tails. Prominent colours are black, green and brown.

Adult: Great variety (includes crane flies, house flies and mosquitoes among others); rarely important to fish.

» **WHAT TO LOOK FOR**

**Chironomid
(midge) pupa**

As the pupae break through the lake's surface to become adults, they leave behind an almost transparent husk or shell, called the pupal shuck. Watch the water carefully for these shucks—a sure sign midges have been or are hatching. Bulging surface rises in spring signal fish taking midge pupae just beneath the surface.

» **LIFE CYCLE**

Midges are found in virtually every lake, pond and tarn in B.C. During the larval stage they are bottom dwellers, inhabitating all zones from shoreline shallows to depths of 70 metres and deeper. Mass migrations can occur in spring and fall when larvae look for new homes or move into deeper water to overwinter. The fish respond accordingly. The pupal stage is normally the most heavily preyed upon. When the

pupae are fully formed, they begin a
rather awkward migration to the surface, frantically wiggling their worm-
like bodies from side to side, but achiev-
ing little upward movement, although
trapped air beneath the pupal shuck
helps lift them upward. At the surface
the pupae have difficulty breaking
through and may hang suspended just
beneath the surface film for some time.
Finally, the pupal shuck splits along the
back and the adult emerges, taking
wing very quickly in search of a mate.
Females return to lay their eggs on the
lake's surface; the eggs sink to the lake

**Chironomid
(midge) adult**

bottom and the cycle is repeated. For most species the entire life cycle is completed within one year.

» **WHEN TO FISH**

Immediately after ice-off in the spring, midge pupae begin their journey to the surface and adulthood. They provide trout with the first real feast of the year. While there
will always be some midges hatching through the ice-free
months, nothing equals the frenzied activity of early spring.
Mid-May to mid-June is peak midge-fishing time.

» **HOW TO FISH**

Fishing Chironomidae pupae sounds like high-tech fly
fishing, but in reality it is not much different from light-line
fishing with hook and worm. Using a floating line and long
leader, with the boat anchored bow and stern, a suitable
pupal imitation is cast with the wind. The angler does nothing more; wind and wave action will normally impart life-
like action to the imitation. If too much wind moves the fly
in an unrealistic manner, find a more sheltered spot to fish.
It is important to maintain a direct link with the fly: keep
the line as straight as possible and hold the rod tip down,
pointed at the water. A strike indicator attached where line

and leader meet can be a big help, as the take is very soft and can easily go undetected. When a fish is felt it is vital to set the hook lightly or risk breaking off. Do this by lifting only the rod, leaving the line free. Known as a slip strike, the technique is not difficult but requires practice; the instinct to tightly grip the line must be overcome.

» **HINTS**

During the heat of summer and again in late fall, trout will take midge larvae on the bottom. In many interior lakes these larvae are deep red in colour because they possess hemoglobin—the famous "bloodworms" of the interior lakes. Suitable imitations can be fished near bottom with sinking lines. Retrieve the line very slowly, a series of two-centimetre strips followed by a long pause can be effective. Takes are extremely delicate so the key is absolute concentration. Think of this type of fishing as a form of meditation.

The Mayflies

Order: Ephemeroptera **Family:** Baetidae **Genus:** Callibaetis

» **IDENTIFYING FEATURES**

Nymphs: Distinguishing features include three fringed tails of equal length, long antennae and large abdominal gills. Colour is pale green or mottled olive, also light to dark gray. They are capable of rapid movement marked by quick flips of the tail propelling them forward in 15-centimetre bursts. Active through the year, they are most available to fish during their emergence swim.

Adults: There are two stages: the dun and the sexually mature spinner. Duns are duller in colour than the glossy spinners, which

Callibaetis **(mayfly) nymph**

emerge once the duns have shed their outer skin. Wings of both are held upright on the water and are often likened to small sailboats.

» WHAT TO LOOK FOR

Large mating swarms of spinners congregate between mid-morning and late afternoon either over the water or over open areas nearby. Bird activity provides good clues. Female spinners return to the water to lay their eggs, dipping the tips of their abdomens to the water to release their eggs, normally without coming to rest. Bulging rise forms during emergence of duns on the surface indicate trout are feeding on nymphs just subsurface. Splashy rises indicate fish are feeding on adults.

» LIFE CYCLE

Much has been made of the mayfly, but the cycle is simple; it is the fishing which becomes complex. Mayflies can survive almost anything and are found in all lake types. Nymphs prefer the near-shore or shallow water zones and are rarely found deeper than about six metres. Dense mats of aquatic vegetation are the preferred habitat. They become most active prior to emergence, often swimming far from cover, and thus become available to fish some time before emergence. Final emergence swim is rapid and transformation to duns is also quick, often occurring between midmorning and early afternoon. Transformation from dun to spinner is accomplished in about 10 hours. Males die a few days after mating; females die after egg-laying and will be seen on the water with outstretched wings.

Callibaetis **(mayfly) Dun**

» WHEN TO FISH

Mayfly nymph imitations are a good bet any time for probing water in the absence of surface activity, but are most effective during late May to mid-June when the strongest hatches occur. Depending on altitude, this may last through July, but the most prolific hatches are normally over by mid-July. Fish adults any time mayflies are spotted on the water.

» HOW TO FISH

Parachute-hackled dry flies are now *de rigeur* for the mayfly hatch, but many fish, and especially large, older fish, concentrate on the emerging nymphs for long periods both before and during the emergence. Fishing duns on the dry line is straightforward except for the intricacies of matching the naturals as closely as possible. Emerging nymphs are best fished on dry lines with long leaders or slow-sinking lines; the idea is to retrieve the imitation from near bottom up towards the surface. Creeping along bottom is not desirable. Best retrieve is quite rapid hand-twists or jerky pulls of about 15 centimetres followed by a short pause. Since duns emerge quickly, surface-film fishing of nymphs is less critical than normal, but a nymph imitation fished on a dry line just subsurface can be deadly at times. Such imitations can be twitched very slowly or dead-drifted.

» HINTS

A keen eye is required to keep apace of hatch developments. The odd mayfly popping to the surface with no sign

Callibaetis **(mayfly) spinner**

of fish activity often means the fish are concentrating on the nymphs as they begin their surface-swim off the bottom. Go deep at such times. As the hatch builds, fish will follow to the surface; use the bottom to top retrieve. Splashy rises call for the dry line and adult

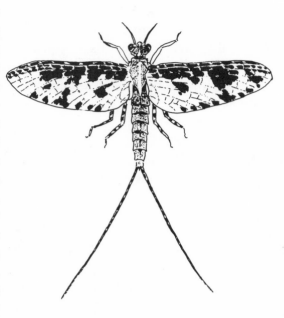

Callibaetis **(mayfly) spinner spent**

imitations and signal the most exciting fishing. Trout response to spent spinners is lazy; watch for sipping-type rises.

The Damselflies

Order: Odonata **Suborder:** Zygoptera **Genus:** Enallagma

» **IDENTIFYING FEATURES**

Nymphs: Easily identified by their long, slender bodies and sculling, side-to-side movement, they have three prominent tails, fan-like gills, and large, and wide-set eyes. Dark olive is a common colour, but colour changes depending on habitat: brown in off-colour lakes, for example.

Adults: Perhaps best known by their slim blue bodies, they are more slender than the dragonfly, and the damselfly's large double set of wings is folded over the body when at rest, unlike the outstretched wings of the dragonfly at rest.

» **WHAT TO LOOK FOR**

Emerging nymphs must crawl out of the water to become adults. Watch for them crawling up shoreline reeds or even anchor lines and the boat itself. Splashy near-shore rises are a good warning that damselflies are emerging. Also watch for split nymphal shucks clinging to shoreline reeds or debris.

» **LIFE CYCLE**

Nymphs develop over a period ranging from a few months to one year, going through several moults or instars during that time and growing larger with each. They remain hidden in dense weed growth throughout this development. Length at time of emergence is usually about four centimetres. When fully developed the nymphs look for something to crawl out on, often shoreline reeds. The shoreward swim takes place near the surface, with nymphs first rising towards the surface then levelling off. Once out of the water and clinging to reeds, the nymph waits to dry; the skin splits and the adult emerges. After the wings unfold and dry, adults take to the air. Females deposit their eggs in the lake. Spent or dead damselflies are rarely taken by fish, but there are exceptions.

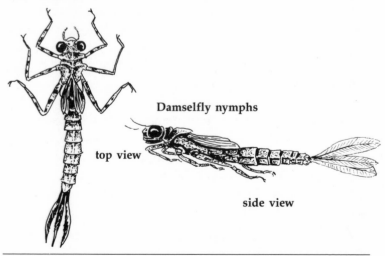

Damselfly nymphs

top view

side view

» WHEN TO FISH

Early June is the peak emergence time for many Kamloops lakes, normally lasting for a period of about two weeks. Again, this is dependent on weather conditions: a late-arriving spring delays the emergence. Altitude also plays its usual role; higher

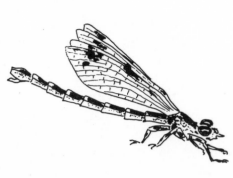

Damselfly adult

lakes are somewhat later than more low-lying lakes. Nymph imitations fished deep over dense weeds can provide fast action for some time before emergence begins.

» HOW TO FISH

Since the subsurface emergence swim is generally shoreward, casting out and retrieving in towards shore makes sense, but this is not always possible nor even desirable if fish are seen feeding close inshore. Anchoring within casting distance of shoreside reeds is accepted practice and not a bad compromise. Dry lines are most often used with sinking patterns, allowing the fly to be retrieved below the surface but not too deep. Long, slow pulls with many pauses is a traditional retrieve, but patterns with large, bulging eyes simulate the side-to-side swimming motion of the naturals when the line is hand-twisted.

» HINTS

The just-below-surface swim of the emergers highlights them for trout looking up from below. This brings a swift and often savage response even from more cautious older fish: do not set hooks hard as the weight of larger fish will instantly pop tippets. Any indication of large numbers of flying adults should send anglers shoreward for signs of emerging nymphs.

The Dragonflies

Order: Odonata **Suborder:** Anisoptera **Family:** Two are important: Aeschnidae and Gomphidae

» **IDENTIFYING FEATURES**

Aeschnidae nymphs are what many anglers think of when they mentally picture a nymph. Also known as the green darner or devil's darning needle, Aeschnidae nymphs have an hour-glass-shaped body between two and five centimetres long. Green and brown are typical colours, but coloration is dependent on habitat. Its jet-propelled motion is achieved by taking in water through the rear gill chamber and quickly expelling it in a stream; it is capable of quick successive bursts of motion ranging between eight and 15 centimetres each. It

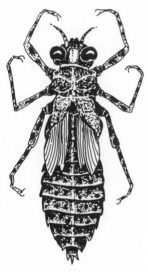

Dragonfly nymph (Aeschnidae or darner)

dwells in dense weedy areas where it is a fierce predator capable of hunting down and capturing even small fish. Gomphidae nymphs are smaller, with a more oval, squat body, but have the same jet-propelled system of movement. They are not as active as the darners and prefer to remain buried in mud bottom or deep in weeds. They are ambush feeders. Light olive green, tan and brown are typical colours.

Dragonfly nymph (Gomphidae)

» **WHAT TO LOOK FOR**

Like the damselflies, dragonflies crawl out of the water to complete their transformation to adults. Unlike damselflies, the shoreward migration is achieved by crawling along the bottom. Watch for them clinging to shoreside reeds or debris. Any sudden appearance of large num-

bers of adult dra-
gons should send
anglers searching
the shoreline.

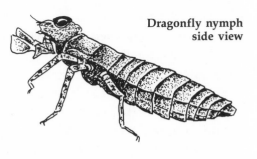

**Dragonfly nymph
side view**

» LIFE CYCLE

Nymphs can take
as long as three or
four years to ma-
ture, evolving through a series of moults, or instars. When
mature, the nymph crawls slowly shoreward along the bottom, seeking something to crawl out on. Once out of the
water it waits to dry, its skin splits and the adult emerges.
Adults remain among the reeds for some time, waiting for
the final transformation to occur. Females return to the water
after mating and deposit their eggs while flying low over
the water. Emergence continues through the hot-weather
months, but the peak normally begins in late May and may
last to the end of July.

» WHEN TO FISH

Dragonfly nymphs are a good searching pattern and can
be fished as close to bottom as possible through the year.
They are the patterns to turn to when there are no indications of any other activity. I prefer Aeschnidae patterns for
most searching work, but the squat Gomphidae imitations
are valuable, especially over mud bottoms.

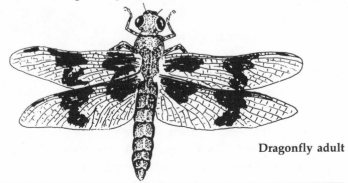

Dragonfly adult

» **HOW TO FISH**

These are another example of patterns which are best fished in the "meditation style" of wet-line fishing. Some anglers use dry lines and long leaders with weighted flies to reach bottom, but sinking lines work well for those who know them and this is the better way to fish dragonfly nymphs. Staying as close to bottom as practical is important as these nymphs rarely stray far from their weedy or muddy homes. Creep the fly along very slowly.

» **HINTS**

Despite their jet-drives, dragonfly nymphs rarely scoot along; the most effective retrieves are the ones which imitate the nymphs' slow creeping stalk among the weeds. Fly colour, as always, should be matched to the waters being fished. Alf Davy notes in *The Gilly* that dragonfly nymphs are a lighter colour immediately following a moult and that trout will often feed selectively on moulting nymphs.

The Caddisflies

Order: Trichoptera **Family:** Limnephilidae (one of many)

» **IDENTIFYING FEATURES**

Caddisflies are better known to B.C. anglers as sedges. Unlike the dragons and damsels, sedges have complete metamorphosis with larval, pupal and adult stages.

out of case

Larvae: Larval cases are built from surrounding material, such as sand, small stones, tiny twigs or bits of vege-

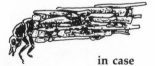

in case

tation. Larvae go through several Caddisfly (sedge) larva moults and build a new home to accommodate each successively larger stage. The larval stage can last from one to two years. Coloration is extremely varied, but green and yellow are important. Sizes range from .5 to four centimetres.

Pupae: Once the final moult is complete, the larvae seal themselves in their homes and undergo the transformation to the pupal stage. Pupae cut their way out of the cases and swim rapidly to the surface. Fully formed adults emerge from the split pupal shuck and rest while the wings dry. To get airborne, they scamper across the surface forming a trailing vee across the water. Colour and size range is as for larvae.

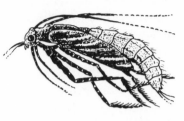

side view

Adults: After mating, females return to the water to deposit their eggs by lowering their abdomens into the water. Usually the females remain in constant motion while laying their eggs. Tan is the most important colour as this is the typical wing coloration. Body colour is varied, but green—everything from forest green to bright emerald—and yellow are important.

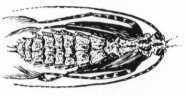

top view

Caddisfly (sedge) pupa

» **WHAT TO LOOK FOR**

Adults are easily recognizable by their moth-like appearance and by the way they carry their wings when at rest. This has traditionally been described as tent-like and the description is apt if an A-frame style tent is pictured. Large moth-like creatures scampering across the water's surface are caddisflies. Larvae are identified easily enough by their cases. Pupae of the types most important to interior waters have a long, dangling set of legs used as oars during the

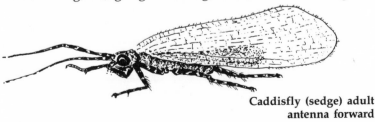

Caddisfly (sedge) adult
antenna forward

surface swim. This and their even longer antennae, laid back across the body, identify them.

» LIFE CYCLE

Much of the caddisfly's life cycle has been covered above, but several important features remain. When the pupae emerge from the larval cases, they are sheathed in a membrane with only their oar-like legs protruding to help them swim. Hatching most often occurs as soon as the surface is reached; the membrane splits down the back and the adult heaves itself free. This may take some time. Adults wing their way to shoreside vegetation to rest. Mating normally follows some weeks later and is most often done in the air. Females of some species enter the water and lay their eggs on the bottom, others drop them while flying over and still others by lowering their abdomens into the water.

» WHEN TO FISH

Again, emergence is a function of elevation and weather, but the last two weeks of June and into early July are typical peak emergence times. They can continue through to September. Late morning to midafternoon seem to be the peak hours for emergence, but late-night hatches are a sedge hallmark. Any sign of sedges on the surface calls for either adult or pupal imitations, especially if the naturals are large. Emergence times on individual lakes vary little from year to year; diaries are the way to keep track.

» HOW TO FISH

The sedges' complex life makes for complicated angling. In still waters the larval stage is generally ignored by anglers.

Caddisfly (sedge) adult

Most effort goes into the pupal and adult stages. Adults provide the most exciting dry-fly fishing of the year on Kamloops trout lakes. The drama of large fish noisily ripping large
flies from the surface would be hard to top anywhere in the
world. Deer-hair flies are used to the exclusion of virtually
all other materials. Cast in the travel path of a surface-feeding
fish and let the fly rest. If no response follows, the fly should
be twitched across the surface after the fashion of the natural
"travelling" sedge. The response to this can be unnerving.
For all that has been said and written about dry-fly fishing
and the sedge, it is often pupal imitations which take the
most fish; the trout will key to them while ignoring the large
adults veeing the surface. Pupal imitations can be fished just
subsurface with dry lines or from top to bottom with appropriate lines. Best bottom to top retrieve consists of a series of short twitchy pulls followed by a pause, then a fairly
long pull, pause and twitch again.

» HINTS

Body colour of adults can be vital, especially once the hatch
has developed to the stage where the fish are well-fed and
fussy. Remember fish look up from below at the sedge, and
body colour is the first thing they see. Pupae struggle might-
ily to free themselves from their shucks; trout often key very
specifically on this stage, a good thing to remember when
fishing the adult amid splashy rises with no results. Even
if no diary is kept, record the time, date and location of any
strong sedge hatch encountered. Next year's hatch will be
a repeat almost to the minute, provided that similar weather
conditions prevail.

The Water Boatmen

Order: Hemiptera **Family:** Corixidae

» IDENTIFYING FEATURES

Water boatmen can be recognized by the two long rear legs
which they use as very effective sweeping oars. They breath
atmospheric oxygen and must regularly travel to the sur-

face to replenish the air supply they carry in a specially-
adapted abdominal pocket.
This gives the abdomen a
silvery sheen. Backs are dark
brown and the undersides
pale yellow to whitish.

» WHAT TO LOOK FOR

Very quick-swimming
beetle-like creatures darting
to the surface, pausing
momentarily, then darting
back out of sight, are sure to
be water boatmen. The very
similar backswimmer is larger and also captures its air in

Water boatman

a special pocket, but they swim on their backs as the name
implies.

» LIFE CYCLE

Unique among aquatic insects, water boatmen do not go
through the remarkable transformation from water-dwelling
nymph to airborne insect. Mature water boatmen are capable of flight, but remain in the water, leaving *en masse* only
during mating. For some boatmen spring is mating time;
for others the season is fall. In both cases mating occurs away
from water with the egg-laden female returning to deposit
her eggs under water. After the eggs hatch, the nymphs
evolve through about five moults before reaching the winged
adult stage. The entire process, from egg to winged adult,
is completed in one year. Wings are held over the back in
beetle fashion.

» WHEN TO FISH

Boatmen are only important to Kamloops trout at specific times, normally when the returning female deposits her
eggs. The favoured time is late September, when most
hatches are finished for the year and the trout will respond

well to this last bonanza. The early spring flight of boatmen may also be important, but chironomids are available at this time and water boatmen do not appear to be a favourite food of the Kamloops. As always, however, a mass movement is likely to trigger a good response and it is best to keep alert for signs of trout taking boatmen during early spring.

» **HOW TO FISH**

Ian Forbes, a master fly fisher and fly-tying columnist for *B.C. Outdoors* magazine, introduced me to a floating water boatman pattern made of styrofoam with rubber legs and coloured with felt pens. This unlikely-sounding pattern solves many of the difficulties involved in successfully fishing boatmen imitations. It floats very well and when fished on a slow sinking line can be pulled under the surface in much the manner of the naturals. After a few quick pulls, it will bob back to the surface and thus will take fish both on the way down and while bobbing back to the surface. Most strikes occur either dead-drift on the surface or on the way down.

» **HINTS**

The grayling-like rise forms of rainbow trout taking water boatmen is unusual enough to provide a valuable clue. Watch for high-arching head and tail rises during early spring, but especially late in September. This activity normally occurs close to shore.

Thompson-Nicola Lakes

*F*ramed by the Fraser River in the west and the Okanagan system in the east, the Thompson-Nicola extends north to Wells Gray Provincial Park and south as far as Spuzzum in the Fraser Canyon. For anglers, the chief attraction is the scattering of small lakes which dot the rolling, forested plateau characteristic of the region. These lovely, woodland lakes nestled in hills of sweet-scented interior pine have long been recognized as producing some of the finest angling in the province. Extensive management has done much to ensure the future of these quality angling waters, but crowding is a problem. Fish populations can and are being maintained through regulation of specific waters, but the angling experience is diminished when anglers concentrate on a handful of proven lakes. As pressure continues to mount on these small lakes, it is incumbent upon anglers to spread themselves out and seek new waters.

The following listing of lakes, while including many time-tested Thompson-Nicola favourites, provides information on a number of less-well-known waters. Most hold large Kamloops trout, and all are worth searching out. The lakes are further organized by the type of angling experience likely to be encountered, rather than by geographical location. Hence, the first heading lists lakes which provide fast fishing. Next comes a listing of lakes known to hold large, difficult fish. This is followed by a select listing of lakes restricted to fly-only fishing. Lakes known for their strong sedge, or caddisfly, hatches have their own heading for reasons which will be obvious to anglers who have fished during the height of a Thompson-Nicola sedge hatch. Finally, there is a short list of lakes to escape to—mostly lakes of higher elevation which provide good angling through the hot-weather months and are less crowded than the popular lakes.

Travelling the backroads which provide access to many of these lakes means digging deep into maps and staying ever alert for the slightest clues. The directions given will allow anglers to locate a given lake, but maps will be required to pin them down. By far the best road map for Thompson-Nicola anglers is the one produced by the Kamloops and District Fish and Game Association (Fishing and Hunting Map of South Central B.C.). These maps provide a good overview of the road network and are available in most regional sporting-goods stores. The association, a member

of the B.C. Wildlife Federation, has done much valuable conservation work in the region, as has the federation province-
wide. Anglers are urged to join affiliated clubs in their home
regions.

Fast-Fishing Lakes

For a variety of reasons the lakes under this heading have
become overpopulated. Aquatic insect populations can become depleted, requiring many years to rebuild unless fish
populations are thinned by anglers. Bag limits are consequently generous, in most cases almost three times greater
than the general six-fish daily limit for the region. These are
good lakes to introduce children to fly fishing. Success rates
will be high and dry flies are rarely refused, providing especially exciting angling for youngsters. Newcomers to fly
fishing should visit these waters to perfect the techniques
required to fish lakes holding larger, more difficult fish. Dryline midge fishing, which provides such fine angling in
spring, can be a frustrating game for the uninitiated, but is
relatively simple once the intricacies have been mastered.
These are the waters to sharpen such skills. The fly fishing
clubs which have annual "fish outs" also would do well to
concentrate some effort on such waters rather than fishing
lakes which already receive too much pressure. Quite aside
from aiding fisheries management, these lakes are pure fun
to fish: light rods and lines, steady action and the day capped
with a panful of small, delicious trout.

» DIXON LAKE—On the Dixon Creek road off Yellowhead
   Hwy 5; located west of Johnson Lake.

» GOOSE LAKE—Near Lynn and Latremouille lakes west off
   Yellowhead Hwy 5 north of Little Fort.

» HALAMORE LAKE—North of Dunn Lake on the same road
   east of Yellowhead Hwy 5 via the Little Fort ferry.

» LITTLE McGILLIVRAY LAKE—A beaver pond requiring a short walk from the west side of McGillivray Lake, reached by crossing the South Thompson River at Pritchard, then the Nisconlith Lake turnoff north to the 24-kilometre post.

» MOOSE LAKE—South and east of Coldscaur Lake; turn west off Yellowhead Hwy 5 at Clearwater.

» SICILY AND ITALIA LAKES—West off Yellowhead Hwy 5 as for Moose Lake, but past Coldscaur and Rioux lakes, then branch north.

» SOUTH BARRIERE LAKE—South of East Barriere Lake; east off Yellowhead Hwy 5 on the Barriere Creek road, then south on Haggard Creek road.

Difficult Lakes

The Thompson-Nicola has many lakes which produce larger-than-average fish. For our purposes here, any Kamloops trout of five pounds and more will be considered larger than average, although the average size an angler might reasonably expect is closer to two pounds. Seasoned veterans will not consider five-pound fish excessively large, but fish of this size are good by any definition. In any event, regulations stipulate anglers may keep only one fish greater than 20 inches (50 centimetres) in fork length. Fish of this length generally weigh in the neighbourhood of five pounds, so the definition pretty much holds with what fisheries managers see as a trophy.

All the lakes under this heading hold larger-than-average fish. Some hold good numbers of them and a few hold really large fish, trout of eight to 10 pounds. For the record, consider these difficult lakes. There may be exceptional times when the angler will have a really good day, but mostly the fishing will be slow. Fooling older fish with any consistency requires a fair degree of sophistication from anglers. Even then, success is never a certainty. Be prepared for many frustrating hours with a better than even chance of no reward for the effort put in. This is the way of such lakes.

In recent years, likely a result of the ever-growing popularity of fly fishing, many anglers have taken to concentrating exclusively on such waters. The thinking seems to be that unless a lake provides the opportunity to catch exceptionally large fish, it is not worth fishing. This is foolish for a number of reasons, but chief among them is the impact on quality angling. Crowded waters, cramped camping and frayed tempers are not consistent with quality angling, no matter how large the fish.

» CAMPBELL AND SCUITTO LAKES—Two personal favourites, they provide similar angling to that found in Tunkwa and Leighton lakes but are less popular. Both are shallow and subject to fierce winds but provided good fishing for very large Kamloops during the mid-1980s. The fish were somewhat smaller in more recent years, but good anglers will still find numbers of fish in excess of five pounds with some larger (fish to 10 pounds). Average size is perhaps two pounds, so the fishing is faster than in lakes with populations of only large, wary trout. As always, it is the angler attuned to the seasons of the fly who will take the largest fish. Spring and fall are the best seasons. Dark, plankton-stained waters and a heavy algae bloom mars the water, but the fish in either of these two lakes make up for whatever else they might lack. Access and camping is on private land thanks to long-suffering co-operation from the land owners. There have been problems and access may be restricted in the future if defacing of nearby heritage buildings and careless handling of garbage continues. Good roads east and south from Barnhart Vale (continue past the Campbell Creek road; take the next branch south) provide access.

» STUMP LAKE—Right on Hwy 5A between Kamloops and Merritt, no discussion of difficult Thompson-Nicola lakes would be complete without mention of this large, shallow, weedy and highly productive lake. Stump has long had a reputation for producing exceptionally large Kamloops and it still holds many fish of six pounds and better with occasional giants which are rarely fooled and all but impossible to bring to the boat. It also holds kokanee and brook trout, but for all that, fishing pressure is not high. There are two reasons: the winds which mercilessly pound the area and its reputation as an extremely moody lake. Those determined to try this tough-to-figure lake might concentrate their fly fishing efforts on the shoals found at both the north and south ends. Low elevation makes spring and fall best; early and late in the day are the best times to avoid the gusty winds.

» HOSLI LAKE—This tough-to-reach quality angling lake is well-suited to fly fishing. Most reports concur Hosli produces Kamloops trout to four pounds with remarkable consistency, but angling acquaintances report this small, all but hidden lake also holds some very much larger fish. Do not expect fast fishing. Spring and fall are best, but the summer doldrum period may be relatively short. Under good conditions, well handled two-wheel-drive pickups can make it in, but for the record consider four-wheel-drive necessary. To get there, turn east off Hwy 5A about 30 kilometres south of Kamloops onto the Roche Lake road. Branch north off the Roche Lake road about nine kilometres from Hwy 5A after crossing a small creek and continue past the north side of Bleeker Lake for about four kilometres to Hosli.

» PETERHOPE LAKE—A well-known favourite with a rich angling history, Peterhope is still a wonderful fly fishing lake which will yield large fish to skilled anglers. Clear water, marl flats and wide shoal areas with a number of "sunken islands" (midlake shoals) mark this exceptional lake. Fish size varies from year to year, and while there is always the chance of taking trout to eight pounds and better, fish of five pounds are more typical trophies, with many smaller fish. The larger fish will not go to inexperienced rods with any consistency. To get there, leave Hwy 5A just past the south end of Stump Lake on a good (signed) gravel road.

» JIMMY LAKE—A small secluded lake long known for quality angling, there are whispers concerning a strong sedge population, but this was not confirmed. To find out try this lake late in June or early July. Altitude is more than 1,300 metres so angling will be good through the prime sedge season and beyond. Current regulations stipulate only one fish may be kept, with catch-and-release for all fish longer than 16 inches (40 centimetres). This, along with a winter-long closure, will assure the lake's population of large fish is not harvested. Canny anglers can expect fish to six pounds and better. Such fish should be played deftly and are best released without being lifted from the water. Barbless hooks are advised and nets should not be used. Nearby Woods Lake (some larger fish) is a better bet for those who prefer to keep their catch. To get to Jimmy Lake, turn south off Hwy 97 on the Ingram Creek road near Westwold (just past the Salmon River bridge). Jimmy lies about three kilometres beyond Woods Lake. The road can be bad when wet.

» AMPHITHEATRE LAKE—This small, moody lake is not particularly scenic or special in any way except for the size of its fish. I recall taking several Kamloops here of about six pounds on a green, deeply sunken dragonfly nymph over the weed beds at the west end and just off the shoal at the east end of the lake. Typical of the lakes under this heading, a full day of fishing was required to take these fish. The west end has a deep-water channel with extensive weed beds on all sides and is probably the best bet, although fishing can be good anywhere in the lake. The deep-water channel runs through the middle of the lake.

Anglers met on the lake reported catching a number of fish in the eight to 10-pound class and while this may be possible, four to six-pound fish might more reasonably be expected. In my experience, patterns fished deep just over the weeds take larger fish than dry flies even when fish are seen rising freely. This is often true of lakes holding larger fish. Quickest access is off the South Thompson River road (leave Hwy 1 at Pritchard) then the Niskonlith Lake road up a series of switchbacks with stunning views. Watch for a small creek crossing just past the posted 12-kilometre mark then take the first road left (west). This passes beside the lake. Good roads all the way.

» LEIGHTON AND TUNKWA LAKES—These are also long-time Thompson-Nicola favourites with established angling histories. Tunkwa, aside from yielding its fish very, very grudgingly, is also a large lake, making it difficult and daunting for the fly fisher. Leighton is several times smaller, not as subject to windy conditions and gives up its fish less reluctantly. Naturally, Leighton's trout are smaller, say three to four pounds, compared to Tunkwa's six and eight-pound fish. Fooling Tunkwa Lake trout requires real fishing smarts and landing a good one is by no means a certainty. Kamloops in Tunkwa and Leighton seem to be both especially difficult and strong. Spring and fall are best for both. The early June damselfly emergence is well-known for its intensity. These are popular lakes; long weekends are best avoided by those who prefer uncrowded conditions. Access to both is off the paved Logan Lake to Savona road (about 15 kilometres north of Logan Lake).

Fly-Only Lakes

Aside from the artificial flies restriction, there is not much to distinguish these lakes from those under the Difficult Lakes heading. Like the difficult lakes, they are managed as quality waters, but have been set aside for fly fishers. People do cheat, however, and it is not unusual to see trollers working these lakes with worms and gang-trolls. Fly fishers are urged to use the Observe, Record and Report program to help thwart these lawbreakers. B.C.'s Conservation Officer Service is chronically underfunded; concerned anglers should help wherever possible

Again, because these waters provide quality angling for larger trout, there can be overcrowding difficulties. I recall fishing Island Lake in the Highland Valley when a fly-fishing club descended on the lake. Island is a small lake. Six to 10 boats makes for comfortable angling; 24 or 30 ruins the experience, puts undue pressure on limited camping space and damages fragile vegetation. I moved camp to nearby Bose lake. In two days of fishing at Island Lake, I had managed to fool but one fish, a 24-inch beauty. During the next two solitary days at Bose, I lost count of the number of fish hooked and released. None were as large as the Island Lake fish, but all were good fish of between two and three pounds. Returning to camp one evening, I put out both the dry and wet line for a slow troll to shore. A two-pound Kamloops took the wet line almost immediately and even before I could reach for the rod, the trailing dry fly disappeared in a neat boil of water. This kind of fast fishing is not unusual on lakes like Bose. They provide a welcome relief from hours of fruitless "technical" fishing. By all means try the difficult lakes and the fly-only lakes, but remember there are many nearby lakes which offer rewarding angling in uncrowded conditions.

» ISLAND LAKE—Also known as Big OK Lake (nearby OK Lake, like Bose, provides a ready alternative), Island is now managed as a fly-only catch-and-release lake. This will help relieve some of the pressure, as well as assuring the survival of its exceptionally large fish. It's a small lake with a sunken island (midlake shoal) surrounded by rich weed beds. All the usual aquatic insects are present and there is a sedge hatch, but I have never seen it at its height so cannot report on its strength. Scud and leech patterns will do well late in the day and in the fall. The midge hatch is strong and black patterns seem to work best, but a slip strike (see the section on aquatic insects in this chapter) is vital to keep from breaking off these often very heavy fish. Five and six-pound fish do not earn bragging rights. There is no spawning stream, but gravel has been provided at the south end and in spring anglers can see spawning fish, some in the 10-pound class, near the gravel. This may well be the only time such fish are seen, as Island's larger trout are notoriously difficult. A good gravel road leading south off the paved Ashcroft to Logan Lake road at the open-pit copper mine goes to Island, OK and Calling lakes.

» BLUE LAKE—Reports vary concerning the size of fish available in this small gem of a lake, but all agree the fish are large and very difficult. Exceptionally clear water and extensive marl shoals with a deep-water middle section makes long, fine leaders and gentle hands a must. Like Island Lake, there is no spawning stream so fish numbers remain relatively stable. This makes for very large fish. Good anglers can expect fish of five pounds with many larger. There is a sedge hatch which likely provides the best opportunity to fool the largest fish. Water boatmen provide good fall fishing. Expect to spend many fishless hours for every fish taken. To get there, take the Douglas Lake road off Hwy 5A then go north on the Glimpse Lake road. Blue lies just northwest of Glimpse, which is the lake to try if you're frustrated with Blue. Alternate access is via Peterhope Lake.

» ERNEST LAKE—Only a few rough kilometres beyond Black and Bog lakes in the Roche Lake area, the drive to this quality angling lake seems to go on forever due to the rutted, extremely bumpy road which may be all but impossible in wet weather; it definitely requires four-wheel drive. As with many of the lakes under this heading, the "riddle of the day" will have to be solved before Ernest Lake's trout can be caught with anything approaching consistency. I have yet to talk to anyone who claims to have had a big day on this small, secluded lake. Spring and fall are best, although the fishing is said to hold for much of the summer with only a relatively short period when high water temperature slows angling to a virtual standstill.

» PASS LAKE—Patience is a necessary virtue on this small lake holding Kamloops trout to at least six pounds and probably much larger. Pass is known as a moody lake, but I suspect it can provide very good midge fishing for larger trout early in the season, notably for anglers who have perfected their techniques. It would be a good lake to try after sharpening midge-fishing skills on one of the fast-fishing lakes; if nothing else it will drive home the need to offer patterns which match as precisely as possible the naturals hatching in the lake—a seemingly insignificant detail can make a world of difference to success. The lake's tough-angling reputation and the fly-only restriction make it less popular than it might otherwise be. Low elevation means good early-season angling, a long slow summer and good fishing again later in September. Late September and October likely offer the highest chance of success. To get there take the Lac du Bois road north and west from North Kamloops; Pass is about 20 kilometres in on a good road.

» SALMON LAKE—Long a mecca for fly fishers, Salmon remains an excellent fly fishing lake with good numbers of medium to large Kamloops which are not as difficult as those in some of the other lakes under this heading. It's a shallow, silty-bottomed lake with good weed beds; most anglers concentrate on the weed beds at the western end.

The summer algae bloom on this lake puts some anglers off, but I have had success fishing below the soup with a sinking line, as have many others. The count-down method helps in finding the clear water below the algae, where fish often cruise. A leech works well, but bright green damselfly patterns seem to do particularly well. There are some larger fish taken every year, but four- to five-pound fish are typical trophies with a good number of fish in the two-pound class. Access is possible either south from Westwold off Hwy 97 or east and north off Hwy 5A as for Glimpse and Blue lakes. The Douglas Lake road runs right beside the lake and access is via a private lodge.

» WARREN LAKE—Another personal favourite, this exceptional angling lake with extensive weedy shoals also has a history of producing very large trout. Today, trophy-sized fish are most often between five and six pounds and although I have never caught one larger, I suspect this lake holds a number of trout in the double-digit class. In any case, it is a lovely lake to fly fish despite the presence of cabins which detract somewhat from its wilderness flavour. The Kamloops trout in this lake seem in especially good condition; it is not unusual to lose two fish for every one brought to the boat. Elevation is more than 1,200 metres, so it is somewhat later getting started and lasts longer into the summer. Some attempt has been made to block the final access to the lake, but four-wheel enthusiasts seem intent on circumventing any effort to make Warren a walk-in lake. It is possible to drive in, but walking actually takes less time as the final bit of road is very rough and may in any case become impassable in wet conditions. To get there, turn north off Hwy 1 at Pritchard and cross the South Thompson River to the Paul Lake road. Warren is to the west off this road; watch for a branch road turning west five kilometres south of Hyas Lake (just before a small bridge). The first road to the right (north) off this branch road is the Warren Lake access road. The Paul Lake road can also be reached by turning east off Hwy 5, five kilometres north of the South Thompson River.

Sedge Lakes

The sedge, or caddisfly, provides the most exciting dry-fly fishing of the year in the Thompson-Nicola. Seasoned Thompson-Nicola anglers tend to be secretive about lakes which hold good sedge populations, and they have reason for keeping mum. The sedge is one of the most fragile of aquatic insects and like the mayfly, its populations can easily be destroyed by anglers who persist in using outboard motors on lakes which are easily traversed by oar, paddle or float-tube. The scummy residue of oil left behind by outboards is devastating to these creatures, as indeed it is for many of the aquatic insects. Also, lakes with good spawning tributaries, a minority in the Thompson-Nicola, tend to overpopulate. The result is a large population of smaller fish which soon deplete aquatic insect populations. The caddis in particular has difficulty recovering from such depredations. So while the reasons may be many, the result is the same: sedge lakes are easily ruined, especially in the small angling lakes typical of the Thompson-Nicola. Anglers are encouraged to leave their outboards behind and dig out the oars or electric motors on all such lakes, but especially the sedge lakes. With mounting pressure on all Thompson-Nicola waters, this seems only reasonable. There is now little doubt that unless anglers become informed and adjust their behaviour accordingly, the next generation of anglers may never know the nerve-tingling excitement of fishing during the height of a strong sedge hatch.

» LAC LE JEUNE—This large popular lake complete with provincial park is about 35 kilometres south of Kamloops on a paved road, so anglers should not expect uncrowded conditions. The lake itself is long and narrow with many points and bays and enough shallow water to make it a good fly fishing candidate. Heavy angling pressure makes stocking mandatory and while most fish are small by Thompson-Nicola standards, fish of between two and four pounds come regularly enough to keep fly fishers keen. Watch for emerging sedges in late June and early July, which is a fairly typical emergence time throughout the region. Remember also that fish may be feeding on sedges in deeper water for some time prior to the emergence.

» ROCHE LAKE—This very popular lake with an upscale lodge noted for its fine dining room holds some exceptionally large Kamloops, fish to eight pounds, but the average is probably around two pounds. Trolling is very popular, but anglers who anchor and cast and are tuned to the season might expect a consistent catch of fish in the four-pound class. The sedge hatch, which may be in some jeopardy due to extensive use of outboard motors, is known to start a little earlier, say mid- instead of late June. Roche is a good lake for both serious anglers and family outings. A string of surrounding lakes, normally requiring four-wheel drive to reach, makes Roche an excellent base for longer trips. Brook trout lakes are discussed in chapter six, but Bog and clear-water Black Lake deserve mention here both for their proximity to Roche and the exceptional sizes of their brookies. To get there take Hwy 5A south from Kamloops (or north from Merritt) then a good gravel road (signed) east from the north end of Trap lake.

» HAMMER LAKE—Most of the angling attention is focused on nearby Bonaparte Lake, where plug-trolling fishers seek Kamloops trout in the 10-pound class. Hammer lies to the south off the west end of the large lake and was once known to hold fish as large as those in Bonaparte. Typical catches today range from two to four pounds with the occasional heavy fish, but power boats are banned and this bodes well for the lake's reportedly still strong sedge population. It is a good lake for fly fishers. Access is west off Hwy 97 from near 70 Mile House. (For more information on Hammer, see also chapter six, South Cariboo section of the lakes listing.)

» LUNDBOM LAKE—This very rich lake was once a legend, its name a whispered secret, with many fish to eight pounds and good numbers in the magic double-digit class. Today it is too popular to rank as a quality angling lake, although its rich waters still produce numbers of four- to five-pound fish despite the heavy pressure. Extensive use of power boats likely means its very strong sedge population will dwindle rapidly. Still, the late June/early July emergence is reportedly prolific, at least for now, and a midweek trip to this once-legendary lake at this time is worthwhile for anglers wishing to witness a strong sedge hatch at an easily reached lake. Otherwise, try mid-September with scud or leech patterns, but weekends are still best avoided. A good (signed) gravel road east off Hwy 5A southwest of Merritt provides access.

» BADGER AND SPOONY—Both of these dark-bottomed lakes were once fly-only lakes and were noted for large fish. Today, although closed to winter fishing and limited to single-hook fishing with the use of bait banned, they typically produce fish of between two and four pounds with some very much larger fish for wily, patient anglers. Some reports indicate the sedge hatch begins as early as the first week of June, but anglers with limited time are probably better off waiting until the middle of the month. As for all of the lakes under this heading, hitting the hatch just right will involve several trips over a number of seasons. To get there, take Yellowhead Hwy 5 north of Kamloops. A number of roads branching east provide access; the Knouff Lake road or the Heffley Creek road both approach from the south. Small Spoony Lake lies just west of Badger and is not named on most maps.

» MURRAY LAKE—Not reputed to be a rich lake, Murray produces Kamloops to about two pounds, but the sedge hatch is said to be very strong and may continue well into mid-July. Once reached by the Coldwater River road south from Merritt and a very rough final spur, access is now possible off Coquihalla Hwy 5. Look for an exit shortly after crossing Juliet Creek in the vicinity of Coldwater River Provincial Park (day-use only).

» ANTLER LAKE—There are only sketchy reports on this remote lake, with differing opinions regarding the size of its fish. Some say the fish are small, to about 1.5 pounds; others claim Antler produces fish better than five pounds. Nearby Billy Lake also has a muddied reputation, but most sources say its fish grow to between four and six pounds. In any case, Antler is said to have a good sedge hatch and other nearby lakes in the seven-lake Chataway group would also be worth probing during the prime sedge season. To get there, leave Spences Bridge/Merritt Hwy 8 at Lower Nicola, turning north on a gravel road which is reported good as far as Chataway Lake. Four-wheel drive is needed for the spur to Antler and a short walk is required.

» HIHIUM LAKE—Although relatively large, this is an excellent fly fishing lake with good weed beds and rocky shallows; there are prolific hatches of all the main aquatic insects. Reports are the sedge hatch can be hit and miss; some years provide very strong hatches while others are low-key. Elevation is more than 1,200 metres so emergence time may be somewhat later than for more low-lying lakes. Both Hihium and Lac le Jeune were called Fish Lake back in the early days due to their incredible abundance of large Kamloops and both have a long angling heritage. Past Savona on Hwy 1, turn north on the Deadman Creek road;

a steep (greasy when wet) pipeline road climbs the final 16 kilometres to the lake. (For more information on Hihium, see also chapter six, South Cariboo section of the lakes listing.)

» PLATEAU LAKE—Like many lakes in the Thompson-Nicola, Plateau is subject to periodic winterkill. When several seasons go by with no winterkill (see the section on reading lakes in chapter five), its trout will grow to exceptional sizes. For anglers this makes the lake a hit-and-miss proposition. When all goes well for three years or more, fishing for larger trout can be good; otherwise the fishing can be poor to fair. Learning to gauge the severity of the preceding season is valuable in planning trips to such lakes. Most recent reports indicate fish of between two and three pounds with good sedge hatches perhaps somewhat later than the norm. Plateau is generally best fished a little later in the season; the best angling is normally had just as more low-lying lakes begin to turn off. It is ideally suited to fly fishing. The lake is reached over a rough road west off Hwy 5A from the north end of Stump Lake.

Escape Lakes

The lakes under this heading are almost all small, high-elevation lakes which provide good fishing through the hottest months of summer. Generally they are lightly fished lakes holding smaller trout, but there are exceptions. Hikes or short walks are required to reach some of them, which also helps keep the crowds at bay. These are lakes to escape to, either from the crowded conditions of the more low-lying lakes or the heat of high summer. They are not described in detail and the best advice is to keep mum about any gems discovered.

» PARADISE LAKE AREA—There are six small lakes in the high country southeast of Merritt of which Paradise is the largest. Boot and Island lakes are reached over the same road as Paradise, south off Hwy 5A near Quilchena. Skunk, Reservoir and Walker are reached from the same road, but the final access road is farther to the west. All provide good fishing with Reservoir perhaps yielding slightly larger trout.

» MEADOW LAKE AREA—A scattering of small lakes northwest of Little Fort off Yellowhead Hwy 5, then north off the Bridge Lake road, are high in altitude and offer good angling. Some of these lakes yield surprisingly large fish, notably Lost Horse, Grizzly and Gammarus. Others to look for include Lorenzo and Deer lakes.

» WELLS GRAY PARK LAKES—There are a number of excellent fishing lakes in the park, but small, secluded Placid and Sedge lakes are the ones which concern us here. Both require short hikes to reach and provide good fishing for trout to about two pounds. Contact the Parks Branch for trail information.

» RIDGE LAKES—A rough road from Lac le Jeune provides access to these two high-elevation lakes with good fishing for trout to two-pounds-plus.

» BLACKWELL LAKE—Just west of Pratt Lake this small gem is south and west off Hwy 97 from Monte Lake.

» BLUE EARTH LAKE—Look for a logging road branching west off Hwy 1 near Ashcroft Manor, south of Ashcroft. Good-surface gravel to the lake.

For more information contact:

Fisheries Branch
1259 Dalhousie Drive
Kamloops, B.C.
V2C 5Z5

High Country Tourist Association
Box 962
Kamloops, B.C.
V2C 6H1

CHAPTER FOUR

The Okanagan

*T*ourists lured by sunshine and sandy beaches will no doubt take umbrage, but for anglers it is the Okanagan's varied angling challenges which make the region special. Sunny summer days are a bonus, but are in no way necessary. More often than not, anglers will find themselves wishing for less rather than more of the Okanagan's much-celebrated sunshine. The same sparkling summer sun which draws increasing numbers of tourists each year casts a pall over low-elevation lake angling. Rainbow trout are the backbone of the region's sports fishery; when water temperatures climb, trout tend to sulk and fishing becomes a slow, dreary affair. But here the Okanagan's incredible diversity comes into play. In the neighbouring Thompson-Nicola, anglers escape the summer doldrums by seeking lakes of higher elevation. The Okanagan offers similar high lakes, but its broad range of fish species ensures good low-elevation angling through the hot-weather months.

Both largemouth and smallmouth bass inhabit the southern Okanagan, with the best fishing in Vaseux and Osoyoos lakes. The angling literature which has grown up around these fish invariably stresses spring and fall as the best times to target bass. This is no doubt true. Both the largemouth and smallmouth bass (see the section on bass in chapter seven) are spring spawners which guard their nests and remain in shallow water for some time following the spawning period, when angling becomes so easy as to verge on the unsporting. Fisheries managers have responded by closing some bass waters during this time to protect the fish from overharvesting. In the fall bass, like trout, again become active, indulging in a close-of-the-season feeding spree. So spring and fall are the best fishing times, no doubt, but summer bass are not nearly as sulky as hot-weather trout. Midday fishing slows, to be sure, but early morning and late evening bassing can remain good through the summer. Some of my most memorable bass-fishing adventures occurred under the mad-dog sun of midsummer, proving once again that angling has few if any iron-clad rules.

Okanagan bass lakes tend to offer advantages beyond monster-sized fish. Vaseux Lake, one of the province's top bass waters, is a prime example. To the north lies Skaha Lake of sandy-beach fame and the Penticton to Kelowna tourist strip; to the south lies Osoyoos Lake, another fine bass-fishing lake, but also home to water-skiing and powerboating mania. By Okanagan standards, Vaseux is a lonely lake with a Canadian Wildlife Service ban on power boats. The ban is a tip-off to the incredible diversity of waterfowl which use this lake. Even if the bass prove elusive, poling a canoe or punt on this quiet lake will prove a special experience for the angler-turned-naturalist. Rainbow trout and kokanee are also present, but numbers are thought to be low. Largemouth bass are the main draw for serious anglers, who should be prepared for fish in the 10-pound class, although average size will be considerably smaller. Still, five to six-pound largemouth bass are nothing to sneeze at, providing splashy, weed-rolling action that will strain line-test to its limits. Any of the weeded shallows should provide good action, but flies or lures should sport weed protection in order to fish amid the heavy cover these fish favour. Jumbo-sized yellow perch, a fine table fish, are also found in this unique lake, as are some of the largest carp in B.C. (see chapter two for carp-fishing tactics).

Many, if not most, B.C. anglers still shun spiney-rayed

species such as bass and perch, and while I find this view limiting, the Okanagan offers fish to suit all tastes. The far northeastern portion of the region provides fine mixed-stock fisheries for several species. Char, not normally associated with the Okanagan, are found in a number of northeast Okanagan lakes, lovely Mabel Lake chief among them. I am not inclined towards large lakes, but Mabel is beyond doubt one of the province's most beautiful waters. At almost 6,000 hectares in area, Mabel is large enough to handle its reputation as a popular holiday destination. In addition to the resort facilities, there are four Forest Service campsites, as well as 182-hectare Mabel Lake Provincial Park with more than 80 campsites. Do not expect solitary camping, but out on the waters of the big lake there is always room enough to find a spot of one's own. Char fishers will find this more difficult than others as lake trout tend to hold at very specific locations. This concentrates the fishery to some degree, but I have discovered a lake trout trait which avoids the merry-go-round trolling style required in crowded conditions.

Very early in the mornings, well before sunlight touches the water, lake trout often move into shoreline shallows to hunt. This is probably more true in spring and fall than it is in summer, but I have caught lakers in shallow water as late as July, so height-of-the-season shoreline trolling for char is by no means out of the question. Deep trolling is the most popular method for char, either with wire lines or down-riggers, but it has been my experience that char dredged up from the depths are a lacklustre fish. They seem less adept at compensating for pressure changes than rainbow trout or salmon and I think this goes a long way towards explaining the lake trout's generally poor performance as a game fish.

Lake trout taken in shallow water are an altogether different fish. Long, line-melting runs and smashing takes not normally associated with lakers are to be expected with this style of fishing. Anglers may still opt to use at least some lead, but I have had good success using no weight, and while I have not yet tried surface-trolled bucktails, I think such lures could prove quite effective. My favourite shallow-water char-trolling lures are Apex Hotspots in a variety of sizes and colours, but this is strictly a personal choice. Any of the lures commonly fished in deeper water for this species should do well in shallow water as well. As sunlight touches the lake's shoreline, the char retreat to deeper water, calling for the more traditional techniques, but for anglers looking for a different char experience, I would definitely try Mabel Lake's shallows in the predawn hours.

Rainbow trout are Mabel Lake's premier game fish and these fish can grow to large sizes, to eight pounds and better, thanks largely to the kokanee which also inhabit the lake. In lakes of mixed stocks such as Mabel, trolling is generally the most effective tactic for rainbow trout, but fly fishers need not put up their rods altogether. Creek-mouth fly casting, notably in spring, can yield surprising results, either for larger rainbow trout or Mabel Lake's other char species, the Dolly Vardens. Dolly Varden numbers are believed to be quite low, so consideration should be given to catch-and-release fishing for this species at least.

One does not have to travel far from holiday-destination Mabel to discover the diversity of experience available to Okanagan anglers. Nearby Kidney and Liver lakes, reached over a rough spur road north of Mabel Lake, are small, semi-wilderness style lakes offering good angling for larger-than-

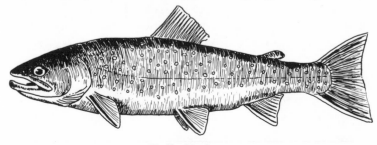

Dolly Varden

average rainbow trout. Fly fishers will delight in these secluded lakes ideally suited to float-tubes and small boats. Scenic
Kidney holds rainbow trout to four pounds, while reduced
stocking in Liver should produce larger fish over the next few
years. Management of these two small lakes, as with many
of the Okanagan's smaller waters, has been fairly intense, as
reflected by the reduced stocking of Liver. Such waters must
be treated with respect if they are to survive ever-growing
angling pressure. More than 500,000 freshwater fishing li-
cences are now sold each year in B.C. It takes only a few un-
caring or ignorant fishers to ruin the carefully groomed quality
angling available on so many small B.C. lakes.

Cross the Okanagan Valley to the plateau country on the
west side and the mountains give way to rolling forested
hills where angling changes from mixed-stock fisheries to
match-the-hatch-style fly fishing in waters dominated by
insect-eating rainbow trout. These fish are entirely different from the generally larger rainbow trout found in the
mixed-stock lakes. Mabel Lake rainbow trout, like the rainbows of Okanagan Lake itself, are highly piscivorous, sub-
sisting chiefly on a diet of kokanee and other forage fish.
But cross the valley to the west side and we find a different
strain of rainbow trout, the famous Kamloops rainbow of
Thompson-Nicola fame (see chapter three). This is not at
all as unlikely as it may at first appear. Much of the Okanagan's western half is an extension of the plateau and pot-
hole lake country normally associated with the Thompson-

Kokanee salmon

Nicola. Canny fly fishing is required to take the best fish with any consistency. Pinaus Lake, south of Falkland off Hwy 97, in many ways epitomizes this type of Okanagan lake.

Long known as a fine angling lake, Pinaus's early glory days of 10-pound-and-better rainbow trout are long past, as they are for so many of the plateau's rich lakes. Intensive stocking (50,000 rainbow yearlings annually) and the lake's natural aquatic riches combine to produce good-to-excellent angling for fish in the two-pound range, although knowledgeable fly fishers regularly take fish of four pounds or slightly better. The lake has many shoals, ledges and drop-offs which are virtually impossible to learn during the course of a single visit. Those who take better fish with consistency, always the mark of a top-class angler, are those who have taken the time to become familiar with the lake's many nuances. In this lies one of the great secrets of successful lake angling, if secret is the right word. Returning to the same lake for a number of years during various seasons will increase anyone's success rates. More importantly, anglers with intimate knowledge of a given lake often play lead roles in conservation and management efforts. Their detailed, on-the-spot knowledge of a lake's dynamics is invaluable to fisheries managers. Clearly, the need for such concerned and informed anglers is directly proportional to the ever-mounting pressures on the resource. It is no longer enough for anglers to be concerned; they must be informed, knowledgeable and organized if their views are to be counted.

Pinaus's popularity means a wide variety of fishing styles will be in evidence on any given day. Trollers, unintentionally for the most part, tend to trespass within casting distance of anchored fly fishers. Fly fishers may find this disconcerting, especially when the dry line is in use for, say, Pinaus's fine spring chironomid hatch. Fortunately, a number of smaller nearby lakes offer quieter settings for fly fishing. Little King Lake, just off Pinaus's western end, is susceptible to winterkill (see the section on reading lakes in this chapter), but produces good numbers of fish. Lakes with a tendency to winterkill are often highly productive and Little King is no exception. In good years the lake produces fish as large as those found in Pinaus.

The transition zone between dry grasslands and wetter pine and fir forests is found south of the Pinaus Lake area and is yet another aspect of the Okanagan. This appealing, semi-open parkland setting takes in lakes such as Kentucky, Alleyne and Bluey, which lie about as far west as it is possible to get in the Okanagan. Located east of Hwy 5A and south of Aspen Grove, this group of lakes offers fair fishing with some chances of taking larger fish. Stocking experiments at Alleyne are aimed at producing large rainbow trout, making this a lake to watch. Bluey, smallest of the three and the most difficult to reach, is probably the best bet for serious anglers with fair numbers of fish in the four-pound range. Fishing can be good at all three lakes, but it is their suitability to family fishing and camping which makes the group special.

The many marshes and ponds on the road/trail around Alleyne make for pleasant family outings with good opportunities for wildlife viewing. For the more adventuresome, scenic Quilchena Falls lie hidden in the scrub timber of a canyon north of Alleyne Lake, about a 15-kilometre round trip. Canoes or small boats will be wanted to explore the reedy marsh at the north end of Alleyne Lake, home to a variety of waterfowl and shy, bewhiskered muskrats. A finer place to introduce children to nature would be difficult to imagine.

Bluey lies south of the other two lakes over a rough four-wheel-drive access road which is probably better walked by family groups. Walking time is about one hour. Both Kentucky and Alleyne contain good numbers of gammarus shrimp and vast chironomid populations (see chapter five for gammarus, chapter three for chironomids), making them capable of producing large, well-conditioned fish, but most stocked fish are harvested the same year they are planted. The unassuming-looking ponds between the lakes often yield surprising results, providing lightly fished habitat where fish can live long enough to grow to larger sizes. Children left to fish these ponds have been known to land the largest fish of the day, much to the chagrin of many a parent.

This chapter barely scratches the surface of this complex, multilayered region. But perhaps it will serve to whet appetites and arouse curiosity for the Okanagan and its special blend of diverse angling challenges.

Closeup: Reading Lakes

*R*ivers are obvious, offering a neat, set-piece design of lyrical water. Eddies, chutes, flats, boulder gardens, bends occur in endless combination but remain constants, familiar touchstones for angler and paddler alike. Lakes are subtle, their songs muted. Well-known lakes are comfortable, like old friends. We cherish the familiar haunts, relish the ever-changing guises, anticipate the rediscovery of secrets. New lakes are like strangers, their moods unknown, the patterns undiscovered. They attract and repel at the same time. Commitment and study are required to unravel the many subtle nuances, the shades of meaning obscured beneath the mirror of surface water.

Trolling, it is often said, is the best way to begin the process of discovering a lake's secrets. Agreed, but aimless wanderings are not the way. If a motor is used, shut it off. Rowing, except for the largest lakes, is better, a slow quiet circling with senses finely tuned. On the large lakes, motor until interesting water is reached, then shut down. For most anglers the exploration ends with the first fish snatched from the depths. An examination of stomach contents, clues to the unseen predator-prey warrings unfolding below, ends the search. Matching lure or fly pattern is tied on and casting begins. It is a relief, a settling back into well-worn ways and an end to disquieting probing of unknowns. But lakes are not formless puddles. Beneath the surface, subtle dynamics shift and rearrange unseen variables. To unravel the web of interconnected threads and discover the larger pattern requires a working knowledge of lake dynamics, the hidden constants which hold from lake to lake. Trolling until a fish is blundered upon provides valuable clues, but only that.

Lakes can be divided into two broad categories, eutrophic (nutrient-rich) and oligotrophic (nutrient-poor). Mentioning these terms to anglers regularly results in glazed-over eyes and stifled yawns, but recognizing a lake as being either eutrophic or oligotrophic is the first step towards understanding its hidden dynamics. For the most part, the lakes in this book are eutrophic. They are the best waters, growing larger fish faster than do oligotrophic lakes. Virtually all the small lakes of the Thompson-Nicola are eutrophic, rich in the essential nutrients required to foster aquatic life forms. The Okanagan offers such diverse angling largely because it offers a mix of both lake types. The cutthroat trout lakes of the Lower Mainland and Vancouver Island are mostly oligotrophic, low in nutrients and capable of sustaining low numbers of large, slow-growing fish. Biologists have arrived at complicated methods of determining whether a lake is nutrient-poor or nutrient-rich, but the angler standing on the shores of a new lake can make an educated guess by knowing the basic indicators.

The shape of a lake is often a good clue. Lakes with regular shorelines unbroken by bays, points and islands tend to be oligotrophic. Lakes with irregular shorelines offer more protection against the destructive action of wind and waves. Aquatic plants find more suitable habitat and the entire cycle leading to rich angling waters has a chance to become established. Erratic shorelines also mean more of the lake's area falls within the rich shallow-water zone. When new roads first provided access to the Omineca-Peace's Grassham Lake, just south of Stuart Lake in the Camsell group of lakes, one look at the maps would have been enough to get a canny angler's pulse racing. The lake has an incredibly convoluted shoreline with a multitude of bays and a number of islands. For the fly fisher this means more productive water to search with the fly; for spin-fishers it means more exciting casting and less mind-numbing trolling. In this case the guess would have been a good one; Grassham holds numbers of large, wild northern rainbow trout.

Weed growth is another good indicator. There are still anglers who avoid heavily weeded lakes or weeded areas of lakes. Anglers should not fear losing lures to weeds. A costly but cardinal angling rule says those who regularly hang up are the ones who regularly take the best fish. Extensive weed growth normally means great fishing. Most coastal lakes have very limited weed growth, an indication of their basic inability to foster rich aquatic life. Such waters can still offer good angling, but not if there is any pressure. Once the larger, older fish are harvested, many years will be required to replace them. If angling pressure continues during the rebuilding period, the fish never again reach optimum sizes. The lake char waters of the Skeena and Omineca-Peace regions, as well as those in the Okanagan, are prime examples of this dynamic. Char prefer pristine waters—clear, cold and essentially sterile lakes. They adapted to oligotrophic waters successfully enough to survive the age of glaciation, but not the predations of man. Like the lake-resident coastal cutthroat, once anglers have harvested the oldest, largest fish, there is no way to replace them short of closing the lake to fishing.

There are too many types of aquatic vegetation to delve into here, but a general understanding of broad categories is often enough for anglers wanting a quick indication of a lake's potential. The bottom-hugging weeds, such as the rich chara beds of the southern plateau lakes, are tip-offs to better-than-average angling waters. These weeds foster the aquatic insects upon which trout feed. The bottom weeds provide both habitat and feed for a plethora of aquatic creatures. When such vegetation grows in extensive mats, covering entire shallow-water bays and extending out from shore for some distance, expect rich waters. Some lakes have only limited areas of such growth. Palmer Lake in the Chilcotin is a prime example. Most of its shoreline is steeply-shelving and the bottom consists mainly of large cobble, fist-sized rock. A midlake shoal acts like a magnet for most fishers, but there is a solitary shallow-water bay which is covered from end to end by chara. Fly fishing this bay is like fishing one of the rich Thompson-Nicola pot-hole lakes, but anglers must be well enough versed in how lakes function to make the connection when they troll by the bay's entrance. None of the trollers I saw bothered to turn in. To them the water looked too shallow and weedy to fish successfully and thus they missed the lake's best fishing spot.

Weeds which extend out of the water are important to a variety of aquatic insects (chapter three explains how this works), but if the bottom-hugging varieties are not present as well, chances are the lake is oligotrophic. Lakes with lily pads, especially those marked by dark water, are generally poorer fishing waters, although far and away better than lakes with no or little weed growth. I know of at least one such lake which supports incredible numbers of fish, but the lily pads cover most of the lake and there are likely good areas of bottom-hugging weeds as well. Pond weeds, the long, tentacled weeds with small leaves spreading on or near the surface, are also an indication of poorer angling waters. Waters sporting such growth are not be dismissed out of hand. Kennedy Lake on Vancouver Island has the most extensive pond-weed beds of any lake I've ever seen and offers good fishing by coastal lake standards. Pond weeds provide prime stickleback habitat and cutthroat trout prefer three-spined stickleback to virtually all other prey fish, so Kennedy nurtures good numbers of cutthroat trout, some of impressive size. The trick is to place the lake within its broader biological context. A lily-padded southern interior lake will yield poorer fishing than a nearby lake with extensive chara beds, but a northern lake with lily pads or pond weeds likely holds bigger and better fish than similar lakes with no or little weed growth.

Extent and type of weed growth is a clearly visible indicator, but under the surface, unique unseen dynamics work at shaping a lake's biology. All but the shallowest lakes contain four distinct layers. Each layer is flexible, expanding and contracting with changes in temperature. This layering is vital to fish. For short periods in spring and fall the layers break down completely, resulting in what is called lake turnover, a thorough mixing of all waters from top to bottom. For many of the richest lakes, this mixing of the various water layers can result in massive fish kills. Decomposing vegetation robs the water of oxygen during the course of a winter. In heavily weeded lakes, the eutrophic waters, all remaining oxygen is concentrated in a narrow band near the surface against the lake's icy ceiling (hence, the best late-winter ice fishing is found near the surface where fish will be concentrated for the oxygen). When the ice melts and surface water temperatures change, turnover occurs and the layer of life-giving oxygen is dispersed throughout the lake and may be too low in concentration to support fish. Even when this catastrophe is avoided, lakes in the throes of turnover are in a state of turmoil. A period of seven to 14 days is normally required for a lake to recover from turnover. Fishing during this period is a waste of time; the fish will not return to active feeding until the lake has stabilized. For anglers, a working knowledge of the various layers and how they interact within the mini-universe of the lake is indispensable fishing lore.

Starting at the top and working down, the first layer is the surface itself, called the surface film by anglers and the meniscus by biologists. This is the lake's micro-thin skin, created by tension on the water, the resistance of lake to sky. For some aquatic creatures it is a floor they skate across, for others it is a ceiling they must break through and this is what will interest anglers. Tiny life forms such as the chironomids (see chapter three for a description of the major aquatic insects and their habits) must struggle to break through the surface tension. As they wriggle and writhe against their ceiling, they become vulnerable to fish. If enough insects are thus trapped, a frenzy of feeding fish follows. The caddis remains partially buoyed in the surface film as it metamorphoses from aquatic swimmer to flying insect and is thus also vulnerable to predators from below. Once tuned to the strange nether zone of the surface film, anglers will want to add butterfly nets to their arsenal of fishing tackle. They are used to collect the creatures trapped by surface tension, which can then be identified at least well enough to be imitated.

The epilimnion is the lake's top-water layer. It conforms to shoreline irregularities and thus contains the food shelf or littoral zone. This zone is the shallow-water area where sunlight penetrates and the magic of photosynthesis takes place. Normally the littoral zone extends to a depth of four or five metres, but may extend to depths of 10 metres in very clear waters. This, of course, is the area most frequented by trout. During the day they cruise its edges, darting in to snatch some morsel, then out again, but always with watchful eyes on the food shelf. As light fades they make everbolder forays into the shallows until near dark, when they hunt the shallow water with abandon. The epilimnion heats up quickly in the spring and thus spurs fish activity, but it is also the warmest layer and this is where algae blooms in summer. Anglers tend to shy away from lakes experiencing such blooms, but the green soup of micro plant and animal life rarely extends beyond three metres and fish often cruise its borders. Salmon Lake in the Thompson-Nicola is a prime example; I have taken good fish there simply by concentrating on depths immediately below the soup.

The thermocline will be familiar to many anglers. It is the middle layer where the temperature shift between the lake's upper and lower zones is most pronounced. In late spring and summer, water temperatures above the thermocline can be uncomfortable for fish. So they haunt its edges, staying clear of the uncomfortable epilimnion, but close enough to prey on surface-bound insects or small forage fish which are there for much the same reasons. Finding the thermocline is difficult without a thermometer, but possible by using the count-down method until fish are located. The major drawback to fishing the thermocline is the faith required: it's hard to believe fish are lurking at mid-levels when experience teaches that the littoral zone is the most productive water. The canny angler taking fish on a hot day when everyone else is working on their tan is likely fishing the thermocline.

Which leaves only the hypolimnium, the dark, murky reaches of the bottom itself. Lake char spend much of their lives in this cold, gloomy zone, but for trout it is important mainly in early winter, when warmer water sinks and enriches the bottom layer's supply of oxygen. (In July and August, oxygen supply is greatest in the epilimnion where circulation remains good.) At the bottom of shallower lakes, stagnation results in depleted oxygen supplies. Fish will stay clear, but since water temperatures in the oxygen-rich epilimnion are too high for comfort, fish concentrate in the narrow band between the layers, the thermocline.

Reading lakes is an intuitive process for many experienced anglers. They take in everything, adjust, react and continue without conscious thought. Others are doggedly determined. They cruise the edges, stopping to jot notes or make small maps. Their process across the lake is erratic. A shoreline is followed only to be abandoned; one bay is minutely probed, the next bypassed altogether. These are different approaches to the same end. One gathers the clues intuitively, automatically comparing, sifting, rejecting here, accepting there. The other demands concrete evidence, squiggly lines drawn on water-splashed paper. In both cases a picture is formed, an understanding reached. Slowly the bits and pieces accrue, each new lake adding its embellishments, its own variation to the broader theme. It is a game without end, nature's grand open-ended puzzle. The reward lies in the understanding gained, the answers angled for and the mysteries touched.

Okanagan Lakes

*F*or the purposes of this lakes listing, the Okanagan has been divided into east and west sections based on the natural north/south line formed by the Okanagan Valley. The West Okanagan takes in the parkland country west of Okanagan Lake, while the East Okanagan extends east of the big lake as far as the Monashee Mountains. To make lake location easier, both east and west portions of the region have been further divided along north/south lines centred on the city of Kelowna. Hence, Christina Lake is found under listings for Okanagan East/Southern Portion, while Mabel Lake is found under listings for Okanagan East/Northern Portion.

Okanagan East Lakes/Northern Portion

Waters east of Okanagan Lake and north of Kelowna are found under this heading. As always, the emphasis is on small angling lakes, but the area also holds a number of large lakes offering mixed-stock fisheries.

» WAP LAKE—Nestled in the narrow Wap Creek valley between the Monashee Mountain's Hunter and Mabel ranges, this small lake is known primarily for its medium-sized rainbow trout, although it also supports a large population of Dolly Varden char and whitefish. Mixed fish populations make trolling an effective method, both for char and trout. Best Dolly fishing is in the fall. Access is either south off Hwy 1 at Three Valley Gap; east and north from Enderby along the west side of Mabel Lake, or north from Lumby up the east side of Mabel Lake. A high-clearance vehicle is required.

» KIDNEY AND LIVER LAKES—See the introduction to this chapter for full details. Kidney has the larger fish, good numbers of rainbow trout in the four-pound class; fish in Liver are about half the size. Together with nearby Wap and Mabel lakes, these lakes would make a good destination for anglers interested in sampling a variety of Okanagan angling experiences. Access is as for Wap Lake, but the best approach is from Enderby over the Kingfisher Main logging road, then the spur road east about 35 kilometres north of Hupel. Best camping is at Kidney.

» HIDDEN LAKE—This relatively large, scenic lake holds rainbow trout to six pounds and better, although the larger fish, as always, are difficult. Spring and fall are the best fishing seasons, but do not expect solitary angling on this popular lake with three Forest Service campsites. Trolling is the most popular method, but there are reports of good fly fishing for those who take the time to explore; creek inlets as well as the outlet stream at the northern end are worth probing both for fly fishers and trollers. Good road all the way east from Enderby (Mabel Lake road), then south near Hupel. Alternately, turn south off Mabel Lake road at Ashton Creek, then east on good gravel to the lake.

» MABEL LAKE—See the introduction to this chapter for full details. Mixed-stock fishery; rainbow trout to eight pounds, lake trout to 15 pounds-plus. Kokanee, Dolly Varden char and whitefish are also present. Access is over the Mabel Lake road from Enderby with four Forest Service campsites and lodge facilities at the lake.

» HOLSTEIN AND KATHY LAKES—These two lakes in the Silver

Hills between Mabel and Sugar lakes are small, secluded lakes with good gravel road access. Fish size was reported as small at time of writing, but this may change as management strives to increase fish size. Holstein holds rainbow trout, while Kathy holds both rainbows and brook trout. Access is north from Lumby on the Mabel Lake road, then east on a branch road near Ireland Creek.

» BISSON LAKE—A small lake with a reputation for large rainbow trout, to four pounds and better. It is suited to fly fishing, but is popular with trollers, which may make fly fishing difficult depending on the number of boats trolling. To get there, leave Hwy 6 south of Monashee Pass (past Cherryville) on the gravel Kettle River road, then go north on a spur road to the lake.

» ECHO (LUMBY) LAKE—A take-your-breath-away lake with some very large fish but heavy angling pressure. A fishing lodge, store and 154-hectare Echo Lake Provincial Park (limited camping) make this a good family-fishing lake. Trolling is the most popular method, but canny fly fishers should do well, notably over the shoals along the north side and the western end. The lake holds a good population of gammarus shrimp, accounting for the large size and superb condition of the fish (see the section on scuds in chapter five). The lake was stocked with late-spawning Gerrard-strain rainbows (see chapter seven) in 1987. These fish grow to larger sizes before reaching maturity, but heavy pressure likely means few will survive to reach exceptional sizes. Kokanee numbers are low, but run to very large sizes. Lake trout are also present, which helps explain the popularity of trolling on this lake. Average size of rainbow trout is around the two-pound mark. Deep-trolling accounts for most of the really large fish. East of Lumby on Hwy 6, turn right on a signed, good-surface gravel road. Echo is 21 kilometres in on this road. Spring and fall are best fishing seasons.

» KEEFER AND HOLMES LAKES—These two small lakes make a good family-fishing destination, with lodge facilities available at Keefer. Holmes provides more secluded angling for those seeking an escape. Neither lake holds particularly large fish—a good fish might go two pounds—but the fishing can be very fast and children are rarely concerned with fish size. In addition to rainbow trout, both also hold brook trout (see chapter six). The brookies make for exciting fishing in the fall months when they don their spectacular spawning colours. They are also more aggressive at this time, making them easier to catch. To get there, leave Monashee Hwy 6 south of McIntyre Lake on the gravel road going up the Kettle River.

» SUGAR AND KATE LAKES—Dolly Varden char in the five- to 10-pound range and Gerrard-strain rainbow trout to about four pounds are the main drawing cards to Sugar, a large trolling lake. A number of good creek inlets are candidates for the fly, mainly forage-fish patterns fished on the sinking line. Sugar also holds kokanee and burbot. The best fly fishing is in the river channel at the north end. Angling for whitefish is excellent, both in size and numbers, notably during early April and especially in the river above and below the lake. Nearby Kate Lake, reached by walking about three kilometres on a very rough road from the Sugar Mountain lookout, holds good numbers of medium-sized to small rainbow trout. This small lake is suited to fly fishing; float tubes or canoes are a good idea. To get to Sugar, turn north off Monashee Hwy 6 at Cherryville on gravel road for about 16 kilometres.

» BEAR LAKE—This tiny lake holds some fair-sized rainbow trout, but while numbers are low, there is a good chance of having the lake to oneself. The fish are wild, as opposed to stocked, a matter of no small importance to many fishers. Maximum size is about two pounds, but the wild streak will be noticed by those canny enough to fool these fish. To get there, take Hwy 6 to Coldstream, then the gravel Oyama Lake road south; the last few kilometres may be very rough and require a walk.

» OYAMA LAKE—The very rough road in to this super fishing lake requires a truck at minimum, but the rewards are great for those who persevere over the 15 kilometres of rough road east from Oyama. Relatively large in size (260 hectares), Oyama is nevertheless known as a fly fishing lake and reportedly holds good numbers of fish in the six-pounds-plus range. A fishing camp provides most facilities.

» DEE LAKES—Four interconnected lakes, Crooked, Deer, Island and Dee, make up this chain of fast-fishing lakes. Dee is said to hold the largest fish, rainbow trout to about four pounds, but there is no reason to suppose fish of similar size are not present in the rest of the chain. All are excellent fishing lakes suitable to either fly fishing or trolling. A number of other small lakes are accessible from these lakes: the two Flyfish lakes, Loon Lake and Brunette Lake (with larger rainbows), are among those worth probing. Public access to the Dee chain is probably best at the Island Lake Forest Service campsite; a lodge is located on Dee Lake. To get there, take the Vernon Creek road (good gravel) east from Winfield for about 27 kilometres.

» DOREEN LAKE—This quality angling lake has been restricted to fly fishing only for many years and holds good numbers of fish in the four-pounds-plus range. These fish are notoriously moody; anglers can expect frustrating hours with large fish showing just often enough to keep interest high. Doreen is a match-the-hatch lake after the fashion of Thompson-Nicola lakes. It is also a very nice camping lake. To get there, continue past Dee Lake for about two kilometres.

» POSTILL LAKE AND WALK-INS—Postill is a very popular lake with all facilities less than 20 kilometres north of Kelowna. The lake holds both rainbow trout and brook trout, but neither species grows to exceptional sizes; typical fish run from 1.5 to two pounds. Seven small lakes (Glen, Hereron, Meadow, South and Twin are among the best known) can be reached by trail from Postill. These lakes typically produce small to medium-sized rainbow trout but offer rewarding angling in uncrowded settings. The lodge at Postill maintains boats on a number of these lakes.

Okanagan East Lakes/Southern Portion

Lakes under this heading lie east of the Okanagan Valley and south of the city of Kelowna. Main roads are Hwy 33 east and south from Kelowna to Rock Creek (at the junction with Hwy 3) and the Christian Valley road up the Kettle River.

» BROWNE LAKE—This small lake, like nearby Hydraulic Lake (McCulloch Reservoir), is subject to drawdown for irrigation purposes, but it does have a reputation for producing rainbow trout to about four pounds. Browne probably provides the best angling in the group of lakes, which includes Pear, Minnow, Idabel and Haynes, as well as Hydraulic. Most of these lakes produce smaller rainbow trout, but the fishing can be fast at times. A number of lodges and facilities are available. To get there, take Hwy 33 east from Kelowna for about 40 kilometres to the Hydraulic Lake road; Browne lies about two kilometres beyond Hydraulic Lake on a good gravel road.

» COPPERKETTLE LAKE—A small fly-only lake nestled in its own side valley high above the Kettle River requiring a short (three-kilometre) hike to reach. Fish size is not large, to about two pounds, but solitude and a nice setting provide ample compensation. To get there take the Christian Valley road north from Westbridge at the Hwy 33 junction. Copperkettle is about 63 kilometres in on this gravel road. The trailhead is located just south of the Forest Service campsite at Damfino Creek. Alternate access is from Beaverdell off Hwy 33 on the Beaverdell Creek road.

» SANDRIFT AND STATE LAKES—The Sandrift group consists of three small lakes well suited to fly fishing, while nearby State is a fly-only lake reached by a short (two-kilometre) walk from the State Lake road Forest Service campsite south of the Sandrift group. Fish size tends to be small, but rainbow trout in the Sandrift group can reach large sizes. State is said to provide excellent fishing for rainbow trout to about two pounds, with average size between one and 1.5 pounds. Road conditions can be very rough, requiring four-wheel drive for the last 15 kilometres or more. To get there, take the Beaverdell Creek road off Hwy 33 at Beaverdell, then take a spur road located 10 kilometres past the Forest Service's Sago Creek campsite. The lakes are about 15 kilometres in on this spur road.

» JOAN, LASSIE AND CUP LAKES—All three are within 40 kilometres of Beaverdell on Hwy 33 and provide good fishing for smaller rainbow trout. Cup Lake rainbows tend to be larger (to about two pounds) than those found in the other two lakes, but Joan Lake rainbows, while somewhat smaller, are wild fish. A walk is required to reach Joan; the trailhead is found beyond Cup Lake on a branch road past Lassie Lake's northern end. Otherwise, directions are as for Sandrift Lake.

» THONE LAKE—At more than 1,250 metres in elevation this small, high lake should provide good angling through the hot-weather months. Maximum size of its rainbow trout is about two pounds, but they come to the fly readily. To get there, take the Christian Valley (Kettle River) road north from Westbridge for about 25 kilometres to a branch road leading east across the river. This good-surface branch road provides access to the lake.

» CHRISTINA LAKE—Large holiday-style lakes lying adjacent to major highways are not normally listed here, but Christina, despite the crowds, is special. This large, 2,600-hectare lake is very productive and provides good angling for a variety of species, including large rainbow trout, smallmouth bass, small kokanee and whitefish. Trolling accounts for most of the large rainbow trout, but a good fly fisher working shallow water early and late in the day might expect exciting angling. Smallmouth bass are found in shallow bays and can be taken with spinning gear or flies. Best whitefish season is fall. All facilities are available. Christina is located east of Grand Forks on Hwy 3.

» JEWEL LAKE—Long known for its large rainbow trout, this productive lake will quickly win the hearts of fly fishers. A good Jewel Lake rainbow will run to five or six pounds (although the average size is considerably smaller) and these fish come to the fly very willingly. Extensive areas of emerald green aquatic vegetation beg for the careful working of submerged nymphs (dragonfly patterns are known producers) and there is almost always an evening rise to hold anglers on the water until after sunset. High elevation makes for good fishing through the hot months. To get there, watch for a railroad underpass east of Greenwood on Hwy 3. Turn north on a paved road and continue for about 10 kilometres to the lake, which offers full facilities and a lodge.

» XENIA LAKE—This small, remote lake north of Grand Forks on the Granby River road is regularly stocked with rainbow trout which grow to about two pounds. A nice fly fishing lake, but the road can be very rough and four-wheel drive is likely required. From Grand Forks on Hwy 3, take the road on the east side of the Granby River for about 30 kilometres, then a rough branch road east for about five kilometres.

» OSOYOOS LAKE—This is another large lake (4,000 hectares) lying beside a major highway (Hwy 3), but is included due to its productivity and the variety of species available. Believed to be Canada's warmest lake, with average summer water temperatures of 24 degrees Celsius, Osoyoos lies in the most northerly extension of Mexico's Sonoran Desert, Canada's only true desert. Much of the desert country surrounding this 19-kilometre-long lake is under irrigation. The lake's sandy beaches, massive, draping willow trees and nearby desert combine to evoke the feel and flavour of a strange, exotic world. Rare wildlife, such as burrowing owls, painted turtles, pygmy horned toads and even scorpions, do nothing to detract from the lake's otherworldly feeling. The variety of fish species is also exotic by B.C. standards. There are 12 different fish species, including largemouth and smallmouth bass, perch, black crappie, kokanee and some very large rainbow trout. The rainbow trout can run to 10-pounds-plus, although fish between four and five pounds are more typical. Best trout fishing is in the spring, with trolling by far the most popular method. Kokanee fishing holds up well through the summer. Best fishing for the more exotic species is found in the oxbows and shallow bays and in the river channel at the lake's northern end.

» VASEUX LAKE—See the introduction to this chapter for full details on this lake's one-of-a-kind bass fishery, which boasts largemouth bass to 10 pounds, and an average size between five and six pounds. (See also the section on bass in chapter seven.) Jumbo-sized yellow perch, a fine table fish, are also found in this unique lake, as are some of the largest carp in B.C. (see chapter two for carp-fishing tactics). The lake lies alongside Hwy 97 about five kilometres south of Okanagan Falls.

Okanagan West Lakes/Northern Portion

Lakes under this heading lie to the west of the Okanagan Valley and north of an imaginary line based on the city of Kelowna.

» GARDOM LAKE—This is a very popular lake complete with regional park, but Gardom has long been known as a good producer of larger rainbow trout. Heavy angling pressure has sharply reduced chances of taking large fish, with most of the year's annual stocking of rainbow yearlings caught during the same year. Still, this may change and the lake does have a long-standing reputation for rainbow and brook trout in the four- to five-pound class. Gardom is easily reached by travelling northwest from Enderby on Hwy 97B for about 10 kilometres to the park access road which branches west off the highway.

» SQUARE LAKE—This tiny dot of a lake produces rainbow trout to about two pounds, but careful Fisheries Branch management may result in larger fish in the future; it is a good fly lake which bears watching. To get there turn off Hwy 97 about 10 kilometres west of Falkland on the road to Pinaus Lake. Square lies immediately east of Pinaus.

» PINAUS AND LADY KING LAKES—See the introduction to this chapter for full details. There are reasonable chances of taking fish to five pounds, and good chances of taking fish to two pounds. There are a number of nearby small angling lakes, including Lady King. The road in to these lakes is treacherous when wet, but easy going in dry weather. Best access is off Hwy 97 on a gravel road about 10 kilometres west of Falkland.

» DRINKIE LAKE—This small, scenic hike-in lake is in the process of being groomed to produce large rainbow trout. The effects of these management efforts should be noticeable within the next few years; it is definitely a lake worth watching. To get there, take the Lambly Creek logging road north of Westbank on Okanagan Lake's west shore, then a branch road located just south of Christie Lake. A final spur branches off this road to the lake and requires a walk of two kilometres or more, depending on road conditions and the vehicle used. A truck or four-wheel drive is required.

» JACKPINE LAKE—Another well-known favourite, Jackpine produces rainbow trout to about three pounds or slightly better, although average size is much smaller. Lodge on the lake provides directions to two nearby walk-in lakes, making Jackpine a candidate for family outings. To get there, take the Last Mountain road from Westbank, then watch for a sign about 10 kilometres past Last Mountain. Can also be reached from the Lambly Creek road.

Okanagan West Lakes/Southern Portion

Lakes under this heading are located to the west of the Okanagan Valley and south of an imaginary line based on the city of Kelowna.

» HEADWATERS LAKES—There are four lakes in the group, all used as irrigation reservoirs and all subject to drawdown, making them less appealing angling lakes than might otherwise be the case. The chance to catch rainbow and brook trout in the same lake mitigates this somewhat, and there are reports that both species can reach weights of four pounds in these small lakes. Headwaters 1, the largest of the group, is said to provide the best brook trout fishing, for both size and numbers. To get there, leave Hwy 97 at Peachland; take the Peachland Creek road for 10 kilometres, then the Greata Creek road to the lake.

» TEEPEE LAKES—Tough to reach without four-wheel drive, these three lakes, Friday, Saturday and Sunday, are collectively known as the Teepee Lakes and provide fast fishing for medium-sized rainbow trout. Saturday and

Sunday lakes are reached by short walks from Friday, where a lodge provides services, including a private jeep access road to the group. All are excellent fly fishing lakes. Access is also possible from Peachland by continuing past Headwaters Lakes, but time and trouble are saved by going through the lodge.

» KENTUCKY, ALLEYNE AND BLUEY LAKES—See the introduction to this chapter for full details on these excellent family-destination lakes. Bluey Lake holds rainbow trout to about four pounds with average size between one and two pounds. Coarse fish in Alleyne were killed off in 1956; Kentucky Lake coarse fish were removed in 1959. Both contain good numbers of gammarus shrimp and vast numbers of chironomids (see chapter five for gammarus, chapter three for chironomids), making them capable of producing large, well-conditioned fish, but fishing pressure is heavy. To reach these lakes, turn east off Hwy 5A immediately south of Aspen Grove on the signed Bates Road (good surface) which leads to the lakes.

» BOSS, DAVIS AND TAHLA LAKES—A group of small lakes which makes a good family-fishing destination with increasingly good chances of larger fish. Davis, most southerly in the group and the first reached by road, is said to hold the largest fish, rainbow trout to about four pounds. Boss, just north of Davis, is being groomed to produce larger fish, while Tahla, most northerly and smallest of the group, provides fast fishing for smaller rainbow trout. All three have Forest Service campsites and are suited to fly fishing. From Hwy 5A, just south of the turnoff for Kentucky/Alleyne lakes, turn west on a gravel road, then take the first branch road north to the lakes.

» ANDYS LAKE—A tiny, get-away-from-it-all lake with wild rainbow trout, which requires a short hike to reach. The fish tend to be small, but there is a good chance of having this lake to oneself. Nearby Brook Lake is reached by trail from Andys and provides similar angling as well as a good excuse for a short hike. Access is as for Boss, Davis and Tahla, but carry on past the turnoff to these lakes for another 15 kilometres to a branch road turning south. The trailhead to Andys is about 12 kilometres in on this rough road, which will likely require a pickup truck or high-clearance vehicle.

» GREEN, HARVEY HALL, LODWICK AND THALIA LAKES—These lakes are located amid a scattering of about 14 small lakes just off Hwy 5A north of Allison Lake (about 30 kilometres north of Princeton). Fish size varies from lake to lake, but typically ranges from two to four pounds. Green is the only one of the group on the east side of Hwy 5A and holds rainbow as well as brook trout, with some larger fish. Harvey Hall also holds brookies and rainbows, while Lodwick and Thalia are rainbow lakes. The number of lakes compressed into a relatively small area and a circuitous, looping road network make getting lost all too easy, but there is a lake at the end of each branch road and the exploring can be fun, even if one is never quite certain which lake one is fishing. Thalia is furthest in and the road can get rough; two-wheel-drive vehicles should turn around before bogging down.

» CATHEDRAL PARK LAKES—A number of fine fishing lakes located within this wilderness park are perhaps best suited to experienced hikers/fishers who do not mind stretching their legs to get to good fishing waters in spectacular settings. Alternately, there is a private lodge within the park, with a private jeep access road directly to the alpine lakes. Contact the Parks Branch for information on the lodge and transportation arrangements. From the lodge at Quiniscoe Lake, four other turquoise-coloured lakes in alpine meadows can be reached over a trail network. Fishing is fast for small alpine rainbow and cutthroat trout. The Haystack Lakes can be reached over the Ewart

Creek Trail along the park's eastern boundary. A hike of about 20 kilometres is required to reach this group of small alpine lakes.

For more information contact:

Fisheries Branch
3547 Skaha Lake Road
Penticton, B.C.
V2A 7K2

Okanagan Similkameen Tourist Association
104-515 Highway 97 South
Kelowna, B.C.
V1Z 3J2

CHAPTER FIVE

The Chilcotin

Once off the beaten track west of Williams Lake, which is to say anywhere off the main road to Bella Coola (Hwy 20), forget all about marking time in terms of hours. Forget even any notions of day trips. Think in terms of days, even weeks, because this Chilcotin country is an eyeful of what the best of B.C. is all about. Small alpine tarns, glittering fiord-like lakes, rushing streams and snow-capped peaks are all rolled into one impossible panorama. At such junctures time has no meaning—at least not until it runs out. And the awful truth is, nowhere does time slip by more quickly than in the meandering byways of the Chilcotin.

This entire sweep of country, both north and south of Hwy 20, is remote, sparsely settled backcountry with much of it qualifying as out-and-out wilderness. Most services are available along Hwy 20 and there are small lodges tucked away here and there in the hinterlands, but exploring anglers should be self-sufficient and must be properly equipped for backroad travel. In some areas snow can be expected during any month of the year: I recall a July outing called short due to snow. In the main, however, the Chilcotin is notoriously dry country, and dust, not rain or snow, is most often the bane of backroad exploration. Still, it is wise to be prudent: a Chilcotin backroad easily travelled during dry weather can become an impassable quagmire given a little rain.

In recent years high-volume logging has come to the Chilcotin. No matter where one stands on this hotly debated issue, anglers must now take logging trucks into consideration when travelling off the main road. For specific information, stop at any of a number of small stores or service stations along Hwy 20 before branching off. The local folks will know where and when logging traffic is running, or be able to provide further sources of information. In a region of slow-growing trees with questionable commercial value, clear-cut logging seems like sheer madness, but it appears the die has been cast and we will have to learn to live with this brand of despoliation. On the positive side of the ledger, the Chilcotin is a vast region and, for now at least, anglers will have little difficulty finding unscarred settings in which to fish.

The fishing itself is best described as dramatic, given the spectacular backdrop provided by the Coast Range mountains and the still largely unspoiled woodland vistas of the Chilcotin Plateau. The primary quarry is, of course, rainbow trout, but there is also a better-than-even chance of landing trophy-sized Dolly Varden char. Eastern brook trout have been introduced to a handful of lakes, some of which produce large fish. Like the Dolly Varden, brook trout, despite the name, are members of the char family. The lake-

Ian forbes

resident Dolly Varden char, as opposed to the river dwellers, will appeal primarily to anglers who prefer conventional trolling, since they are almost exclusively piscivorous (fish-eating). Brook trout will readily take a fly and are famed for their willingness to rise to the dry fly, even in the absence of any major hatch or other surface activity. As well as these species, there are cutthroat trout in the far western Chilcotin, mainly in the hike-in or air-access lakes of Tweedsmuir Park. Salmon and steelhead are found in a number of rivers tributary to the Fraser as well as in the rivers which meet tidewater at or near Bella Coola, although these seagoing species are beyond the scope of this book.

It is the rainbow trout which lures most anglers to the Chilcotin and a variety of angling opportunities exist for these prized fish. Scattered throughout the region are lakes which hold the larger, wily fish sought by serious anglers. In some cases these lakes have been carefully managed by provincial fisheries biologists to produce exceptional angling; in others the large fish are due entirely to natural causes, often thanks to the presence of *Gammerus limnaeus*, the tiny freshwater shrimp known as scuds (explained in a later section of this chapter). Aquatic insect life is often poor in the region's largest lakes. In such lakes rainbow trout have adapted by becoming piscivorous, forcing fly fishers to adopt the heroic efforts required to fish deeper water with minnow patterns. Spinning tackle and trolling gear is, of course, ideal for such lakes. In the smaller lakes characterized by the heavy weed growth which fosters aquatic insects, fly fishers will do well with much the same style and patterns employed in the famous Kamloops trout lakes found further south. Bait and hardware fishers will find themselves at a disadvantage in such waters.

Fly-in lakes are often described as the ultimate Chilcotin fishing experience and, truly, one would be hard-pressed to find a fishing trip which offers more in terms of a soul-satisfying experience. The trout in these remote lakes are generally smaller fish, but they are as wild as the settings in which they are found. Catching them is most often merely a matter of placing some offering in the water—these are not, rest assured, sophisticated fish. Some remote lakes do offer larger trout, and even those which hold predominantly smaller fish will occasionally yield a few giants. In the main, however, the fishing is fast and furious for trout averaging one to 1.5 pounds. Charter air services are available from a number of points along Hwy 20 (Nimpo Lake is something of a mecca) and these operators or nearby lodges will have specific seasonal information on the kind of angling to be expected at a range of lakes within reasonable flying distance (the listing of lakes at the end of this chapter also has information on these lakes).

Packhorse fishing trips are offered by a number of outfitters scattered across the Chilcotin. The horses used for such trips are, in the main, mild-mannered mountain ponies which will follow along nicely no matter how inexperienced the rider. I have little or no affinity for horses and even less riding experience, yet still managed the rigours of a 10-day Chilcotin packhorse trip without mishap or unbearable discomfort. The rewards, even for dubious riders, are great. The horses can access waters no four-wheel-drive vehicle can ever hope to reach and even some which are beyond the landing requirements of floatplanes. There is, without question, no better way to experience the Chilcotin's remote alpine terrain than on horseback. However, only a select few outfitters specifically gear their operations to fishing. For the serious angler it is important to distinguish between outfitters who offer fishing as an adjunct to sight-seeing rides and those who make fishing a primary goal. Ask for precise details on the nature of the trip and how much time is allotted for fishing each day of the trip. References should be willingly given; avoid those not forthcoming in this regard.

Generally speaking, the fishing is best in the spring and fall, something which is true almost anywhere in the province with the exception of far northern waters. There are, however, a number of mitigating factors. In the Chilcotin, spring does not arrive as early as in more southerly regions and the heat of summer is slower in building and generally not as intense. Consequently, the fast fishing of the spring/early summer months lasts much longer than what southern anglers have come to expect. The slow fishing of the summer doldrums may span only a period of several weeks as opposed to two or even three months farther south. Altitude also plays a role. Generally, the Chilcotin Plateau slopes upward towards the Coast Range mountains to the west. The farther west one travels, the greater the likelihood of encountering good fishing through the heat of high summer, a result of the increased altitude which makes for moderate heat during the day and cool to downright frigid evenings. The opposite is, of course, true of the fall months: fall comes earlier and water temperatures, a major factor influencing fish activity, drop sooner than in the south.

September and October are my personal favourite months in the Chilcotin, but this is purely subjective—I like the snap of fall in the air and most lakes are empty of other anglers by then. This is important to those who enjoy solitude with their fishing, and the quiet days of fall seem tailor-made for solitary reflection over a fishing rod. I have fished as late as mid-October in the more low-lying eastern parts of the Chilcotin and experienced quality angling for large fish. Truthfully, though, the large fish caught at this time tended to be somewhat lacklustre, and I'm convinced this was due to low water temperatures. Still, eight-pound rainbow trout, even if a tad slower than normal, are big, exciting fish: getting them to the boat is no trifling matter, even if they don't display the incredibly long, heart-stopping runs one expects of larger-than-life-sized rainbow trout. Normally, provided temperatures have not taken an unseasonal plummet, the fish of September still provide such sizzling runs.

The Chilcotin encompasses all the superlatives normally applied to B.C. in one grand sweep of country. Quality angling in such settings is a bonus all anglers should strive to maintain. Seriously consider practising catch-and-release fishing with barbless hooks. This is not always easy when confronted with a wilderness of plenty, but this wealth of the wild country is a tenuous thing, one which is easily depleted. The opportunity to catch large wild fish in unmanaged or natural waters grows less with each passing year and once gone is lost forever. Groomed waters with stocked fish are a poor substitute for the genuine article. It is incumbent on the present generation of anglers, likely the last to be confronted with the choice, to ensure wild fish in wild waters will be there for the future.

Closeup: The South Chilcotin

*F*or the uninitiated, the sheer vastness of the Chilcotin can be overwhelming. My own early explorations, while always spiritually satisfying in the way of the backcountry, did not regularly result in pulse-quickening angling for just this reason. There was always so much to explore, so much wild country beckoning, that fishing often took a back seat. When angling did remain a primary goal, exceptional waters were often unwittingly bypassed in favour of harder-to-get-to but ultimately less-productive lakes. Not that I regret a moment of those early trips. Still, as both wilderness and quality angling become increasingly rare, it seems a real missed opportunity not to take advantage when the two are offered in combination.

For the angler this is the Chilcotin's special attraction—pristine waters, unparalleled natural settings and quality angling for large trout. Finding them all in one place is no simple feat, even in the Chilcotin. Secondary roads branch out in all directions and lakes abound on all sides. The possiities, it would seem, are as limitless as the Chilcotin's endless horizons. Where, the angler might well ask, does one start? To help limit the possibilities, following is a guide to one of my favourite regions of the Chilcotin, the big lake country of the south.

This slice of country lies south of Hwy 20 between Hanceville and Tatla Lake. Three great lakes backed against the highest peaks of the snow- and ice-crusted Coast Range dominate the region's geography: Taseko to the east, Tatlayoko in the west and shimmering Chilko, set with jeweler's precision to lie gleaming in between. In the hills, draws and side valleys between the big lakes lie countless hidden alpine meadows rich in game and strewn with the wildflowers of the high country. At every turn there are waters designed to waylay wayward fishermen—from solitary wilderness lakes ringed with the tell-tale rise-forms of surface-feeding rainbows, to sparkling rivers holding the promise of large Dolly Varden grown heavy on the eggs and fry of spawning salmon.

It is a country of contradictions, wild and remote in its mountains, sparkling waters and the very smell of wilderness; close and tame in the deceiving ease with which it can be travelled during the dry months. A combination of good-surface backroads, old wagon roads, cart tracks, abandoned mining roads, and just about every variation in between criss-crosses this slice of the Chilcotin. It would be the easiest thing in the world to swing south from Hanceville in the spring and re-emerge at Tatla Lake only when the snows drive the game out of the high country. Since most of us count our backcountry time in terms of days, not seasons, a few signposts will help.

It is possible to drive overland from Hanceville to Tatla Lake and touch on all three big lakes (Taseko, Chilko, Tatlayoko), but it is the small-lake country in between which makes the trip special for anglers. A pickup truck or similar high-clearance vehicle is required to make the entire circuit. How much of it can be tackled by two-wheel-drive vehicles depends on the weather and the skill and nerves of the driver and crew. The road from Hanceville south and west is easy going for two-wheel-drive vehicles, even family sedans, as far as Chilko Lake (the final drop to the Forest Service campsite at Chilko may be rough, but passable with reasonable care). That's the good news. From Chilko the road north to Tsuniah Lake is rough and the going slow and wearying as far as the bridge crossing the Chilko River. For the record, consider four-wheel drive necessary to making this portion of the trip.

Covering the entire circuit in one bone-jarring, hard-driving day is conceivable. Road distance from Hanceville to Chilko Lake is about 117 kilometres, or three to four hours driving time, but don't consider that remotely realistic, not if fishing and exploring are part of the plan. From Chilko Lake to the bridge crossing the Chilko River things get a little fuzzy. The actual road distance is about 50 kilometres, but driving time will depend on how wet the roads are. From the bridge out to Tatla Lake, the road is good and the distance easily covered, but save a few days for the dog-leg south along the upper Homathko River to Tatlayoko Lake, also on good road.

Cross the Chilcotin River just after leaving Lee's Corner (Hanceville) and it is soon clear why the minimum driving time is so improbable. Ascend the series of switchbacks to the bench above the river, and there the road forks for the first time. The west (right) fork runs across the plateau to Taseko and the country beyond. The south fork dips to Fletcher Lake, Big Creek, Kloacut Lake and some of the finest fishing in the Chilcotin. The Fletcher Lake/Big Creek road is a detour from the circuit, but if fishing figures among the reasons for meandering through this country, take the left fork south.

Fletcher Lake/Big Creek to Kloacut Lake

Fletcher Lake has long had a reputation for holding large

trout, fish up to 10 pounds, with many between two and six pounds. My own somewhat limited experience on this lake has never resulted in taking fish anywhere near the magic double-digit mark. Most of the fish I caught were about two pounds in weight, with the largest between two and three pounds. However, Fletcher is not known to give up its largest fish to the fly. Trolling hardware seems to account for most of the large fish taken each year. Best places to fish are in the area around the reed bed clearly visible from the small roadside Forest Service campground (there is also a small lodge with rental cabins). Fish all around the reed bed, concentrating on the deeper water off either of the two points formed at the narrow ends of the weeds. This is where the larger fish are most often caught.

The chances of catching large Fletcher Lake rainbows is expected to improve in the next few years. The provincial Fisheries Branch, in conjunction with Ducks Unlimited, has recently improved water supply to the lake through diversion projects and construction of a dam at the outlet, as well as making improvements to spawning habitat. Returns on this effort are just beginning to show, but hold promise for the years to come. Even now the fishing at Fletcher is fast. Taking a limit of two-pound-and-better trout should not be difficult and the chance of a truly large fish is always there. Unlike so many Chilcotin lakes, Fletcher is not remote; private cabins ring much of the lake and there are almost always some anglers out probing its waters, notably in the spring and early summer months and in the fall when fishing is at its peak.

Nearby Mons Lake, reached by taking a side road to the east shortly after Big Creek (look for the rural mail boxes; Big Creek is not a town) is more suited to the fly fisher. Fish average between one and 1.5 pounds although there are also enough fish in the three- to four-pound class to make for exciting angling. This lake runs hot and cold for reasons which remain a mystery. Some days the fishing is stupendous, with fish taking on virtually every cast; on others it is as if there were no fish in the lake.

Willan Lake, visible on the north side of the Big Creek road a few kilometres beyond the Mons Lake turnoff, is subject to winter kill and is a poor bet, but Kloacut Lake, a few kilometres farther along and reached after crossing a grazing lease (be sure to shut the gate after passing through) is a personal favourite which holds exceptionally large trout. This is a bright, clear lake with extensive shoals and weed growth, making it a fly caster's delight and a troller's hell. There is no organized campground and there are several private cabins, but angling pressure appears to be light, probably because the lake winterkills from time to time. Water levels have been good over the last few years and the fishing at Kloacut has been excellent as a result. Best times to fish Kloacut are early and late in the season; expect fish to average about 24 inches in length.

Besides these lakes there are a number of smaller, pond-like lakes accessible by four-wheel drive over the secondary road network which branches south in the vicinity of Willan Lake. Some of these lakes hold exceptional trout, but all are subject to periodic winterkill so one is never certain what to expect. For those with adequate vehicles and a yen to explore, this road network, often little more than cart tracks, can lead to a real bonanza . . . or not, depending on conditions over the previous winter.

Scum/Haines Lake Chains

On the Taseko Lake road (backtrack almost to Hanceville from Fletcher Lake) the next decision comes shortly after crossing McDermott Creek near New Meadows. A rough road branching off to the right leads north to the little-fished Scum and Haines chains of lakes. These are a chain of pond-like lakes best fished early in the summer and again in September, but don't even contemplate the road unless equipped with four-wheel drive. Newly developed logging roads are said to now swing past the Haines Lakes close enough to make access possible. Inquire at the general store in Hanceville if tempted by this possibility. The Scum Lakes give up small rainbow trout, average size between one and two pounds, while the Haines Lakes produce fish of between five and seven pounds and receive almost no pressure. The Haines Lakes are deeper than the Scum Lakes and have higher oxygen levels, which reduces the chances of winterkills. These lakes are difficult to get to, but the rewards can be great. They are ideal fly fishing lakes. There is an air strip and a Forest Service campsite at Scum Lake.

Taseko Lake

The first real view of the Coast Range mountains comes about 65 kilometres from Lee's Corner, shortly after the steep, switchback crossing of Tete Angela Creek. Less than 10 kilometres from here the road makes its switchback descent to the banks of the Taseko River. Despite the rough campsites between road and river and the large Forest Service campsite near the Davidson Bridge, there is an inescapable feeling of wilderness. The wild, rushing silt-laden river is partly responsible, but knowing the little-travelled Taseko Lake country is just a short distance away really imparts the feel and flavour of wilderness. From the Armed Forces-built bridge to the shores of Taseko Lake is less than 35 kilometres, but it is dicey for two-wheel-drive vehicles and impossible when wet. Go at least as far as the lake and the old ford across the Taseko River if at all possible; the view down the lake is worth the tortuous drive. There is a Forest Service campsite at Fish Lake, reached by taking a side road to the east shortly after the Davidson Bridge; the fishing for small but plentiful rainbows is good all season. Another spur of the road just past the Taseko outfitters' camp dips to the shores of the lake at a good spot to rig camp. I have not fished the outlet of the lake and the river immediately downstream, partly because the water is so heavily silted, but this is reported to be a prime location for large Dolly Varden. The original old wagon road is visible across the Taseko River at the ford.

Vedan, Elkin, Chaunigan Lakes

After crossing the Davidson Bridge over the Taseko River, still on good-surface road, the next decision must be made shortly after passing Big Lake. Lee's Corner is now about 80 kilometres and a world or two away. To the south, spectacular 3,061-metre-high Mount Tatlow should be visible and there will shortly be a fork in the road which leads north to Vedan, Elkin and Chaunigan lakes. Unlike most of the side roads encountered so far, the road into these lakes is good two-wheel-drive surface. Boats, accommodations and Forest Service campsites are available. All three lakes contain rainbows and Dolly Varden. The Dollies come big, to 15 pounds; rainbow trout in Vedan and Elkin lakes average between 1.5 and two pounds with some in the five- to six-pound range. Fishing in these lakes is fast: expect consistent action. Chaunigan Lake is a fly fisher's dream with its many shoal areas surrounded by quick drop-offs, ideal for the careful working of various nymph patterns. Rainbow trout have done exceptionally well in this lake; eight-pound-and-better fish are taken regularly. Fisheries Branch staff are contemplating a bait ban and single hook restriction to help preserve this lake's spectacular fishery—check all regulations carefully.

Gunn Valley/Yohetta Valley

Immediately after the Vedan Lakes turnoff there is a road forking to the south (left). This is the old Lord River Development Road which may be passable for two-wheel drive during long spells of dry weather, but more often is strictly limited to four-wheel drive. The rough road is well worth the trouble, since it leads to the Gunn Valley's chain of three mountain-ringed lakes and provides access to the Yohetta Valley trailhead. I have fished the Gunn Valley lakes for small to medium-sized Dolly Varden char, but the real allure of this region is the unsurpassed scenery and easy hike-in access to the alpine country of the Yohetta Valley, often described as the single most scenic valley in the Chilcotin. Lovely Yohetta Lake holds small but plentiful rainbow trout, but the fishing is merely a bonus: it is enough just to be there and experience the wild country. It would be easy to pass the entire summer exploring the country off this road.

Nemaiah Valley/Konni Lake to Tsuniah Lake

After the Lord River turnoff the main road quickly drops to the grasslands of the Nemaiah Valley. This open valley with its ranchlands, native settlement and post office comes as a surprise, but such backcountry settlement seems typical of the Chilcotin. Konni Lake in the heart of the Nemaiah Reserve has a good population of larger fish—average between five and six pounds—and receives very little pressure. This lake does not winterkill, so fish populations are more representative of various year classes. Expect both large and small fish. Beware, however, of sudden afternoon squalls which can be dangerous to small boats. There is no organized camping except at the end of the valley, where a left-hand fork in the road (marked) drops to the Forest Service's Chilko Lake campsite within a couple of rough kilometres. The main road carries on to Tsuniah Lake and beyond, but without four-wheel drive, this is the point to turn around and head back to Lee's Corner, even though the rough section is only 50 kilometres long. For those continuing, expect slow going over ruts, mud holes and all the rest. The consolation is the lodge at Tsuniah Lake, complete with cabins, boats and fast fishing for small but incredibly abundant rainbow trout. There is a Forest Service campsite shortly after the lodge.

Tsuniah Lake to Tatla Lake

The rough road out to the Chilko River from Tsuniah Lake seems to go on forever because the going is so slow, but actual road distance from the campsite to the bridge is only about 25 kilometres. The Chilko River crossing is of prime interest to anglers as the first 30 kilometres of the river down from the lake are said to contain the best fishing water. Expect rainbows to six pounds and Dolly Varden in the 10-pound-plus range. An old wagon road follows the river out to Hwy 20 and the Chilko's junction with the Chilcotin River, but don't attempt this drive unless equipped with four-wheel drive and, in wet weather, nerves of steel.

After the Chilko River bridge the road is good-surface all the way to Tatla Lake. There is a Forest Service campsite at the east end of Choelquoit Lake. Fishing pressure on this lake set amid rolling grassland is light, and it is reported to contain exceptionally large rainbow trout. Just past Cochin Lake, only a few kilometres from Choelquoit, the road forks again, south to Tatlayoko Lake and north to the historic settlement of Tatla Lake back on Hwy 20. The road is good in either direction. The Tatlayoko Valley provides the best road access and most spectacular views of the Coast Range mountains anywhere in the Chilcotin. From the south end of Tatlayoko Lake the Homathko River flows barely 80 kilometres to tidewater. Several outfitters guide into this area. One last hint: make a point of stopping in at the old Tatla Lake roadhouse. The restaurant's home-style cooking is renowned throughout the region.

Discovering the Scud

*O*f all the aquatic life forms important to trout in British Columbia, one clearly stands out above the rest. These are the small freshwater crustaceans known as scuds. More than any other single factor, these tiny shrimp-like creatures account for the excep-

tional size, colour and sporting qualities of the province's
rainbow trout. They inhabit
virtually all our best trout
lakes, are eagerly sought by
the fish and, providing the angler has a nodding acquaintance with their habits, are not
at all difficult to imitate.

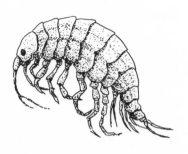

Scud *(Gammarus)*

High in food value and readily available in good numbers
throughout the year, this small, seemingly insignificant
crustacean plays a major role in shaping the incredible fishing to be had in B.C.'s best interior trout lakes. It has become
a recognized maxim that any lake which holds good numbers of scuds—whether in coastal Alaska, the Chilean high
country or Tasmania's central plateau—will provide quality
angling for large, superbly conditioned trout. In B.C. we are
particularly fortunate in this regard: virtually every good interior trout lake contains vast populations of scuds. When
conditions are right, as they are in all of our best lakes, these
crustaceans can be likened to an infestation—populations
as high as several hundred per square metre of lake bottom
have been recorded.

Two members of the scud family are of particular importance in B.C., the small *Hyalella* and its larger cousin *Gammarus*, specifically *Gammarus limnaeus*. Of the two, *Gammarus*
is by far the more important to both trout and anglers, but
the smaller *Hyalella* may also play a crucial role. Trout in
scud-rich waters imprint on scuds early in life, starting with
Hyalella as fingerlings and switching to *Gammarus* as they
gain in size.

It is almost as if scuds were expressly developed to foster
large, exceptionally well-conditioned fish. They are a recognized staple on the Kamloops trout menu, one which is available to them from their earliest days and continues to provide
a rich source of protein as the fish mature, thanks to the vary-

ing sizes of scuds available. Their importance to fish can hardly be overstated. Yet many anglers remain unconvinced scud imitations will regularly fool larger trout, or even that scuds are an important part of the trout fisher's arsenal.

The reasons for this go back to the days when scud imitations were based more on imagination than reality. Usually red or orange in colour and invariably tied on curved hooks to mimic the humped appearance of shrimp in a can, these early patterns fooled few fish. In nature, scuds are never red, pink or orange and display the characteristic "hump" associated with saltwater shrimp only when at rest. Even then the hump is no more than a slight curve of the body. Small wonder these imitations failed so miserably and that early scud patterns remained little-used by anglers.

More recently, several excellent scud patterns have been developed, and these have attracted a significant following among B.C. anglers. Still, anglers tend to reserve scud patterns as a measure of last resort. I confess to having held this view for a number of years, although on reflection it now seems my prejudice against fishing scud imitations—scudding, as this type of fishing is called—was based more on vague intuition than any consideration of the facts. Then a fishing story I was researching took me to Palmer Lake in the rolling forest country of the Chilcotin Plateau. That trip forever changed my views on *Gammarus limnaeus* and large trout.

Some lakes are just plain secretive and Palmer is one of them. The bottom consists almost entirely of fist-sized cobble which plunges from view within a few paddle strokes of shore. It is deep, weedless and essentially sterile from a trout fisher's point of view, especially a fly fisher. There is some weed growth hard by the Forest Service campsite, but it is thin, sickly-looking stuff, not the thick submerged mats which harbour a rich abundance of aquatic life and are a hallmark of all the better lakes.

This was a major disappointment. I had been lured to

Palmer by its reputation as a big-fish lake and fully expected to be fishing the traditional fare of such lakes in B.C.—dragonfly nymphs, damselflies, chironomids and so on. Now it appeared I had hit on a lake which fosters large trout thanks to its population of forage fish. This is not at all unlikely once north of the southern interior, notably in the larger lakes of the Cariboo. Judging by what I had seen of its aquatic environment, Palmer appeared to be one of these lakes. Such lakes can be successfully fished with fly gear and often provide exceptional angling for truly large fish. Fur and feather forage fish imitations abound and many fly fishers have learned to use such imitations with great success, but it has always seemed to me a wrong-headed approach. A variety of lures designed to be fished on either spinning or trolling outfits do a much better job of imitating baitfish and seem the right tackle for this kind of fishing. I was prepared to fish minnow imitations with my fly rod, but only as a last resort. As things turned out, however, I could have left my minnow imitations in their dusty corner of the tackle bag. It was a handful of patterns tucked into an equally little-used nook of the fly box which would be called upon to unlock Palmer's puzzle.

A fisher could cruise Palmer Lake for a long time without ever discovering the one bay which is entirely different from anything else on the lake. I'm convinced the dynamics at work in that one deep, shallow-water bay—the first major left-hand bay on leaving the campsite—go a long way towards making Palmer the super fishing lake that it is. Frustration led to its discovery. I had grown weary of aimlessly hunting the near-shore area, alternately trolling and casting various minnow imitations with no luck. (Minnow imitations are neither easy nor particularly pleasing to cast, even with an eight-weight fly rod.) It took several hours, but finally I was frustrated enough to set the rod aside and explore without the hindrance of a trailing fly line. And so I discovered Palmer Lake's secret.

As soon as the canoe rounded the point formed by one arm of the bay I knew I was on to something important. Not only was the water shallow, between three and four metres deep—perfect for bottom probing with fly gear—but instead of the fist-sized rocks which made up the bottom everywhere else I had explored, here were the thick mats of bottom-hugging weed growth I had expected from the start. I anchored near the first large weed mat, exchanged the minnow imitation for a favourite dragonfly pattern and cast myself into a lather, convinced that this was where the fish would be and that a morsel as tempting as my dragonfly could not possibly be ignored by hungry rainbow trout. I was wrong.

Not until I had shifted position several times, always working deeper into the bay, did I tumble to what was happening. Each time I changed location, a small cluster of weeds clung to the anchor and was deposited in the bottom of the canoe. Soon I had amassed a fair collection of these weeds and noticed a small greenish-grey wiggling among the sodden pile at my feet. Rooting about in the weeds I soon had the wiggler in my hands. There is no mistaking a scud for anything else and that's what I held in my cupped hand: a perfect example of *Gammarus limnaeus*. A quick search revealed I had six never-before-used imitations in my bag, at least three of which were close enough in size and colour to the original to, hopefully, fool the fish. This time I was right.

The first cast snaked out over the weed mat and even as the fly was settling I felt a sharp, solid bump. I missed the first, but at the second cast I was ready. Again that solid bump just as the fly settled over the weeds and this time the hook went home. Suddenly the quiet little corner of the bay erupted in silver as a 26-inch Palmer Lake rainbow burst to the surface and sizzled off on one of those incredible runs exclusive to rainbow trout. At such moments it is easy to be convinced there is no other fish anywhere quite like the

B.C. version of the rainbow trout, as indeed may very well be the case.

That lovely first fish, so large it was later cut into steaks for a campfire dinner with my companions, proved to be the start of an unforgettable day of scudding. I hooked and released six more rainbows that day without ever moving from my now thoroughly familiar spot. All the fish were about the same size—giants—and I lost count of the number which came unbuttoned at some point during the ensuing mayhem. The superb condition of these fish, their exceptional size and colour, in a lake which, outside of one relatively minor bay, displayed poor fish habitat serves as a striking example of the importance of *Gammarus limnaeus* in the aquatic environment. Clearly, a basic understanding of scud habits is vital to anyone serious about fishing for trout in British Columbia.

Scuds do, in fact, look somewhat like shrimp and, like all crustaceans, have a hard exoskeleton formed of calcium absorbed from the water. This exoskeleton must be shed in order for scuds to grow; abandoned exoskeletons are often found floating on the surface of lakes—a sure sign that scuds are present. *Gammarus* range in size from one to 2.5 centimetres in length; *Hyalella* grow to a maximum size of about one centimetre. This size difference is the easiest way to distinguish between the two and explains why *Gammarus* is the more important to both fish and anglers: the larger size makes it more valuable to feeding fish (energy gained per unit of output) and easier for anglers to imitate. While the bodies do tend to be somewhat curved or humped, scuds swim with their bodies completely outstretched. This is important, even vital to success, as any scud pattern tied on a curved hook will be badly out-fished by those tied on regular hooks.

As to colour, the best bet is to capture a few naturals and match their colour in the imitation, something which may require blending dubbing material such as seal fur to achieve the desired hue. *Gammarus* come in a range of colours, including greys, browns, olives and even brilliant turquoise, but combinations of light olive, tan and grey are common in B.C. and are probably the most important to anglers. It is important to remember that in nature *Gammarus* are never red or pink, although they may turn pinkish red when dead and females carry their young in a brood pouch visible as a bright orange spot. Other distinguishing features include abdominal gills and longish dangling legs located along the underside of the body and at the thorax.

Gammarus can range to depths of 15 metres if weed mats are present, but prefer lake margins and shoals, with the heaviest concentrations found in depths of between one and three metres where there is good weed growth. They are omnivorous scavengers, meaning they'll eat just about anything, plant or animal. They are also prolific, breeding many times during the April-to-December fertile season.

Unfortunately for anglers, scuds are nocturnal, meaning they tend to hide in their weedy aquatic jungles during hours of daylight, emerging to forage in great numbers only under cover of darkness. It is important to note, though, that darkness does not necessarily mean night; scuds may be out in force on cloudy, overcast days or even along lake margins where weed mats lie in hard shadow, as was the case at Palmer Lake. Scuds are also especially active in the fall, a fact worth remembering (my Palmer Lake bonanza occurred in September). As the upper layers of water cool prior to freeze-up, oxygen is trapped. This upper oxygen-enriched layer then sinks, mixing as it goes and resulting in well-oxygenated water which increases aquatic activity, including that of scuds, and triggers feeding behaviour in the fish.

Besides colour, size and habitat, successful imitation of the scuds' movements are crucial to fooling fish, especially large, older fish. In this we are fortunate, since the movements of scuds can best be described as erratic. For the angler this means just about any retrieve, or combination of retrieves, will work at some time. Still, some general guidelines are handy to know. What will surprise many anglers is the speed at which scuds rip along, especially if they're chasing something down or taking evasive action. To get a feel for this, capture a few scuds (normally just a matter of pulling up a handful of weeds) and carefully release them out of a cupped hand—the scud will immediately streak for the bottom, seeking refuge in the darkness of its weedy home. This gives a good indication of both how fast scuds can move and their body shape when scudding along flat out.

Scuds are also known for their seeming aimlessness, darting rhythmically in various directions only to stop, settle briefly, then burst ahead or sideways a few centimetres, only to settle again. These are apparently entirely erratic, aimless movements, but only a scud would know for certain.

At Palmer Lake the most effective retrieve, one which has subsequently proven itself in several interior lakes, was simply a combination of finger-twists followed by three or four short, quick pulls and a brief pause. Most takes seem to come on the pause following a series of quick pulls. Keeping a keen eye on the line for any unusual movement and the rod tip pointing down at the water is essential. Sinking tip lines or dry lines with sinking leaders are a good way to go, although a full sinking line is entirely adequate provided you feel comfortable about sensing subtle takes. Twice at Palmer the scud pattern was taken dead drift while waiting for the line to sink, pointing out the need for a nicely placed line. Those unable to deliver the flyline in one neat, wave-free line should develop the habit of pulling the line taut the moment the fly has landed. This greatly increases chances of detecting takes soon enough to set the hook.

The heaviest concentrations of scuds are found in shallow water, and fish feeding on them tend to be easily spooked; since water is a far better transmitter of sound than air, the thrumming of an outboard, the splash of a carelessly released anchor, the metallic thud of a foot against the bottom of a tin boat or even the slicing splash of a poor cast are enough to scatter feeding fish for a long time. Stealth, both in terms of water-transmitted sounds and placement of the boat, is essential to successful scudding.

There is no reason why a careful, stealth-conscious fisher shouldn't be able to successfully fish scuds in any interior lake at just about any time of year. You don't hear about scuds in the same awed tones anglers use to describe the big sedge hatches or the June migration of the damselfly, because these are special once-a-year events; whereas a big rainbow quietly browsing on scuds is just a day like any other—until the scud it takes is the one tied to your line.

Chilcotin Lakes

The listing of Chilcotin lakes has been divided into four quadrants centred on Puntzi Lake, about 60 kilometres west of Alexis Creek. The eastern boundary is the Fraser River; the western edge extends to Tweedsmuir Park. To the north the area covered stops at the Blackwater (West Road) River and to the south the region extends as far as the southern reaches of Chilko and Taseko lakes. An imaginary north-south line based on Puntzi Lake puts Chilko Lake into the southwest quadrant, while Taseko Lake lies in the southeast quadrant. An east-west line based on Hwy 20 provides the north-south division.

Northeast Chilcotin

The northeast section is characterized by the rolling woodlands of the Chilcotin Plateau. Access is via Hwy 20 west from Williams Lake and a number of backroads which branch off to the north. Alternatively, access is also possible west across the Fraser River from Quesnel towards the Blackwater River. A number of backroads spread south from this river to give access to the northern portions of this region.

» BUCKSKIN LAKE—Known to consistently deliver rainbow trout in the four- to five-pound range, this is an intensively managed lake which requires a provincial Fisheries Branch aeration program to maintain its population of fish. Fly fishing is best, although small spinners should also produce action. From Hwy 20, take the Meldrum Creek road north at McIntyre Lake and continue due north beyond Till Lake for about 20 kilometres to the lake. Alternatively, take the Mackin Creek road by following the Soda Creek road north from Williams Lake and crossing to the west side of the Fraser on a bridge near Hargreaves. The last six kilometres to the lake may be impassable to two-wheel-drive vehicles in wet weather.

» RAVEN LAKE—This lake is subject to heavy angling pressure both winter and summer, but its mixed population of rainbow trout and stocked brook trout appears to be holding up remarkably well. The larger rainbow trout run to about five pounds but are notoriously difficult to catch. They make good quarry for the technical fly fisher who enjoys a challenge. Similarly, the lake's biggest brookies, averaging two pounds and better, are most often taken by anglers who have learned to imitate specific aquatic insects. Try large dragonfly imitations; a muddler minnow fished to represent a dragonfly may do very well. Access is over the Palmer Lake road, found about 25 kilometres west of Riske Creek and turning north (right) off Hwy 20. Raven Lake is about 20 kilometres north on this road. Good campsites and a gravel launching ramp help make the lake popular.

» BEAVER LAKE—Consider this shallow lake inaccessible to two-wheel-drive vehicles, as the last 10 kilometres to the lake off the main Palmer Lake road are extremely rough. The turnoff to the lake is found about 40 kilometres north of Hwy 20 off the Palmer Lake road (see last entry above). It is best to avoid this lake in the heat of summer as high water temperatures will slow fishing to a standstill, but in spring and fall it can produce exceptional rainbow trout. Expect fast fishing for large fish at this time. Nearby Stum Lake and White Pelican Provincial Park are home to the pelican rehabilitation program which brought this species back from the brink. Wildlife enthusiasts will want to see these spectacular birds. Contact the B.C. Parks Branch for further information.

» PALMER LAKE—See the section on scuds in this chapter for details. The last six kilometres in to this lake off the main Palmer Lake road are rough; wet weather makes two-wheel-drive access impossible, and even in dry weather caution and care are required on this steep road. The turnoff is found about 70 kilometres north of Hwy 20 from near Riske Creek. Fishing for rainbow trout heavier than two pounds is consistent, with many larger fish. Best fly fishing is found in the shallow-water bay on the left after leaving the campsite. Trolling, concentrated on the mid-lake shoal some distance from the campsite, is the conventional way to fish this lake, and while this method accounts for many good catches, fly fishers can do as well or better by matching their imitations to the predominant aquatic insect activity at the time. An excellent lake.

» TWO LAKE—This is actually two lakes locally known as One and Two lakes. A narrow strip of water navigable by canoe connects the lakes. Heavy winter angling pressure on these lakes has reduced success rates, but rainbow trout to five pounds and brook trout to two pounds and better are still present in sufficient numbers to make for special fishing. There is a small Forest Service campsite. To get there, turn north off Hwy 20 on the forest access road found about 10 kilometres west of Alexis Creek. The lake is about 30 kilometres up this road, just beyond Alexis Lake.

Southeast Chilcotin

The southeast Chilcotin consists largely of the rolling forest lands of the plateau and is best accessed via the Taseko Lake road south from Hwy 20 at Hanceville. However, an alternate route is possible via the Farwell Canyon road which heads south shortly east of Riske Creek on Hwy 20. This is a good-surface road and provides access to the Big Creek/Fletcher Lake area and hooks up with the Taseko Lake road just south of Hanceville. There is no real advantage to taking this alternate route, except that it crosses the Chilcotin River at the visually stunning Farwell Canyon, where sheep can be seen by those with sharp eyes. For those who relish dramatic scenes, the Farwell Canyon is a must. Be sure to take a spotting scope or good binoculars.

» FLETCHER LAKE—See the section on the south Chilcotin in this chapter for details. Fletcher produces fairly reliable numbers of rainbow trout in the magic 10-pound class, with consistent fishing for two-pound-plus fish. Trolling accounts for most of the large fish, but this may be only because most anglers use trolling gear. The reed bed visible from the Forest Service campsite is the most-fished area of the lake. This is also good fly fishing water. Recent Fisheries Branch improvements bode well for this lake's future. To get there, turn south (left) off Hwy 20 at Hanceville; it is about 30 kilometres on a good gravel road. Accommodations and some services available.

» KLOACUT LAKE—See the section on the south Chilcotin in this chapter for details. Rainbow trout in this relatively shallow, heavily weeded lake run to at least eight pounds with a strong likelihood of even larger fish. It is, however, subject to periodic winterkill and may turn off during hot weather in summer. June and September would be ideal times to target this exceptional lake. It is ideally suited to the fly fisher (leech patterns are deadly in the fall). To get there, continue south from Fletcher Lake (see above) then southwest from Big Creek past Willan Lake. A tur-noff to the south just past Teepee Heart Ranch (accom-modations/horses) passes through a grazing lease to emerge at this lake. There are no facilities and no or-ganized camping, but camping is possible. An excellent lake.

» SCUM/HAINES LAKES—See the section on the south Chilco-tin in this chapter for details. These are best described as adventure lakes, as the road in is extremely rough and those who have fished them are inordinately tight-lipped about the fishing. Fisheries Branch sources say the small Scum lakes produce fish of between one and 1.5 pounds with amazing consistency, while the Haines lakes produce large rainbow trout (five-pounds-plus) just as regularly. To get there, turn south off Hwy 20 at Hanceville on the Taseko Lake road for about 40 kilometres, then turn north on a very rough road (four-wheel drive only) for about five kilometres. There is a Forest Service campsite at Scum Lake.

» CHAUNIGAN/ELKIN/VEDAN LAKES—Chaunigan produces the best rainbow trout fishing of the three with fish to eight pounds taken regularly. This lake is ideal for fly fishing (see section on the south Chilcotin in this chapter) and its population of large fish is due entirely to natural causes—no stocked fish or extensive management. A very special lake—anglers should willingly practise catch-and-release fishing with barbless hooks to help preserve its magic. Elkin and Vedan lakes produce good numbers of rainbow trout in the 1.5 to two-pound class with some larger trout, but these lakes are best known for their large (15-pound) Dolly Varden char. Since these char are easi-ly fished out, anglers should look on the chance to catch these larger fish as a special privilege. To get there, take the Taseko Lake road south off Hwy 20 at Hanceville for about 85 kilometres. Turn north off the Taseko road shortly after passing Big Lake. There are Forest Service campsites at Vedan and Chaunigan, which also has boat rentals, accommodation and some services. Pressure on Chaunigan has been relatively light to this point.

» TUZCHA/FISHEM/YOHETTA LAKES—These lakes have been included due to their remoteness and the mountain-ringed settings in which they are found. The Yohetta Valley is likely the most scenic valley in the entire Chilcotin, if such distinctions are possible. Fishing on Yohetta Lake is good for smallish rainbow trout, just right for the campfire frying pan. Tuzcha and Fishem lakes, in the Gunn Valley, provide fair angling for small rainbow trout and Dolly Varden char. By crossing Tuzcha Lake over the creek at the lower end, it is possible to access the alpine country overlooking Taseko Lake to the east. This day hike is well worth the effort, but the walk up from Tuzcha is steep and hikers should be reasonably fit. Meandering horse trails make access less difficult. To get there, take the Taseko Lake road south off Hwy 20 at Hanceville as far as the old Lord River development road, found immediately west of the Elkin/Vedan turnoff (see above). Two-wheel drive might make it in, but four-wheel is best and absolutely necessary in wet conditions. Access to the Yohetta Valley is by foot over a good trail starting near the lower end of Tuzcha Lake.

» KONNI LAKE—This lake in the heart of the Nemaiah Valley does not give up its largest fish easily, but it does hold a good population of rainbow trout in the five- to six-pound range. It is a wild lake in that its fish have not been stocked, although it is in the middle of the Nemaiah Reserve. Various year-classes are well represented so anglers can expect small as well as large fish. Technical fly fishers will enjoy this lake's manifold challenges. Afternoon squalls are common, presenting a possible danger to small boats. The wind also changes fish activity patterns and anglers should be alert enough to react by changing location with the change in wind direction or velocity. There is no organized camping, but the Chilko Lake Forest Service campsite is only a short distance to the west (care is required on the final drop down to the lake). To get there, stay on the main Taseko Lake road (see above), continuing west past the Lord River road turnoff. The road follows the lake's north shore. Distance from Hanceville is about 110 kilometres.

Southwest Chilcotin

The southwest Chilcotin is dominated by Chilko and Tat-layoko lakes and the incredible vistas provided by the meeting of the Chilcotin Plateau with the Coast Range mountains. For those who have a yen for mountain scenery with their fishing, this is the section of the Chilcotin to visit. Access is via a network of backroads which swing south of Hwy 20 from Tatla Lake, although the lower Chilko Lake Forest Service campsite (about halfway down the lake on the eastern shore) is best accessed from Hanceville over the Taseko Lake road (see the section on the southern Chilcotin). The road from the north via Tsuniah Lake is extremely rough going from the Chilko River bridge south.

» CHILKO LAKE—This large, fiord-like lake of sparkling waters and mountain scenery is one of the province's most visually stunning lakes. Large rainbow trout and Dolly Varden char are present, but angling pressure in recent years has risen dramatically. Since these are wild, slow-growing fish, the future, at least so far as angling is concerned, does not look good for this one-of-a-kind lake. In fact, Fisheries Branch staff have issued a plea asking anglers to spread themselves out on the region's many smaller lakes instead of concentrating on this lake. When feeding, the fish target creek in-flow areas, making them easy prey for anglers. Also, when salmon are running in the Chilko River, lake-resident trout and char move into the river to take advantage. Fishermen who have learned this secret naturally follow, further increasing pressure on an already beleaguered population of wild fish. By all means visit this lake, but bear the catch-and-release philosophy in mind. The road in to the Forest Service campsite at the north end, complete with launching ramp, is easy going; from Tatla Lake on Hwy 20, go south as far as Cochin Lake, then east around Choelquoit Lake and south to the campsite. The mid-lake campsite (see above) is best reached via the Taseko Lake road, but is not suited to those pulling trailers. Larger boats are required for this often-windswept, 85-kilometre-long lake; shore access is limited.

» CHOELQUOIT LAKE—This lake, set in a mix of rolling grassland and forested hills, is subject to strong afternoon winds which can chase anglers off the water. It is a wild (unstocked, little management) lake with a little-known reputation for exceptionally large rainbow trout. Reedy edges and the presence of submerged aquatic weed growth will appeal to fly fishers. Although easily reached over good roads, the lake receives virtually no pressure. To get there from Tatla Lake on Hwy 20, take the Tatlayoko Lake road south for about 20 kilometres to Cochin Lake, then turn east on Choelquoit/Chilko lakes road which passes Choelquoit's north shore before cutting south to the big lake. A small Forest Service campsite is found at the east end of Choelquoit.

» MOSLEY CREEK LAKES—A number of small lakes, Horn, Sapeye and Bluff being the best known, make up the headwaters of this creek which drains into the Homathko River. All these lakes are set in magnificent mountain scenery which of itself makes the trip in worthwhile. The fishing, however, can be as spectacular as the settings. The combination of spell-binding scenery with good fishing and relatively easy access makes these lakes very popular; do not expect wilderness solitude. Reports vary, but generally Sapeye is said to have the largest rainbow trout with fish to six pounds and averaging over two pounds. Sapeye also has Dolly Varden char averaging about six pounds. Bluff lake has a reputation for large Dolly Varden, to 10 pounds and better. Horn Lake is probably the most popular, with consistent fishing for rainbow trout averaging about 1.5 pounds as well as Dolly Varden char averaging about the same as at Sapeye. Forest Service campsites are found at all three. As with all mountain lakes, anglers must be cautious of sudden winds which can result in whitecaps within a matter of minutes. To get there from Tatla Lake on Hwy 20, take the Tatlayoko Lake road, branching off to the west on the Mosley Creek road after about five kilometres. This road accesses all of these lakes and is generally good, although the final access to some of the lakes is steep and narrow.

Northwest Chilcotin

The northwest quadrant is essentially wilderness country with few backroads, although Hwy 20 swings north near Kleena Kleene to provide access to the western edge. In the area between Nimpo Lake and Anahim Lake a number of backroads provide access to the wilderness fishing lakes west of Hwy 20 and backed against the eastern edge of Tweedsmuir Park. In the main, however, fishing the backcountry of this region requires charter air services, available at Nimpo Lake. Details on the kind of fishing to expect are provided in the lakes listing for the northwest Chilcotin and in the opening section of this chapter.

» NIMPO LAKE—This lake, aside from being the main base for floatplane operations serving the backcountry and the centre of the region's lodge activities, supports good populations of rainbow trout in the three-pound class with fish of five pounds and better not uncommon. At last count, five lodges were based on this lake, all with either their own floatplanes or connections with one of several charter air outfits operating from the lake. The ready availability of all services, as well as good fishing, makes this an excellent choice for a family fishing holiday. While trolling is the favoured method (Flatfish and Hot Shots are popular lures) of catching these wild (not stocked) fish, the lake also offers quality fly fishing, notably during the mid-June emergence of the sedge, or caddisfly. Various sedge imitations (both pupae and adult) are very good at this time. Other popular patterns include the venerable Doc Spratley and scud patterns (see the section on scuds in this chapter). Prolonged spells of hot weather will slow the fishing. The lake is beside Hwy 20, about 290 kilometres from Williams Lake. It is also possible to fly in, either from Williams Lake or Vancouver, to the airport at Anahim Lake; lodges supply transport from there.

» ANAHIM/ABUNTLET LAKES—Generally the fish are smaller in these lakes than those chosen for inclusion in this listing—although Anahim Lake has some fish in the three-pound class—but drifting the river from Anahim to Abuntlet Lake is a unique experience for fly fishers. At normal flows, with a 10-hp outboard, it's possible to make the return trip without effort. Fish in this section of river, reserved for fly-only fishing, will go to two pounds. Best fly fishing on Anahim Lake is where water flows in from Little Anahim; best fly water on Abuntlet is at the outflow into the Dean River. Anahim Lake, complete with lodges and public campsite, is about 30 kilometres from Nimpo Lake on Hwy 20.

» HOTNARKO LAKE—The large, wild fish for which this lake has long had a reputation have made a comeback in recent years. Fish of five pounds and better are taken regularly, with some much larger. In fact, this vehicle-accessible lake produces fish to match anything available in the more remote fly-in lakes reached by charter air from Nimpo

Lake. Fly fishing is best, but spinners also produce well. Strong winds represent a danger. To get there, branch south off Hwy 20 on a road located just west of the Little Anahim Lake Forest Service campsite, found about five kilometres west of the town of Anahim Lake. A very rough 18-kilometre-long road reaches the lake; access to the lakeshore is rougher yet. Alternatively, fly-in access is available from Nimpo Lake.

» CHARLOTTE LAKE—This large lake, 20 kilometres long and six kilometres wide, holds some exceptional wild rainbow trout. Native rainbow trout weighing between four and five pounds are the norm, with much larger fish to be expected. A Forest Service campsite is found at the southeast end, but the best fishing is at the opposite end of the lake in the narrow bay to the northwest, where the Atnarko River flows out (draining through Little Charlotte lake). Winds are a problem on this lake, so those intending to make the long crossing are advised to proceed with caution. Just before the northwest bay narrows, lies another bay with a good in-flowing stream from Whitton Creek and a handful of unnamed lakes to the south. This location is also a good candidate for anglers. To get to Charlotte Lake, take the Pine Point road west from Hwy 20 for about 10 kilometres before branching south for another 20 kilometres. Enquire at Nimpo Lake for details on road conditions; access to the lake itself can be rough.

» TURNER LAKES—This lake chain set in Tweedsmuir Park, the largest in the province at 981,000 hectares, offers incredible fishing for pan-sized cutthroat trout. These small, colourful trout are not, however, the reason I've included this lake chain. For the angler who enjoys untrammeled mountain scenery at least as much as fishing, this chain is a must. Full details are available from the Parks Branch, but suffice to say this string of seven interconnected lakes at an elevation of 1,100 metres offers some of the finest mountain-lake scenery anywhere. Canoe-camping is the way to go on these lakes (Junker Lake makes a good base camp). Nimpo Lake lodges provide air access, although hike-in access is possible over a gruelling trail, with canoe rentals available at the wilderness camp on Turner Lake (Stewart's Lodge at Nimpo lake will supply food, air services and canoe gear for a flat fee). The view of spectacular Hunlen Falls, plunging 259 metres from Turner Lake to Hunlen Creek, alone makes the flight worthwhile.

» ELIGUK LAKE AND THE FLY-INS—Most Nimpo Lake lodge operators have secret fly-in lakes which they swear produce larger-than-life-sized rainbow trout. This may well be true as Chilcotin rainbow trout will grow to exceptional sizes when conditions are right, often thanks to the presence of freshwater shrimp. In the main, however, these remote backcountry lakes produce small to medium-sized rainbow trout in large numbers. Eliguk Lake in the headwaters of the Blackwater (West Road) River is typical. A fly-in trip to this lake will undoubtedly result in very fast fishing for fish of between one and 1.5 pounds. It is not unusual for all anglers to have a fish on at the same time, usually within minutes of wetting a line. It would be a shame, though, to concentrate all one's efforts on fishing: the air-access corners of the Chilcotin offer some of the finest undisturbed wilderness country in the province. However, a word of warning: fly-in wilderness destinations quickly become habit-forming.

For more information contact:

Fisheries Branch
540 Borland Street
Williams Lake, B.C.
V2G 1R8

Cariboo Tourist Association
Box 4900
Williams Lake, B.C.
V2G 2V8

CHAPTER SIX

The Cariboo

Traditionally the Cariboo has been lumped together with the Chilcotin as one out-sized region, and provincial fisheries managers still treat both as a single unit. But for angling purposes, the region is best divided into separate areas based on the natural boundary formed by the Fraser River. The Chilcotin lies to the west of the big river while the Cariboo extends east as far as Bowron and Wells Gray provincial parks. While both are characterized by rolling plateau country and backed by lofty mountain peaks (the Coast Mountains in the Chilcotin, the Cariboo Mountains in the Cariboo), the Chilcotin seems a wild and distant land compared to the civilized comforts of its eastern neighbour. To some extent this is misleading. The Chilcotin has its lodges and popular angling meccas, just as the Cariboo holds a number of fine wilderness waters. It is on the backroads that the difference between the two is most noticeable. Once off Hwy 20 in the Chilcotin, the traveller enters remote country with few services, but turn east off Hwy 97 onto the meandering byways of the Cariboo and the traveller is greeted by a wealth of resorts, lodges, general stores, small settlements and even the odd golf course. The Chilcotin suits those with a yen for adventure, while the Cariboo is one of the finest family-holiday destinations in the province.

Large, often highly productive lakes have made the Cariboo famous in angling circles, notably the waters of the easily reached Interlakes District, with access by way of paved Hwy

24. Sheridan Lake is the most famous of this group of lakes, offering excellent angling for both trollers and fly fishers. While much of the region's angling effort is concentrated on the large lakes, many if not most of the Cariboo's small, quality angling lakes go unnoticed by visiting anglers. Given that the Cariboo is the province's third most popular fishing destination, this will likely change over the next few years, especially as pressure continues to mount on the better-known lakes of the Thompson-Nicola. For now, however, the small lakes of the Cariboo receive relatively light angling pressure and the fish often grow to incredible sizes.

The fact that the Cariboo offers the best small-lake angling in North America is, for now at least, one of the best-kept angling secrets in the province. The small, relatively unknown lakes of the Cariboo provide exceptional angling in terms of fish numbers, sizes and uncrowded conditions. However, the fish of these shallow lakes often have a distinctive muddy flavour and are not generally suitable for the table. This can be a bane or a boon, depending on the point of view. For those primarily interested in eating the catch, it is a disaster; for the dedicated angler it means quality angling for large fish in uncrowded settings. The lakes listing at the close of this chapter concentrates on the Cariboo's small, quality angling lakes. Although a number of them provide fish of good table quality, the larger, deeper lakes are more reliable producers of such fish and are generally better suited to family fishing holidays. But small-lake anglers should not bypass the larger lakes altogether. The resorts and lodges found on these lakes are the best sources of local angling information, and a number provide charter air services to remote small waters. A good compromise is to use the large-lake lodges as a base of operations for exploration of nearby small waters.

Trollers will want to concentrate on the larger lakes, as small, shallow, weedy lakes are rarely suited to trolling. Fly fishers, on the other hand, may want to try their luck on large lakes such as Sheridan. Located just 50 kilometres east of 100 Mile House on Hwy 24, Sheridan remains a highly productive lake despite heavy angling pressure, estimated at almost six per cent of total Cariboo angling effort. Incredibly, for a lake with such heavy use, average fish size is close to four pounds. Trollers who probe the depths might reasonably expect fish of 10 pounds and better. The largest fish are rarely available to the fly fisher, but Sheridan's still prolific July/August sedge hatch will bring even the largest fish within reach of a dry line. With more than 160 kilometres of shoreline and an area of 65 hectares, trollers have a distinct advantage in locating fish. The lake's southwest bay is relatively shallow and weedy with prolific populations of aquatic insects, making it a logical choice for fly fishers. Exceptionally clear water, typical of large Cariboo lakes, means long, fine leaders are mandatory, both for fly fishers and trollers. The lake holds vast populations of scuds (see chapter five), which helps explain its continuing productivity despite heavy angling pressure. Brook trout are also present, mainly in the western end, and grow to respectable sizes, but these fish have proven to be notoriously difficult, with relatively few taken in a given year. The following section on brook trout gives a comprehensive listing of the province's best brookie waters.

If Sheridan is the jewel of Interlakes angling waters, lovely Lac Des Roches is the district's overlooked diamond-in-the-rough. Barely 10 kilometres beyond Sheridan, Lac Des Roches receives only a fraction of Sheridan's angling pressure. There is no logical explanation; fish sizes are similar, averaging between two and three pounds with good numbers in the five-pound class, and its waters are equally suited to both fly fishing and trolling. A shallow, narrow channel divides the lake into two separate basins. The smaller basin offers shelter from the winds which regularly force Cariboo anglers to seek shelter. Moose and deer use the channel to cross the lake, making it an ideal location for viewing wildlife. Fall is probably the best time for wildlife viewing and fishing. Cooler temperatures spell relief from stinging insects, the surrounding aspens are in full colour and the fish respond with typical season-end vigour. A variety of rainbow strains have been stocked into Lac Des Roches, including the famous late-maturing Gerrards (see chapter seven). For fly fishers, the lake offers a number of shoals, good spring chironomid fishing and one of the most prolific mayfly hatches (see chapter three) in the Cariboo. The mayfly hatch normally starts towards the end of May and continues into June.

North of the Interlakes District, large lakes such as Canim and Horsefly provide good angling for rainbow trout and lake char, but are less well suited to fly fishing. Full services are available at both, but boaters must take care as sudden storms are a fact of life on these big waters. Horsefly, while more than 50 kilometres long, is not wider than about three kilometres and often escapes the winds which plague other large Cariboo lakes. Still, it is a large, deep lake best suited to trolling. The small boat-access-only Forest Service campsite at Horsefly's Suey Bay involves a long boat trip, but offers good shelter and trail access to Quesnel Lake by way of tiny Suey Lake, a good prospect for adventuresome fly fishers seeking lightly fished waters with the promise of larger rainbow trout.

Finally, the two provincial parks, Bowron and Wells Gray, deserve special mention for their wilderness qualities, although angling is generally not as good as that found in managed Cariboo waters outside the parks. The fish of the parks are all wild stocks and while sizes tend to be small, the fishing can be very fast, notably for fly fishers using small patterns on the dry line. Murtle Lake in spectacular Wells Gray Park produces excellent numbers of rainbow trout in the 1.5 to two-pound range. The best fishing at Murtle is found in a lagoon on the outlet stream. Called Diamond Lagoon, this secluded piece of water is found just past a section of boulder garden riffles in the outlet stream and entails a lengthy paddle down the lake. The fishing, however, is typical of difficult-to-reach wilderness waters with two-pound rainbow trout possible on virtually every cast. Murtle's Fairy Slipper Island, besides offering a wonderful campsite, is home to rare fairy slipper orchids (*Calypso Bulbosa*) which bloom in July. The park itself is known primarily for the incredible diversity of its landscapes, everything from extinct volcanoes to glaciers, big deep lakes and waterfalls such as impressive Helmcken, fourth highest in Canada.

Bowron Lake Provincial Park is home to one of B.C.'s oldest and most popular canoe routes. The entire circuit covers 116 kilometres with a minimum of six portages and rapids to grade two in the connecting rivers. Covering the circuit normally requires between seven and 10 days and should not be attempted by inexperienced canoe trippers. The popularity of the route means reservations are essential and canoeists' departure times are staggered to help prevent crowding. Camping outside designated camping areas is not permitted. Fishing is generally poor, with Isaac and Indian Point lakes likely offering the best angling for rainbow trout, kokanee, Dolly Varden and lake char. I would not recommend the circuit to dedicated anglers seeking a wilderness angling experience. The Cariboo's Blackwater River (also known as West Road) offers much better angling, freedom to choose one's own camping places, and far fewer people. This trip requires honed tripping skills and should not be attempted by inexperienced canoeists. The fishing, however, is spectacular for rainbow trout in the two- to three-pound class.

Closeup: The Brook Trout in B.C.

*B*C.'s brook trout lakes rank among the finest brookie waters in North America. This should come as no surprise. Brook trout are much like rainbow trout; stock them into waters which produce trophy-class rainbows and the results are predictable enough: football-shaped brookies that would thrill most eastern anglers. There are literally dozens of such lakes in the province, enough so that what is considered once-in-a-lifetime fishing by eastern standards is mere commonplace in B.C.

Comparing eastern and western brook trout waters is hardly fair, a bit like comparing apples and oranges. The one is a remote fly-in river fishery for wild fish in north-country settings; the other involves driving to the shores of often easily reached lakes and launching the cartopper for a few hours of fishing. Still, when it comes to sizes and numbers of fish available, B.C. brookie waters need take a back seat to none. In fact, if B.C. anglers were as conscious of line-class records as their eastern counterparts, there is little doubt one or more B.C. brook trout would have made the record books by now. I know of anglers who have taken B.C. brook trout weighing better than six pounds and firmly believe much larger fish yet are available. What will astonish B.C. anglers unfamiliar with these wonderful fish is their short body length compared to their weights. A six-pound B.C. brookie typically measures 18 inches or less. Small wonder their body shape is often likened to a football.

So why is it that brook trout, celebrated as a minor deity in other parts of the country, haven't caught on in B.C.? The most common explanation one hears is that B.C. anglers

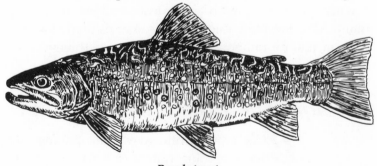

Brook trout

suffer from a rainbow trout/salmon fixation: if it isn't silver-bright and doesn't take to the air when hooked, it isn't much of a fish. Besides, brook trout aren't naturals. There wasn't a brook trout in the province until the first 35,000 were introduced from Quebec in 1908. They're not "real" trout, either, despite the name. Brook trout are members of the char clan, along with lake trout, Dolly Varden and arctic char, although it is pretty much accepted that the brookie is the most sporting fish of all the chars.

In the Thompson-Nicola, where brookies have been stocked fairly extensively, biologists have used them in waters considered marginal for rainbow trout. For the most part these are lakes which winterkill due to low oxygen levels and/or high water temperatures (they also tend to be the lakes which grow the largest fish, but more on this later). Use of the fish in such waters has resulted in the nickname "slough shark." This is unfortunate. The brook trout is a fine fish and deserves better. Besides, the logic behind the nickname is faulty.

To set the record straight, there is no evidence in the scientific literature to suggest brook trout survive slough conditions any better than do rainbow trout. Slough is, in any case, something of a misnomer. These shallow, nutrient-rich lakes of the interior grow large fish very quickly, and when rainbow trout survive several seasons in such lakes, as they often do, they are reckoned among the best lakes in the province. Stocking of such waters indicates that brook trout may survive when oxygen levels become too low to support rainbow trout. While this has not been scientifically proven, many biologists feel the brook trout can sometimes survive where rainbow trout fail. If anything then, the brookie is slightly hardier than the rainbow, and according to several experts, is the more difficult of the two to catch.

I'll include myself among the group who thinks the brook trout a more difficult fish to fool than the rainbow trout. Many devoted rainbow trout fishers, which includes just about everyone who fishes fresh water in B.C., will take exception. The rainbow can be an incredibly fussy fish and many are the tales of woe from anglers who had everything right but one seemingly minor and insignificant detail: they had the right fly in the right place at the right time but the colour was off just a tad, or the pattern was just one size too large or too small. We've all had days like that fishing for rainbows, but I'll stand by what I said. If you think rainbow trout can be tough to catch, try fooling a B.C. brook trout during the peak May-to-August fishing season.

Brook trout lakes tend to be moody and that's the way Edith Lake looked last fall when we tested its legendary waters. It is hard to define exactly what creates this impression, but it's something I've felt on every brook trout lake I've ever fished. The absence of surface activity, so different from the rainbow lakes where there is almost always some sign of life at the surface, is certainly part of it. It's eerie, too, to be on a lake known to hold exceptional fish and see no sign of them through the day, not even the splashy near-shore antics of the yearlings. I've been skunked often on such moody brookie waters, but this time things were destined to turn out differently.

Trolling is always a smart move on a new lake. I had the sinking line out and was meandering close to shore, exploring this relatively small lake just south of Kamloops. One of the bays ended in a shallow weed bed and that's where I set the anchor to try some casting. Two hours of trolling had failed to impress the fish; it was time for a change. The sinking line would hang up in the weeds after a count of about 10, so by rights I ought to have changed to a sink tip or even a floater, but. . . .

The first big brookie smashed the big muddler minnow as it crept through the weeds. The tussle which followed was very much like playing a large lake-resident cutthroat— dogged, determined, bulldogish, without so much as an attempt at a surface leap or roll. The big fish ploughed into the weeds and rolled, wrapping the leader with streaming weeds, but the eight-pound leader was equal to the strain and the brightly coloured fish was soon alongside the canoe.

The brookie is a stunningly coloured fish at any time of year, but in the fall, as spawning time nears, the colours are intensified and a deep orange-to-red band edged in black appears near the undersides. This contrasts dramatically with the rich creamy whiteness of the belly. The fins and big square tail also are tinged with red or orange and edged with white. These fantastic fall colours add an element of drama and excitement that no other fish can match. Watching as one of these brilliant fish nears the boat will quicken the pulse of any angler. This is especially true when it happens with some regularity, which is exactly what occurred at Edith.

The fish, very likely schooled in the shallow bay in preparation for spawning, were actively rooting deep in the weed beds, dislodging dragonflies and other aquatic insects from their weedy homes. Rainbow trout are content to wait for their buggy dinners to come to them; brookies, it seems, will go in and drive them out. I caught the football-shaped brookies at will, just about as fast as I could get the line into the water. This fall fishing bonanza is not at all typical of the rest of the year. Brook trout become extremely aggressive around their fall spawning time, especially the big males. They will often hit any large fly pattern or lure they see, so there's no great trick to catching them then. This explains the prevailing theory that any large gaudy pattern will do to fool brook trout—which is true, but only in the fall. The prespawning aggressiveness makes fall the time to test as many brookie lakes as possible. Anglers will get a real feel for the sizes and numbers of fish available. Try going back to these lakes in June or July if you're a technical angler who enjoys a challenge. At this time, when very precise matching of the hatch is required, fishing for brook trout can be a lesson in frustration.

Spring is also a good brook trout season. Brookies respond to the first hatches of the year much in the manner of rainbow trout—aggressively and with less caution than at other times of year. This is also the best time to take them with floating lines as they surface feed for chironomids and mayflies just like the rainbows. Even in the absence of a major springtime hatch, brookies are actively feeding at this time and a sunken dragonfly will rarely fail to fetch some action.

Winter ice fishing has become the most popular time to fish for brook trout in B.C. In the interior there is tremendous interest in this winter fishery. Most biologists feel the brook trout is a more active winter feeder than the rainbow and several hundred winter ice fishers will happily concur. So winter, early spring and fall can be brookie bonanza times, but late spring through summer and even early fall is the time for the technical angler who revels in a good challenge. It is less crowded then; a summer survey of 10 top Thompson-Nicola brook trout lakes turned up only two anglers.

Brook trout sizes vary tremendously across the province and from lake to lake within regions. The largest fish are found in the Thompson-Nicola, the Omineca-Peace and the Cariboo-Chilcotin. The Thompson-Nicola provides the highest numbers of brookie lakes and probably the best chance to boat a real trophy, although the other two regions also offer some very large brook trout. How large is large? Productive lakes—and most brookie-stocked lakes in these three regions qualify as productive—produce two-pound brookies with amazing regularity. That's the average. Four- and five-pound fish are less common, but the chances of catching one or more in this class are good. As is the case with rainbow trout, there are brook trout heavier than five pounds and the persistent angler will find them. Just where B.C. brookies top out remains to be seen, but I've heard about eight-pounders and suspect there are even larger fish swimming around out there right now.

There are brook trout in every region of the province, although sizes are small in the few Vancouver Island and Lower Mainland lakes which have been stocked with brook trout. Following is a guide to the best brook trout lakes in the province.

Cariboo-Chilcotin

There are not many brookie lakes in the Cariboo-Chilcotin, but the fishing in lakes which have been stocked with brook trout is excellent in terms of both numbers and sizes. Average size is around two pounds although there are fair numbers of fish to five pounds. Brook trout have developed a real following among those Cariboo-Chilcotin anglers who have discovered them.

» MILBURN LAKE—On the Nazko Road, 15 kilometres northwest of Quesnel, it holds both rainbows and brookies to two pounds and better.

» ONE, TWO LAKES—These lakes on the Alexis Creek road near Alexis Lake, about 20 kilometres northwest from Hwy 20, provide good fishing for both rainbows and brookies, despite being very popular.

» DUGAN LAKE—About 25 kilometres east of Williams Lake on the Horsefly road, Dugan produces brookies between two and four pounds with the possibility of some much larger fish.

» RAVEN LAKE—On the Palmer Lake road, found north off Hwy 20, 27 kilometres west of Riske Creek. It produces brookies to about two pounds.

» SHERIDAN LAKE—On Hwy 24, 32 kilometres east of 93 Mile House, Sheridan is noted for its exceptional rainbow trout, but also produces very large brook trout.

Omineca-Peace

At least one new brook trout lake is added to the region's growing list each year, and there are a dozen or more good brookie lakes in the Prince George area that are not listed here; check with the Fisheries Branch for information. In some lakes brook trout have been used as a prey species on various coarse fish. The result is reduced numbers of coarse fish and some very large brookies.

» BARTON LAKE—About 65 kilometres off Hwy 16 west of Prince George on the Pelican Lake road. It holds both rainbows and brookies.

» VIVIAN AND VERDANT LAKES—About 26 kilometres west off Hwy 97 on the Chief/Ness roads, found about 10 kilometres north of Prince George. Vivian has the larger fish, with brookies to four pounds and better reported, while Verdant's brookies average about two pounds.

» GANTAHAZ LAKE—Located five kilometres north of Mackenzie, it holds brookies to four pounds and better.

» ONE ISLAND LAKE—Go 35 kilometres south of Dawson Creek via Hwy 2, then 32 kilometres on a gravel road heading southwest from near Tupper. Holds good rainbows and brookies.

» INGA LAKE—Located north of Fort St. John on the Alaska Highway, this may be the most northerly brookie lake in the province. It holds brook trout to four pounds and better.

Okanagan

This region does not produce the large brookies found elsewhere in the province. Anglers target them primarily in the winter months. Okanagan brookies have been stocked mainly in the kind of rich marginal lakes which produce exceptional fish when not subject to winterkill.

» HEADWATER LAKES—Located 27 kilometres northwest of Peachland. Hold both rainbows and brookies to four pounds and better.

» JEWEL LAKE—Located 10 kilometres northwest of Greenwood. It is famous for its large rainbow trout, so there
is no reason why its brookies shouldn't reach the same
six-pound-plus sizes.

» IDABEL, OR CARIBOO, LAKE—Located 37 kilometres southwest
of Kelowna; holds both rainbows and brookies to about
three pounds.

» YELLOW LAKE—On Hwy 3A about two kilometres west of
Trout Lake; holds both rainbows and brookies.

» GARDOM LAKE—This lake 10 kilometres northwest of Enderby is well known for its rapid growth rates, regularly
producing rainbows and brookies in the three-pounds-
plus range.

» BECKER LAKE—Located 26 kilometres east of Vernon;
produces brook trout to about two pounds.

» AGUR LAKE—About 15 kilometres west of Summerland;
produces small rainbows and brookies.

Kootenays

Brookie fishing in the east Kootenay consists chiefly of
smallish fish with larger fish found in the west Kootenay.
The small streams of the Kootenay region are probably closer
than any other waters in B.C. to the kind of fishing typical
in eastern Canada. The fish are small but often plentiful and
fishing can be a real pleasure. For streams holding brookies, contact regional Fisheries Branch offices. Lakes in the
region vary, but generally the brook trout tend to be smaller
than elsewhere, although there are exceptions.

» CAMERON LAKE—About 35 kilometres north of the Arrow
Park ferry; holds both rainbows and brookies to about four
pounds.

» LITTLE SLOCAN LAKES—Located about 20 kilometres from
Passmore or Slocan on Hwy 6 and hold both rainbows
and brookies to four pounds (also larger Dolly Varden).

» SNOWSHOE LAKE—Located north of Hwy 6 near the Needles Ferry and requires four-wheel drive. It holds rainbows and brookies to two pounds.

» MAIDEN LAKE—Located on the Findlay Creek road via Canal Flats, this small, rich lake is said to hold larger brook trout.

» SIX MILE LAKES—About 12 kilometres up a logging road that branches north off Hwy 3A seven kilometres northeast of Nelson. They hold rainbow trout, brookies and Dolly Varden.

» WHITETAIL, OR DEER, LAKE—Located 35 kilometres from Canal Flats via the Findlay Creek road; holds good Gerrard rainbows and brookies.

» BRONZE LAKE—A small lake near the old Bull River townsite on the Fort Steele road; holds brookies to two pounds.

» PREMIER LAKE—Located eight kilometres up a gravel road that branches east from Hwy 93/95 near Skookumchuck; it holds rainbow trout to four pounds with the brookies only slightly smaller.

» SURVEYORS LAKE—Located south of Elkford and holds rainbows as well as brookies, with the brook trout dominant. Expect fish to about three pounds.

Skeena

The vast Skeena is not home to many brook trout lakes but there are a few, mostly small walk-in lakes, worth checking out. Bigelow Lake contains small brookies, but Call Lake produces fish to four pounds, with some larger, and Ross Lake near Hazelton produces fish to three pounds. Access to these lakes requires detailed local knowledge and Fisheries Branch staff at Smithers have prepared handouts which provide the necessary information. Co-op Lake, a small, heavily weeded lake five kilometres north of Hwy 16, about

22 kilometres east of Burns Lake, holds some very plump brookies. Fly fishers will do very well here, taking more and better fish than the bait fishers. Allen Lake, near Dease Lake in the north, was stocked with 10,000 brookies in 1989, and is said to be producing well.

Thompson-Nicola

» ROCHE LAKE AREA—Provides good to excellent brookie fishing in a number of nearby lakes: Black, Bog (some very large fish, but four-wheel drive is required), Rose, Tulip and Horseshoe. Brookies average two pounds, but chances of taking larger fish are good to excellent.

» EDITH LAKE—Mentioned in the introduction to this section, it is off Hwy 5A at Knutsford and about 14 kilometres south of Kamloops. It provides excellent brookie fishing for fish averaging two pounds, with many larger fish.

» KANE VALLEY LAKES—Located off Hwy 5A in the vicinity of Corbett Lake, these waters include a number of brookie lakes. Hamilton Lake is subject to winterkill but provides good fishing for brookies averaging two pounds. Chicken Ranch Lake (Bertoli's Puddle) provides good brookie fishing through the year. Second Lakes (Upper and Lower) provide good fishing for brook trout to two pounds.

» RED LAKE—Located 37 kilometres northeast of Savona; holds brookies to two-pounds-plus.

» McGLASHAN LAKE—South of Campbell Lake on the Barnhartvale road; holds brookies to four-pounds-plus.

Cariboo Lakes

*T*he lakes of this region are grouped into four divisions based on the best access roads off Hwy 97 between Clinton in the south and Quesnel in the north. Hence, lakes found under the South Cariboo heading are found off Hwy 97 between 100 Mile House and Lac La Hache. The South Cariboo is further divided into lakes lying east of Hwy 97, and those lying west of the highway. The Central Cariboo heading takes in all waters east of Hwy 97 from 150 Mile House, and extending north as far as the area around Likely. Lakes east and west of Quesnel are found under the Quesnel Area heading.

South Cariboo

Waters lying east and west off Hwy 97 between 100 Mile House and Lac La Hache are found under this heading. Angling pressure in this portion of the Cariboo is concentrated on larger, better-known lakes such as Sheridan. Generally speaking, the smaller lakes receive far less pressure.

» **HIGHWAY 97 EAST**

» HIHIUM AND HAMMER LAKES—Officially, both fall within the Thompson-Nicola region and are listed in chapter three under Sedge Lakes, but they are also included here since access is over backroads associated with the Cariboo, and most anglers would consider them lakes of this region. Expect fish of four pounds and better from both of these popular lakes. Elevation is high enough for both to provide angling through the summer months. If conditions at Hammer are crowded, try nearby Scot (also Little Scot), Sharpe or Young lakes, all of which provide quality small-lake angling for larger rainbow trout. Hihium can be reached over the Loon Lake road branching east off Hwy 97 south of Clinton. Hammer lies south of Bonaparte Lake's western end and is reached over secondary roads branching east from 70 Mile House on Hwy 97.

» WATCH LAKE—Stocked annually with about 40,000 rainbow trout yearlings, this productive lake produces good numbers of trout in the three to four-pound class, but it is well known and gets heavy use. Try weekdays in spring and fall for best fishing and uncrowded angling, although the lake is said to remain good through the summer. To get there, turn east off Hwy 97 at 70 Mile House on the paved road to Green Lake; Watch lies off Green's northern end.

» CRYSTAL LAKE—There are mixed reports on this small lake just south and west of the Bridge Lake post office off Hwy 24. It holds some larger rainbow trout, fish to four pounds, but most fish are in the two-pound range. Does not stand up well during the hot months; try spring and fall. It is a ready, small-lake alternative to larger and more popular Sheridan and Bridge lakes.

» FAWN LAKE—A highly productive lake which grows good numbers of rainbow trout in the five- to six-pound class. Lake chubb are present, which means some of the largest trout will graduate to prey on these small forage fish. This makes eight- to 12-pound rainbows a possibility. Pressure on this strikingly pretty lake is much lower than at Watch or Hammer lakes. It has great spring chironomid fishing and angling can remain good through the summer. Fawn lies just north of Sheridan Lake's western end (off Hwy 24) and is not shown on many maps—inquire locally at Sheridan Lake, on Hwy 24, 32 kilometres east of 93 Mile House, for location.

» TAWEEL LAKE—Officially, this is another Thompson-Nicola lake, but is included since access is by way of roads associated with the Cariboo. It offers quality angling for fish to four pounds, some larger, and holds up well through the summer. A number of small nearby walk-in lakes, Moose, Jonny, Thelma, Lost, and Lorna, all hold larger rainbow trout and make Taweel a good base for longer angling holidays. It can be reached via Hwy 24 beyond Lac Des Roche, but common access is off Hwy 5 at Little Fort, then north on the Lemieux Creek road.

» HOWARD LAKE—Howard has been discovered and gets heavy pressure, but it is a very productive lake with good numbers of fish in the four-pound-plus class, some much larger. Howard was a barren lake first stocked about 20 years ago and is now stocked annually. Few trollers use the lake, but avoid long weekends unless seeking the camaraderie of other fly fishers. It lies south of Canim Lake, and is best reached from 100 Mile House on Hwy 97 via the Canim Lake road. Branch south off this road just before reaching Canim Lake. The steep, troublesome Howard Lake access road is about eight kilometres in on this road, branching east.

» GREENLEE LAKE—This is one of the best get-away lakes in this area of the Cariboo, with very little angling pressure and exceptional rainbow trout; fish to five pounds and better can be expected at this highly scenic lake offering classic B.C. fly fishing. It lies just off Canim Lake, between Canim and Hawkins Lake; access is via 100 Mile House and the Canim Lake road.

» LAKES TO WATCH—Donnelly and Schoolhouse lakes are two previously barren hike-in lakes in the process of being groomed to provide quality angling in remote settings. Contact the Fisheries Branch for location and results of recent stocking; they are expected to provide excellent angling for larger trout by about 1995. Lorin and Needa lakes, east of Deka Lake in the vicinity of Bowers Lake (Needa is south of Bowers; Lorin north), both hold exceptional rainbow trout.

» **HIGHWAY 97 WEST**

» BIG BAR LAKE—An easy-to-get-to quality angling lake with a longstanding reputation for rainbow trout in the four- to five-pound class. There is good camping at 332-hectare Big Bar Lake Provincial Park. Nearby Beaverdam Lake holds very nice brook trout, fish to four pounds and better. Fishing at Big Bar slows during hot weather, making spring or fall the best bets; try fall for the best brookie colours and faster fishing in both lakes. To reach Big Bar, leave Hwy 97 about 10 kilometres north of Clinton in the vicinity of a railway overpass. Big Bar is part of a group of three interconnected lakes which includes Beaverdam (also Little White Lake), but access to Beaverdam is off Hwy 97 just south of Chasm on a good gravel road.

» VALENTINE LAKE—This lake is the site of a fascinating fisheries study aimed at developing strains of rainbow trout capable of withstanding high levels of alkalinity. The lake is very alkaline, producing exceptionally fast growth rates provided rainfall is sufficient to balance alkaline levels. A two-year-old Valentine rainbow typically weighs four pounds. In good years this lake is capable of producing huge fish; it's always worth probing, but Fisheries Branch biologists will confirm survival rates. To get there, turn west off Hwy 97 at 100 Mile House on the Exeter road, and continue for about 20 kilometres.

» HELENA LAKE—It is known as a very moody lake, but yields rainbow trout to five-pounds-plus for patient, canny anglers. Helena lies tucked away behind (west of) Lac La Hache and can be reached from either end of the large lake lying alongside Hwy 97.

Central Cariboo

Lakes lying east of 150 Mile House and south of Likely are found under this heading. Like the southern Cariboo, it is the large lakes which draw the most attention from anglers. The small lakes of the central Cariboo offer the best angling in the region and rank among the best fishing lakes in the province.

» BLUE LAKE—This lake holds larger rainbow trout, fish to five pounds-plus, but is notoriously moody. Expect slow but steady action in this lake, which was rehabilitated only to see its population of lake chubb make a comeback. Sterile kokanee were stocked a number of years ago to determine growth rates of such fish, but a number proved fertile and kokanee now inhabit the lake as well. The lake's largest rainbows, five-to eight-pound fish, will feed almost exclusively on these smaller fish. June is the top angling month, with slow fishing from early to mid-July through August. To get there, turn east off Hwy 97 at Soda Creek and continue for two kilometres.

» JACKSON AND ELK LAKES—Despite an aeration program, Jackson winterkilled in 1990. It had a longstanding reputation as a quality angling lake and should again be producing large rainbow trout by 1994/5, when great angling can be expected. Elk produces exceptional rainbow trout. Island-studded and scenic, Elk has not yet been discovered; fishing pressure is low and fish size is very good. This is a "best of the best" lake. Both lakes provide better angling early in the summer or later in the fall; spring turnover (see the section on reading lakes in chapter four) can make for poorly conditioned fish for some time following ice-off. To reach these fly-only lakes, turn east off Hwy 97 at McLeese Lake; Jackson lies about 20 kilometres in and just south of this road, Elk is just beyond and to the north.

» DUGAN LAKE—Dugan experienced problems after rainbow trout were added to its established population of brook trout and may have partially winterkilled. It is expected to again be producing brook trout to four pounds by 1992/3. Rainbow trout will not be reintroduced into this highly productive lake, which sees heavy pressure in winter. Dugan is on the paved Horsefly road, which branches north off Hwy 97 near 150 Mile House.

» STARLIKE LAKE—Three different strains of rainbow trout have been introduced to this lake for Fisheries Branch research purposes. The various rainbow strains are all finclipped in different ways; anglers should record which fins are missing and the size of fish caught to aid this ongoing project. Starlike holds numbers of coarse fish as well; when rainbow trout attain about five pounds, they begin feeding on these forage fish. Expect some very large fish in this highly productive lake. To get there, continue east past Dugan Lake on the Horsefly road, branching south on the Black Creek road near Horsefly. Watch for the first access road branching south off the Black Creek road.

» KLINNE LAKE—This is the smallest of a group of four good angling lakes lying just south of Quesnel Lake and reached via Horsefly and the Quesnel Lake road. Spring-fed Klinne produces rainbow trout which average two pounds and offers good chances of taking much larger fish. Jacques Lake, first of the group reached by road, is primarily known for smaller rainbow trout but does yield occasional large trout, fish to five-pounds-plus. Keno Lake provides similar fishing, but Hen Ingram Lake has been known to produce trout in the eight-pound class, although average sizes are much smaller. Fly-only Klinne is the best bet for fly fishers. All are best in June and October, although fishing is said to hold through the hot months.

» BENNY LAKES—A short walk is required to reach this group of three lakes, which includes Freshette and Annette as well as Benny. All three hold exceptional rainbow trout, fish to eight pounds, a tip-off to their high productivity. These were traditionally stocked in alternate years, but stocking has now ceased. The group lies south of Spanish Lake's eastern end (east of Likely); look for a landing on the logging road. Benny is .5 kilometres in on the trail, Freshette another .5 kilometres from Benny's south end and Annette is about the same distance from Freshette.

» WOLVERINE LAKE—Off the beaten track, this little-known lake is said to produce good numbers of fish in the four- to five-pound range. To reach this secluded lake, take the Keithly Creek road branching north just east of Likely; the final access road branches north before crossing the Cariboo River.

» SKUNK LAKE—Very little is known about this secret spot lying north of Horsefly Lake, off the road to Klinne Lake from Horsefly. The lake's poor spawning outlet has resulted in some very large fish. It's definitely worth checking out; there are whispers of very good angling. Skunk is not shown on most maps; inquire locally for best access.

» DOREEN LAKE—There are good numbers of rainbow trout to four pounds, and some very much larger fish in this lake with limited spawning-water access (due to beaver dams). Pressure is very light on this little-known lake, located north of McKinley Lake, off the Horsefly River (Black Creek) road. The final access road may require a short walk.

» FOREST LAKE—This small lake holds the largest rainbow trout in the Cariboo; a number of 20-pound-plus fish have been confirmed. Forest was a barren lake before stocking; it now holds good numbers of fish in the four- to eight-pound range, and there are excellent chances of taking trophy-class trout. It has a good sedge hatch and leech patterns have proven effective. A muddy flavour means fish are not suitable for the table and should be released unless kept for mounting. Forest is located north of Williams Lake and south of Tyee Lake.

Quesnel Area Lakes

Waters lying east and west of Hwy 97 in the Quesnel area are found under this heading. The Quesnel Highlands east of Quesnel contain few lakes and angling is generally not as good as that found farther south. The best waters of this area are found west of the Fraser River and offer the solitude of semi-wilderness, even if fish size is small by Cariboo standards.

» DRAGON LAKE—This lake holds huge rainbow trout, fish to 10-pounds-plus, but is notoriously moody and requires canny, patient fly fishing. But it is an easily-reached lake worth checking out by those passing through. Dragon lies just east of Quesnel on the Quesnel River road.

» BOAT, HANHAM AND BATNUNI LAKES—All three are part of the Euchiniko River chain of lakes reached over the Blackwater River road northwest from Quesnel. Boat, about 30 kilometres west of the Nazko/Blackwater roads junction, offers good fishing for smaller rainbow trout and Dolly Varden char in a highly scenic setting. Expect both species to reach the two-pound range. Hanham, just beyond Boat, offers similar angling but difficult launching; a canoe is best. Batnuni holds kokanee and lake char, as well as rainbows and Dollies; rainbow trout occasionally reach the four-pound class, but they are rare. These are still lightly fished, semi-wilderness waters and should be treated with the respect they deserve.

» BLACKWATER RIVER LAKES—The stories of large trout in wilderness waters are legion from the many lakes of this lovely, canoeable river. In fact, however, the Blackwater's rainbow trout tend to be smaller fish with two- to three-pounders considered trophies. Average sizes, based on Fisheries Branch test netting of 300 fish, are around the 11-inch mark, but the fishing can be very fast—20-fish days are normal—and the settings are wonderful. The headwaters lakes (Eliguk, Tsacha) are reached by air charter from the Chilcotin (see chapter five), but the Euchiniko Lakes, 115 kilometres west of Nazco, can be reached by four-wheel drive. Research has found that the tributary streams are prime habitat for rainbow trout for up to two years, after which they migrate to the main river. This means the best fish are found in the Blackwater and its many lakes. Consideration is being given to limiting these waters to catch-and-release fishing in an effort to maintain this fine wilderness angling experience.

» MARMOT LAKE—There is relatively light angling pressure on this small lake holding some very large rainbow trout, fish to eight pounds, with the average size around two pounds. Marmot is a stocked lake best fished by catch-and-release anglers, as its fish tend to be muddy. It is located west of Quesnel on the Nazko road; watch for the access road south, shortly after crossing the Nazko River.

For more information contact:

Fisheries Branch
540 Borland Street
Williams Lake, B.C.
V2G 1R8

Cariboo Tourist Association
Box 4900
Williams Lake, B.C.
V2G 2V8

CHAPTER SEVEN

The Kootenays

There is a special mystique to the Kootenays reserved expressly for anglers. The long, fjord-like lakes which characterize the region are home to the world's largest rainbow trout. Big lakes hug all the major valley bottoms: the Upper and Lower Arrow lakes lie at the foot of the Monashee Mountains; Trout and Slocan lakes are nestled in the Selkirk Mountains; oceanic Kootenay Lake straddles the Selkirk and Purcell Mountains; and finally there is Koocanusa, with the Purcells to the west and the Rocky Mountains to the east. I have tried to scale down the large lakes' dominance of the region by including small angling lakes in the lakes listing for this chapter, but fishing the Kootenays inevitably means trolling the large lakes for their unique strain of rainbow trout. Known as Gerrard giants, these fish average 20 pounds at maturity. No other strain of rainbow trout grows to these larger-than-life sizes.

Originally found only in Kootenay Lake, this unique strain of fish has been transplanted to lakes around the province, including other large lakes of the Kootenay region, but Kootenay Lake remains the sole source of the Gerrard stock. Back from the brink of extinction in the late 1950s, Kootenay Lake Gerrard rainbow numbers have remained fairly stable since the late 1970s, with about 1,000 fish now showing up at the spawning grounds annually. For some years it appeared all was well with these rainbow trout, and while numbers and sizes are still good as this is being written, the future is far from assured. Kootenay Lake kokanee are in serious decline,

and since the fate of the lake's giant trout is directly linked
to healthy kokanee numbers, a population crash appears inevitable. The fish might yet be saved, but the costs involved
are enormous and the required political will, as in so many
pressing environmental matters, is noticeable chiefly by its
absence.

Like the famous Kamloops rainbows of the Thompson-
Nicola, a unique set of circumstances conspired to produce
the Gerrard strain. Accepted theory has it that sea-run rainbow trout once ran into an early version of Kootenay Lake
with direct links to tidewater. When glacial ice dams gave
way as temperatures moderated about 100,000 years ago,
Kootenay Lake and its sea-run fish became landlocked. The
sockeye salmon which used the lake evolved to become
kokanee and the steelhead became Gerrard-strain rainbow
trout, but as always when dealing with the aquatic environment, the story has a twist.

Spawning season for most rainbow trout coincides with
the spring thaw, which turns many streams brown with
meltwater. In Kootenay Lake good spawning streams of clear
water and stable flows were and remain critically limited.
Only the Lardeau and Duncan rivers at the head of the lake's
vast northern reach provided suitable habitat. Both these
rivers had large lakes in their headwaters which acted as
natural settling ponds for the mud and silt of early spring.
In both cases suitable spawning habitat was limited to short
sections, no more than 300 metres in the Lardeau. Down-

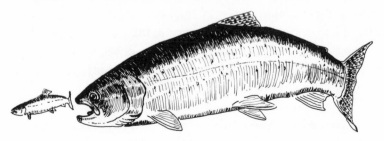

Gerrard rainbow chasing Kokanee

stream of these short reaches, tributary streams again added silt-laden meltwater, which quickly buries river gravel, starving fish eggs hidden in the gravel of crucial oxygen. Competition for suitable spawning habitat was consequently fierce, with only the largest, heaviest fish earning rights to the best spawning areas. Thus a race of fiercely competitive, giant-sized fish evolved. Large body size and aggression became prerequisites of survival.

Anglers who remain unconvinced such trout actually exist can see the evidence for themselves. In May, the Gerrard giants congregate on the Lardeau River spawning grounds just downstream of Trout Lake at the now abandoned community of Gerrard. The second Sunday of May normally coincides with the peak of the run. The fish average 20 pounds, with many heavier than the longstanding Kootenay Lake angling record of 35.5 pounds, but rarely as large as the 52.5-pound Kootenay Lake transplant netted in Jewel Lake. Unfortunately, viewing this spectacle on the Duncan River is no longer possible, thanks to the Duncan dam which effectively cut the fish off from half their spawning habitat. When the dam was built the Duncan River run of giant-sized rainbow trout became extinct. Compensation for habitat lost as a result of the Duncan dam took the form of the Meadow Creek spawning channel, a tributary of the Lardeau. The spawning channel serves the lake's kokanee population, but does little if anything for the giant rainbows.

Long before the dam was built, biologists had established that Kootenay Lake is oligotrophic, low in the essential nutrients which are the required building blocks of a rich aquatic environment. The majority of nutrients are washed into the lake during the spring snow-melt, and the Duncan River had long been thought to be the major contributor of these nutrients. When that relatively rich flow was cut off by the dam, predictions were the lake would become even more nutrient-poor, with serious ramifications for the lake's complex food chain. A further decline in Gerrard numbers seemed inevitable, but a worst-case scenario was forestalled by a wholly unrelated and unforeseen development. Far to the east, at Kimberley on the Kootenay River, the Consolidated Mining and Smelting Company (COMINCO) began manufacturing fertilizer as an adjunct to its industrial operations.

The results of this development were akin to what occurred on the Bow River downstream of Calgary in Alberta. The Bow is ranked as one of the finest angling rivers in the country, but few anglers realize the reason behind the river's fabulously successful fishery: the steady flow of treated sewage dumped into the river by the city of Calgary. The phosphorous contained in treated sewage spurs the growth of aquatic vegetation, thus initiating a chain reaction which works through the food chain. Increased vegetation yields increased numbers of aquatic insects and, eventually, larger and better-conditioned fish. Much the same happened in Kootenay Lake, but the source of phosphorous was pollution spilled into the Kootenay River by COMINCO at Kimberley. When this material made its circuitous way to the lake by way of Montana and Idaho, fishing in Kootenay Lake became wildly successful. Aided by ongoing enhancement efforts and further bolstered by these artificially introduced nutrients, Gerrard rainbow numbers shot up. For almost a decade anglers revelled in what hindsight now tells us was a fool's paradise.

It took the construction of the Libby dam in Montana to reveal the sad truth. This dam, like all dams, acts as an enormous settling pond, or filter, which blocks the flow of nutrients, either natural or man-made. Located on the Kootenai River in Montana, this dam cut off the flow of phosphorous to Kootenay Lake. Having already lost what natural nutrients flowed to the lake via the Duncan River, the true impact of habitat and nutrient losses to Kootenay Lake are just beginning to make themselves felt. COMINCO's phosphorous-rich pollution now gathers in Lake Koocanusa, the reservoir created by the Libby dam, and helps explain that lake's exploding kokanee fishery. But Koocanusa remains an ugly scar on the landscape for much of the year; only in June when it fills with water does it look anything like a lake. In no way does its creation mitigate the loss of Kootenay Lake as one of the province's "best" fishing lakes. Currently, nutrient levels in Kootenay Lake are below what they were before any dam was built and its fishery teeters on the brink of collapse.

Kokanee, which feed on tiny micro-organisms—plankton—for much of their lives, are among the first to experience population declines. The plankton on which they depend require nutrients to grow; any decline in nutrient levels means a decline in kokanee sizes and numbers. But plankton in Kootenay Lake is disappearing faster than warranted even by declining nutrient levels, and in this lies another piece of a complex aquatic puzzle. Enter *Mysis relicta*, a freshwater shrimp introduced to a number of large B.C. lakes during the mid-1960s. This shrimp, yellow-grey in colour and larger than *Gammarus* scuds (see chapter five), was introduced to Kootenay Lake, among others, to enhance kokanee populations. The thinking was that *Mysis* would provide a rich source of protein for the kokanee, allowing them to progress beyond the plankton-feeding stage and grow to larger sizes.

To some extent this is what happened, although *Mysis* became adept at evading the predatory kokanee through vertical migration. During the day *Mysis* remain in deep water, normally beyond the reach of foraging kokanee, migrating to near-surface levels only under cover of darkness. *Neomysis*, a smaller saltwater version of these shrimp which sometimes adapt to freshwater lakes (Kennedy Lake on Vancouver Island is a good example), display similar behaviour to evade the kokanee's saltwater cousin, sockeye salmon. So *Mysis* did not prove to be the factor many thought it would when first introduced. The West Arm of Kootenay Lake, however, proved an exception. Where the lake necks down into the West Arm, deep water meets shallow, causing an up-welling effect which is thought to displace deep-hiding *Mysis* and bring them within reach of the kokanee.

For years this strange combination of factors in the West Arm yielded kokanee fishing unlike anything found anywhere else. Given access to *Mysis*, the kokanee responded as predicted, growing to larger sizes than previously thought possible in freshwater environments. Yet when the Kootenay Lake kokanee crash started, it started in the West Arm. Nowhere is the decline in sizes and numbers of kokanee more apparent than in the big lake's West Arm. And *Mysis* may well be the reason why.

What fisheries managers in both the Okanagan and Kootenay regions are discovering is that *Mysis* may be more of a bane than a boon to fisheries enhancement. Like the kokanee themselves, *Mysis* feed on plankton. *Mysis'* kokanee-evading vertical migrations proved so successful that populations swelled. In both Okanagan and Kootenay lakes *Mysis* populations have reached the stage where plankton levels are now no longer sufficient to support the lakes' kokanee populations. Decreased nutrient levels are only part of the explanation behind Kootenay Lake's decline. We may, in fact, have out-foxed ourselves. By introducing *Mysis* to enhance kokanee populations, we may well have hastened an already established process of decline.

Unlike most rainbow trout, which first spawn in their fourth year, the Gerrard strain does not spawn for the first time until at least their fifth year and often not until the seventh year. This makes them a highly valued source of broodstock, especially in lakes with limited or no spawning streams. In such waters the fish become egg-bound, holding their eggs as they unsuccessfully search for spawning grounds. In some instances the eggs are reabsorbed into the fish's system. In others, gravel placed along lake margins allows the fish to spill their eggs, although they never hatch. In some instances the fish die. The chief benefit of stocking such waters with late-maturing fish is that the fish grow to larger sizes before reaching spawning age, provided angling pressure is light enough to allow at least some fish to survive to their seventh year, a prospect which grows dimmer with each passing year.

The question one must ask, of course, is whether the late-maturing trait is all it takes to qualify as a Gerrard rainbow. I think it fairly obvious that the answer is no. We have already seen how transplanting the Kamloops strain of rainbow trout (see chapter three) outside its home range does not work with anything approaching consistency. Fish are products of their environment; change the environment and the fish change. The Gerrard giants are products of Kootenay Lake. Only the fact they mature later than other rainbow trout sets them apart once they are transplanted. A large, insect-eating trout in a pot-hole lake may well be a fine fish, but it is not to be compared to the deep-swimming hunters which freely roam the long length of Kootenay Lake, even if originally of the same stock.

Artificial fertilization of Kootenay Lake, estimated to cost about $250,000 annually, may reverse the collapse now underway, but quick action is needed and that seems unlikely. For now, anglers may still fish for the giant rainbow trout of Kootenay Lake knowing they have as good a chance of catching one now as they did during the lake's heyday. (A special licence is required; consult regulations.) Spawning returns have not yet indicated a drop in Gerrard numbers. During the summer months they stay deep, following the forage fish, but in winter they come to the surface and can be taken with trolled bucktail flies. This winter fishery certainly ranks among the top angling experiences in the province. Given that the Gerrards are the world's largest strain of rainbow trout, fishing for them is one of the few occasions where the term "world-class experience" might be used with justification. How sad that the next generation of anglers may never see its like.

Closeup: The Bass of B.C.

*B*ass do not carry the regal stamp of trout and salmon, but they are exceptional game fish by any standard, and B.C. anglers are beginning to discover them. The handful of Vancouver Island lakes which support bass now have a small but loyal following and the bass waters found in the Okanagan and Kootenay regions become more popular with each passing year. Still, bass fishing in B.C. remains something of a local secret. The best bass waters, as good as those found anywhere in the country, remain uncrowded and the fish populations, with few exceptions, virtually untouched. This makes for exceptional angling: large trophy-sized fish in typically breathtaking B.C. waters, without the ever-swelling crowds flocking to the best trout waters. That both these fish also take the fly seems too much to ask, but they do, and fly fishers who have not yet discovered them are missing out on some of the best angling in the province.

The fine largemouth bass fishing to be had in the exotic waters of the Kootenay Flats in the Creston area seems the right sort of place to start. Largemouth bass, often touted as the world's most popular game fish, grow to 10 pounds and perhaps better in these warm, shallow, weedy waters. Average sizes are probably somewhere between two and three pounds with fish to five pounds fairly common.

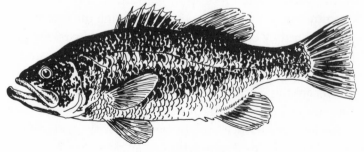

Largemouth bass

By Canadian standards, these are enormous bass and, truthfully, one would have to go a long way south before encountering better, to the famed largemouth bass waters of Florida and Texas where the bass is celebrated as a deity.

Dawn and dusk are the best times to fish for bass and I can think of no finer bass fishing experience than fly casting the Kootenay Flats as the sun steals above the horizon. These are peak activity times for the bass's favourite food fish, the small perch, sunfish and other spiny-rays which call these waters home. Midges and other small aquatic insects bring these fish to the surface and the big, predatory bass lurk under cover nearby, ready to strike. At dusk the small nighttime insects appear and the cycle is repeated. Fish are less cautious when feeding and the bass have learned the trick of catching the feed fish then. For the angler it is a splendid time to be on the water: the fish are eager, the waters uncrowded and the low, slanting light adds a special element of drama to the landscape.

Bass use two types of cover: sanctuarial, the resting places, and predatorial, the ambush spots. Predatorial places have enough cover—shoreside vegetation, under floating vegetation, fallen trees, submerged stumps and so on—to conceal big bass from passing food fish. These are key places to probe, either with the fly or one of the many bass lures available to hardware fishers. Largemouth bass keep their eyes glued to the surface, scanning from cover for signs of small fishes feeding at the surface or hapless grasshoppers, passing frogs, large insects, and even small mammals such as mice. Deerhair mouse patterns, exact down to tiny tails and black eyes, can be very effective bass catchers, especially at dawn or dusk. Veeing such a pattern across the surface in the half-light of early morning or late evening and watching a bulge of water rush in from behind can be an unnerving experience, but it is incredibly exhilarating when the bass blows up from below, scattering weeds and water.

Mouse patterns are just one of a range of strange fly patterns and lures used in bassing. Fly fishers will want to look at patterns such as Dave Whitlock's eel flies, prismatic Mylar streamers and especially the deerhair Most Bug. The venerable Muddler Minnow is easily adapted to bass fishing by adding marabou mane, a Mylar skirt and big eyes. Leech patterns can be very good, especially if top-water patterns fail to attract attention. Large, spent-wing moths are also effective, as are a number of popping bugs, either of cork or deerhair construction. A simple but effective pattern, known as the Whisker Worm, can be concocted using a 10-centimetre plastic worm (purple or black are good) threaded on a number 6 hook and secured with a few lacquered wraps of tying thread. A soft hackle behind the hook eye completes this garish "fly." Generally, the best colours are yellow, white, brown and black.

B.C. hardware fishers will also have to make some adaptations, although the Mepps-style spinners commonly used for trout can be effective for bass as well, both largemouth and smallmouth. Surface plugs, notably in colours which mimic perch and sunfish, are effective largemouth lures and make for exciting fishing. Slim-minnow lures that dive when twitched, then pop back to the surface, are another favourite. Overhead or safety-pin-style spinners are good bets for either large or smallmouth bass, notably in low light conditions and turbid water. Plastic worms should be rigged to be weedless; accepted practice is to cast and wait for the worm to settle to bottom, maintaining enough tension on the line to detect strikes as the worm sinks, a not uncommon occurrence. Set the hook with gusto. Multitailed plastic worms give off more vibrations and are a good bet under low-light conditions. Equally, noisy surface plugs can lure largemouth bass from considerable distances. This is important as largemouth bass may lurk deep in shoreside weeds where casting is impossible. Such fish have to be enticed into clearer water, but expect them to bolt back to cover the moment the hook is set.

Fly fishers do have a few advantages. The largemouth bass' penchant for heavy cover makes them difficult to reach with conventional lures, but the dry line reaches clear pockets amid such weeds, and is easily brought back by lifting the line. Fly fishing also allows faster coverage of a given area because no time is lost in retrieving, a matter of some importance since locating bass is often more difficult than catching them. Finesse is, however, still required. A slapping delivery or chugging pickup will flush bass from ambush cover. Moving closer is better than attempting progressively longer casts. For largemouth bass, an 8.5-foot graphite rod balanced for eight-weight lines is a good choice. A floating line, either weight forward or bug taper, will cover most situations, but a sink-tip will be wanted from time to time. Level leaders are fine, even preferred in many situations. In any event, tippets should be no lighter than 10-pound-test, given that most fish will have to be wrestled out of the weeds. For smallmouth bass the same rods and patterns normally used for rainbow trout will do well, although sinking lines will certainly be required.

By contrast to the largemouth, smallmouth bass rarely leave deep water (spawning and post-spawning are the exceptions), preferring depths to about 12 metres. They are a school fish which relate to structure, sunken rock piles, drowned trees and the like. Accepted practice is to troll until fish are located and then begin casting. Rarely will only one fish be taken from a given location. Trophy-sized

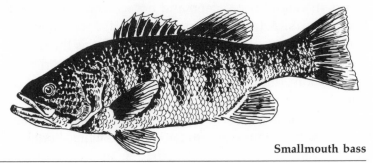

Smallmouth bass

smallmouth are becoming increasingly frequent on such Vancouver Island lakes as Elk, Beaver, Langford, Long, Green and Spider. A Fisheries Branch management program is being developed to ensure the future of this trophy fishery, although indications are the fishery is in excellent shape with both good numbers and sizes of fish available.

Both smallmouth and largemouth bass occur in B.C. due to direct introduction and invasion from the U.S., but as is true elsewhere in Canada, the smallmouth is more widespread. Average length for smallmouths is between eight and 15 inches in Canada. Maximum size in Canada is disputed between a female fish 17.25 inches in fork length and weighing nine pounds, two ounces, or one said to be nine pounds 13 ounces, both taken in Ontario. There are also reports of a Canadian smallmouth weighing 11 pounds, but researchers discount the claim. Maximum age in Canada is about 15 years. Maximum known size for largemouth bass in Canada is a Stoney Lake, Ontario, fish weighing 14 pounds, two ounces. Average size in Canada is the same as for smallmouth, but largemouth get bigger faster—by age three smallmouth bass average between 6.5 and 9.6 inches fork length; largemouth between 9.4 and 11.3 inches fork length.

It is the shape of the snout, rather than the size of the mouth, which most readily distinguishes the two bass. The smallmouth has a deep snout, bluntly pointed and accounting for about 35 per cent of total head length; the largemouth's snout is not deep and not as long in relation to total head size (about 25 per cent). The mouth of the smallmouth bass usually reaches back as far as the front of the eye; in largemouth it goes back to the middle of the eye. The jawbone (maxillary) of smallmouth bass reaches to the middle of the eye; in largemouth beyond the eye. For anglers unfamiliar with bass, the easiest way to distinguish between the two may be to compare the dorsal fins. Both have two connected dorsal fins, the first low and with 10 stout spines. On smallmouth the separation between the first and second dorsal fin is not deep and the two fins appear almost as one. The largemouth's dorsal fins are also joined, but the separation is obvious. To avoid those spines, bass should be picked up by the lower lip in much the same manner used for saltwater rockfish.

Spawning season for smallmouth bass is late spring and early summer, usually between late April and May. A number of lakes are closed to angling during this period. Males are sexually mature at between three and five years of age; females in their fourth to sixth year. Females are thought to spawn every year, but many factors—water temperature and levels, wind, predation—affect reproduction and survival rates resulting in large and small year classes with vastly different contributions to the population.

The male builds a nest anywhere from .3 to 1.8 metres in diameter in one to six metres of water on a sandy, gravel or rocky bottom near the protection of rocks or logs. Males return to the same spot or nearby in subsequent years. Egg number in females varies with size and ranges from 5,000 to 14,000 eggs. The eggs attach to clean stones near the centre of the nest. After spawning, the female leaves the nest and may spawn with another male. The male guards the nest, fans the eggs and guards the young after they hatch. The larger the female and guarding male, the greater the hatching success. Eggs normally hatch in four to 10 days; the young leave the nest after about 17 days, but are still guarded by the male for several days. There is evidence of homing to spawning grounds and summer territory, but movements are generally limited to between one-half and eight kilometres. In winter they school near the bottom, are very inactive, eat little and are rarely taken by anglers. They begin feeding in spring when water temperatures approach 10 degrees.

Crayfish are the smallmouth bass' most important food item, forming between 60 and 90 per cent of the diet for mature fish. However, the relative importance of one food over another depends largely on availability. Other fish are second only to crayfish as a food source and are generally believed to make up between 10 and 30 per cent of the diet. Aquatic and terrestrial insects are third, accounting for about 10 per cent of food volume. The smallmouth takes this food where it finds it, feeding on the bottom, mid-levels or the surface. The largemouth bass seems to prefer other fishes as its most important food and is more cannibalistic than the smallmouth. Estimates indicate up to 10 per cent of food for largemouth bass over eight inches long is fry of the same species. Even largemouth bass smaller than two inches total length have been known to eat other bass just slightly smaller than themselves.

The smallmouth bass' sporting qualities are legendary in other parts of Canada, but it remains little known and little fished in B.C. In eastern Canada it is one of three or four fish that are the mainstay of the region's gigantic sports fishery. Fishing with live bait, usually minnows or crayfish, is the preferred method in other parts of Canada, but is illegal in B.C. (using parts of any fin fish is also illegal). However, smallmouth bass readily take any number of spinners and plugs either cast or trolled. Yellow, brown and black are the favoured lure colours. Smallmouth will take a fly, especially wet flies, much more readily than largemouth bass, but are far less likely to take the floating plugs or poppers designed for largemouths.

Kootenay Lakes

*F*our major mountain ranges—the Monashees, Selkirks, Purcells and Rockies—divide the Kootenay region into distinct parts. This listing of Kootenay country lakes follows the mountains, or rather the valleys between the peaks, from west to east. Hence, the first heading, Monashees to Selkirks, starts on the eastern slopes of the Monashees above the Arrow lakes and ends on the Selkirk divide, with Slocan Lake to the west and Kootenay Lake a glittering blue ribbon in the east.

Monashees to Selkirks

Upper and Lower Arrow lakes, stretching more than 160 kilometres from Revelstoke in the north to near Castlegar in the south, frame the eastern edge of this mountainous area. The Arrow lakes, Trout Lake and Slocan Lake are all large lakes from the angler's perspective and leave the impression that large-lake fishing is the area's hallmark. The large lakes are the focus of most angling interest and trolling is the method of choice. Only a few dauntless fly fishers probe these waters. But there is a scattering of small lakes, most well-suited to fly fishing, which receive less pressure than they otherwise might, due to the popularity of the larger lakes. Fish of the larger lakes will also take the fly, but these are fleeting moments in the season of the lake and one must be lucky to hit them right.

» UPPER ARROW LAKE—This excellent trolling lake yields good numbers of large fish, thanks in no small measure to Fisheries Branch management. Rainbow trout in the five-pound class are said to be numerous and stocking of Gerrard-strain rainbows is paying dividends with ever-increasing numbers of these larger fish being caught (from 40 in 1988, to more than 60 in 1989 and better than 100 in 1990—some tipping the scales at more than 20 pounds). Dolly Varden are also stocked, thanks to a one-of-a-kind Kootenay-region hatchery program. These fish average 10 pounds, with the largest approaching 20 pounds. (Missing adipose fins signal hatchery fish; all such fish should be reported.) Fishing is probably best immediately after ice-off and late in the summer. Creek-mouth fly fishing early in the season is a good bet for fly fishers. Access is at Nakusp, Galena Bay, Beaton and various locations along Hwy 23.

» WHATSHAN LAKE—Almost 30 kilometres long, Whatshan is a mountain-trough-style lake formed by a dam at the southern end. Rainbow trout are said to reach weights of four pounds in this lake, but numbers are low for larger fish. Dolly Varden fishing is slow, but Whatshan char do grow to 10 pounds or better. Kokanee are small. Fly fishing can be good through the early spring, but the fish seek deeper water after about the middle of June. Trolling then becomes mandatory, with early mornings and evenings a possible exception. The lake lies just north of the Arrow Lake ferry at Needles on a good-surface road.

» SNOWSHOE LAKE—A small, secluded lake above the Inonoaklin River, Snowshoe has a mixed population of rainbow and brook trout. Reports are the lake holds good numbers of both, with the rainbows reaching a maximum size of about two pounds, while the brookies are small but plump, not an unusual situation in lakes of mixed rainbow/brookie populations. To get there leave Hwy 6 about 10 kilometres west of Needles on Lower Arrow Lake, branching north on a short, rough road to the lake.

» CAMERON LAKE—This small lake of 16 hectares has a reputation for large rainbow and brook trout, fish to four pounds and better. To get there continue beyond the north end of Whatshan Lake, past Caribou Lake (small rainbows, good fly lake). Turn north at the junction with the Arrow Park Creek road, then take a branch road east just before Arrow Park Lake.

» CATHERINE AND BEAR LAKES—Just past Arrow Park Lake, this much smaller lake of 12 hectares is said to hold rainbow trout to about four pounds, slightly larger than those found in more popular Arrow Park Lake (also known as Mosquito Lake). Anglers fishing Catherine might want to take the walk in to nearby Bear Lake. The size of fish in Bear is unknown, but it likely holds smaller rainbow trout. To get to Catherine, take the Arrow Park Creek road north from Arrow Park for about 40 kilometres, then a short branch road east to the lake and a small Forest Service campsite. Bear Lake lies to the west; take a branch road heading west just south of the Catherine Lake turnoff, then a walk of two to four kilometres depending on road conditions.

Selkirks to Purcells

Travel through the rugged Selkirks is limited to a handful of major arteries: Hwy 31 in the north and down the shores of Kootenay Lake; Hwy 23 along Upper Arrow Lake; Hwy 6 along Lower Arrow Lake to Nakusp and looping south around Slocan Lake; and Hwy 31A connecting New Denver on Slocan Lake with Kaslo on Kootenay Lake. The more populated southern portion is dominated by Hwy 3. Angling highlights include the large rainbow trout of the big lakes, Trout and Slocan; a scattering of smaller lakes with big-fish reputations; and the exotic fish found in the backwaters of Kootenay Lake's southern end.

» TROUT LAKE—Breathtaking Selkirk vistas surround this 30-kilometre-long, deep trolling lake known for its large rainbow trout and sizable Dolly Varden char. Some form of deep-line is required for this lake, either metal lines or downriggers; large plugs or flatfish are the most popular lures. Spring and fall are said to be the best fishing seasons. Draining into Trout lake are Armstrong and Staubert lakes, both lying alongside Hwy 31. Small, shallow Armstrong produces small Dolly Varden and brook trout char, but can be a good fly lake. Staubert is a deep trolling lake holding fair-sized rainbow and brook trout and a small population of Dolly Varden char. Trout lies alongside Hwy 31, with access at Trout Lake village.

» SUMMIT, WILSON AND BOX LAKES—These are three of the best rainbow trout lakes in this part of the Kootenays, with fish size ranging from four pounds to six-pounds-plus.

Box is the smallest of the group and can provide fine fly fishing at times. Summit, in Slocan Lake headwaters, maintains its reputation as a fine rainbow trout lake with reasonable chances of taking fish better than five pounds. The two Wilson lakes are said to hold the largest trout of this group. Box and Summit are on Hwy 6 east of Nakusp; Wilson is on a secondary road branching north off Hwy 6 about 10 kilometres east of Nakusp. Nakusp Hot Springs Park is nearby.

» SLOCAN LAKE—This 45-kilometre-long lake is best known as a trolling lake for very large rainbow trout, fish in the magic double-digit class, although average size is closer to two pounds. Midsummer fly fishing can be productive, notably in the vicinity of creek mouths. It also holds large Dolly Varden char and kokanee. A number of smaller lakes can be reached via a combination of boating and hiking. Two Evans Creek lakes, Beatrice and Cahill, are among the better-known boat/hike-in lakes and provide good fly fishing for small rainbow trout (topo maps are required). The Little Slocan Lakes, reached over secondary roads off Slocan Lake's southern end, are known for good-sized brook trout. Hwy 6 runs down Slocan's east shore; access points include New Denver, Silverton and Slocan.

» CHAMPION LAKES—These are three small lakes in Champion Lakes Park near Fruitvale, north off Hwy 3. Fly fishing can be good for rainbow trout to about two pounds, with some larger fish. Nearby Kerns Lake provides a walk-in alternative.

» ROSEBUD LAKE—This small lake with a longstanding reputation for rainbow trout to about four pounds is located on a branch road just north of Nelway on Hwy 6.

» MONK, NUNN AND BOUNDARY LAKES—These three small lakes hold yellowstone cutthroat trout to about three pounds, much larger than typical for this species in the Kootenays. All are good fly lakes. To get there turn south off Hwy 3 about 25 kilometres west of Creston on the Maryland Creek road. At the first fork, go left (east) for Boundary, right (west) for Monk and Nunn, which require a short walk to reach.

» DUCK AND LEACH LAKES, KOOTENAY FLATS—This fascinating combination of marshy sloughs, backwaters and shallow lakes is one of the best bass-fishing areas in the province. These waters hold a variety of spiny-rayed species such as black crappies and perch, some reaching jumbo proportions. Largemouth bass are the premier game fish, with fish to 10 pounds. Fly fishers can do very well, but appropriate bass patterns are required (see the section on bass on this chapter). Spin fishers new to bass will also want to add new tackle to their arsenals, top-water plugs and the like, although plastic worms are popular, if not as exciting as splashy surface takes. Duck Lake is said to produce the largest bass, but the main and old channels of the Kootenay River south of Hwy 3 also yield rewarding angling. Any mat of floating weeds should be thoroughly probed. Spring and fall are best, but early and late in the day during July and August can also be good. Access is off either Hwy 3 or 3A.

» KOKANEE GLACIER PARK LAKES—Small, brilliantly-coloured cutthroat trout are found in the more than 30 alpine lakes which dot this walk-in wilderness park with stunning alpine vistas. Much of the park is above 2,100 metres in elevation, making mid-July to mid-October the best fishing time. Two cabins are available by reservation. Trails to the lakes are well marked. There are various access roads, but the main one is from Kokanee Creek Park on Hwy 3A, where cabin reservations are taken.

» MIRROR LAKE—This is one of the best smallmouth bass lakes in the region, with fish to four pounds reported. Located just south of Kaslo off Hwy 31.

» FLETCHER LAKES—Most of the small, difficult-to-reach lakes on Kootenay Lake's west shore between Balfour and Kaslo produce small fish, but the lower Fletcher Lake has long held a reputation for larger rainbow trout, fish to four pounds. The upper lake is more typical, producing fish to about one pound or slightly heavier. Both are good fly lakes. To get there, take the Woodbury Creek road south of Kaslo, then the first branch north, to a trail leading to the lake. Walking time is less than one hour.

» KOOTENAY LAKE—This huge, productive lake, long known for its exceptional rainbow trout, Dolly Varden char and kokanee, is experiencing some difficulties (see the introduction to this region), but continues to produce stable numbers of giant Gerrard-strain rainbow trout, fish to 20-pounds-plus. Kokanee are also larger than elsewhere, often attaining sizes similar to their saltwater twins, sockeye salmon, notably in the lake's West Arm. The north end of the big lake is particularly good for kokanee, although they are smaller than those in the West Arm. Fly fishing can be excellent at creek mouths, notably in June. Yellowstone cutthroat trout grow to about three pounds and are most often caught in the lake's southern reach. Hwy 3A follows the eastern shore of the lake's southern half and provides ready access for shore fishers. Boaters who seek uncrowded conditions will want to check out boat-access only Drewry Point and Midge Creek provincial parks on the west shore of the lake's southern reach (the best access is from the public boat launch at Kuskonook). Wind and weather are, however, major factors on this large lake. Crawford Bay, only a few kilometres from the ferry landing at Kootenay Bay, provides shelter from the wind and offers fine fishing for Gerrard rainbows and large Dolly Varden in deep water, largemouth bass in the shallows. Shore fishing is good August through September, but the largest fish are traditionally taken from October to February. Deep trolling is favoured through much of the year, but surface trolling with bucktails during the winter months can be very effective. The Jones Boys Marina at Kaslo is a good source of up-to-the-minute fishing news.

Purcells to the Rockies

This area is bounded by the east side of Kootenay Lake in the west and the Columbia Valley in the west. A relatively small handful of productive lakes provide the best angling. Generally, these lakes are well known to local anglers and the large contingent of anglers who regularly visit from Alberta. Conditions tend to become crowded on these waters during the peak angling season, making spring and fall the times to visit.

» NORBURY LAKES—Located in a scenic area, with 2,774-metre-high Steeples Range in the background, these small, rich lakes produce good numbers of large rainbow trout, fish to four pounds. Fly fishing is demanding at times, with match-the-hatch skills required. From Fort Steele, head south on the Bull River road; the lakes lie alongside this road. A number of other lakes in this area offer angling for larger-than-average trout but all are crowded at peak season.

» WASA LAKE—This popular largemouth bass/perch lake is located north of Fort Steele in 144-hectare Wasa Lake Provincial Park. It holds bass to four pounds and small perch.

» LAKE KOOCANUSA AREA—This large reservoir, created by the Libby Dam in 1972, was accidentally stocked with kokanee and purposely stocked with yellowstone cutthroat and Gerrard-strain rainbow trout. Drawdown reduces the lake to river size until mid-May or June; it is very popular from mid-June through August when it expands again. Rainbow trout numbers remain low, but cutthroat go to about three pounds, and kokanee, the reservoir's main draw for anglers, average 12 inches. Check at Jaffray Sports and

Hardware in Jaffray for up-to-the-minute fishing reports. A number of small, nearby natural lakes provide ready alternatives but now see considerably more pressure due to the number of anglers drawn by Koocanusa's kokanee fishery. Surveyor's Lake, long known as a good brook trout lake, is now a popular swimming lake with a large population of small bass. Hidden Lake is worth seeing for its painted turtles, likely the highest population concentration in the province. Rosen or McBaines Lake near Jaffray was known for exceptional rainbow trout as well as cutthroat; it may still be good. Tiny North Star Lake is said to hold some very large rainbows. Edwards and Loon lakes, farthest south in this group of lakes lying in the uplands above Koocanusa's east shore, maintain their reputation for large rainbow trout, fish to four pounds.

» PREMIER AND QUARTZ LAKES—These very popular lakes adjoining a 662-hectare provincial park hold carefully managed stocks of fair-sized rainbow trout. Fish in Premier run to about four pounds, while those in Quartz are slightly larger. Premier Lake fish are the prime source of broodstock for Kootenay hatchery purposes. There are also some fair-sized brook trout. Fly fishing is good, but the peak season is best avoided due to crowding. About 70 kilometres north of Cranbrook, take a branch road at Skookumchuck east off Hwy 93/95. Wildlife viewing is good for bighorns, elk and deer.

» TAMARACK LAKE—This small fly-only lake has a reputation for good rainbow trout, fish to four pounds. Located just north and west of Skookumchuck.

» WHITESWAN AND ALCES LAKES—Both are contained within a 1,994-hectare provincial park and provide quality angling for large rainbow trout. Stocked with Premier Lake fish, Whiteswan has produced rainbow trout to 18 pounds and was long known for fish to 10 pounds. Average sizes now range between 1.5 and two pounds, with trophies weighing in at about four pounds. Both are very nice fly lakes which might still hold the odd fish in the double-digit class. The best times are early and late in the season. Both are reached by heading south and east of Canal Flats on the 25-kilometre-long Whiteswan Lake road.

» WHITETAIL LAKE—The boat-access only campsites on the lake's eastern shore are the nicest on the lake and worth the effort involved in getting there. Extensive marl flats make for excellent fly fishing on this rehabilitated lake. Expect rainbow trout to four pounds, with some larger. There are good chironomid (pale olive), dragonfly and grey *Callibaetis* mayfly populations. Located west of Canal Flats on the Findlay Creek road.

» LILLIAN LAKE—A small, 25-hectare lake, admirably suited to fly fishing, with rainbow trout to four pounds and somewhat smaller brook trout. Other small lakes nearby are worth probing: Long, Eileen, Enid, and Wilmer, among others. Lillian lies five kilometres west of Invermere on the road to Panorama.

» MOUNT ASSINIBOINE PARK LAKES—Mount Assiniboine, named for the Indians which used the area as a hunting ground, epitomizes the Canadian Rockies; and the lakes nestled below its craggy 3,561-metre peak epitomize Rocky Mountain fishing at its best. Good numbers of smaller cutthroat trout are found in most of the lakes in this hike-in park, but, almost unbelievably, a number of lakes contain giant-sized cutthroat, fish to 10 pounds and better. Catch-and-release Cerulean Lake regularly yields trout to five pounds, with numbers of fish in the 10- to 15-pound range. Sunburst Lake was closed to angling in the early 1970s, but has been reopened and offers similar fishing to that found in nearby Cerulean. Good hiking skills are required to reach these lakes over four different access routes. Contact the Parks Branch in Wasa for information.

» PARSON AREA LAKES—A number of lakes in the Parson area
(south of Golden on Hwy 95) have longstanding reputations for producing rainbow trout in the four-pound range.
Lakes to search for include: Rocky Point, Three Island and
Summit, which also holds brook trout.

For more information contact:

Fisheries Branch
310 Ward Street
Nelson, B.C.
V1L 5S4

Fisheries Branch
106-5th Avenue South
Cranbrook, B.C.
V1C 2G2

Kootenay Country Tourist Association
Site 2-11, R.R. 1
Castlegar, B.C.
V1N 3H7

Rocky Mountain Visitors Association
Box 10
Kimberley, B.C.
V1A 2Y5

CHAPTER EIGHT

The Skeena

T hose who have yet to venture north to the vast Skeena will not believe a word of what follows. The Skeena is a land of angling adventure, a place where our wildest dreams come true. Imagine 20-pound lake trout being average fish, or rainbow trout that look like coho salmon, or strange fish with sails on their backs. The sail-like dorsal fin of the arctic grayling may seem too fantastic to be real and its iridescent, ever-changing colours like nothing else in this world, but the entire Skeena is itself fantastic and other-worldly. The arctic grayling is but one manifestation of this quality. In summer, daylight seems to go forever; in winter, multihued northern lights dance across a black, frozen sky. The landscapes have no end, sweeping on forever over limitless horizons. It is a world where anything seems possible, a place like no other.

There is little point in comparing regions. Each is unique; each has its special qualities and hidden treasures. Let us just say the Skeena occupies prime place in a province rich in natural wonders. For anglers it can seem as if this entire sweep of country was expressly designed for them. The large lakes of the south—only in the Skeena could lakes like Babine or Eutsuk qualify as southern waters—offer unmatched angling for lake trout and trophy-class rainbow trout. Skeena rainbow trout take two radically different forms. One strain has opted for small body size and preys chiefly on insects, aquatic or otherwise. The others have carved out a niche as top predators. These are the large, free-ranging trout of the big lakes, the hunters which seek kokanee, salmon fry and other forage fish. They are not, by and large, fish which come willingly to the fly. But there are times when they do, and the fly fisher who discovers them is in for the experience of a lifetime. The next section in this chapter describes a place where such fishing is not only possible, but expected and even predictable. This is not at all typical. In most waters the predatory rainbows maintain their free-ranging habits and fishing for them is not unlike saltwater trolling for salmon: fun, certainly, but not to be compared with classic dry fly angling. The big char of the same waters are an altogether different fish; they are discussed in the next chapter, as Omineca-Peace waters are also home to this ancient and now troubled species.

Skeena coastal lakes offer one of the few remaining opportunities to fish for large, native cutthroat trout. These are boat-in or fly-in waters and while the logistics of such trips can be formidable, so too are the rewards. I know of no other waters which offer better chances of taking wild, trophy-sized cutthroat trout, fish of 10-plus pounds. Mentioning such waters is not without its qualms: there are still those who kill every fish caught, even if their numbers grow fewer each year. Most who take the trouble to reach such waters seek sport and wilderness, and there is strength in numbers. The more people using the far-flung edges, the more voices are raised when wilderness is threatened.

The entire Skeena is considered north by many, Prince George representing the psychological, if not the physical, demarcation between northern and southern B.C. But the northern area of the Skeena is truly north, its edges spilling into the Yukon, which both Teslin and Atlin lakes penetrate. This great sweep of country, starting at about New Hazelton, is too multifaceted, too much on the grand scale, to be covered in a few paragraphs. Let us instead look closely at one of its finest pockets, the wilderness country of the Spatsizi.

Our trip to Spatsizi Wilderness Park started on the shores
of an alpine lake cradled in the headwaters of the Stikine
River. Moments ago a floatplane had dropped us into the
vast tract of wilderness bounded by the Stikine and Klap-
pan rivers in a remote corner of the Skeena. As the aircraft
vanished in the green-blue wilderness sky, its final
whispered drone gave way to the sounds of wind and water.
We would not hear another mechanical sound for the next
three weeks.

More than a year of planning had gone into the making
of this trip, but despite the attention lavished on every detail, we were not prepared for this moment of first encoun-
ter with Spatsizi Wilderness Park. No one could be. This
headwaters country, kilometre upon kilometre of alpine
stream and meadow, is too big and too visually stunning
to be fully grasped in a few moments. A lifetime may not
be enough. For a long while after the departure of the floatplane we stood staring, utterly spellbound by the Spatsizi's
special brand of magic.

The Spatsizi is wilderness writ large. It will be difficult
for anyone who has never fished rich wild waters to understand this kind of fishing. There was no matching of hatches,
no constant changing of terminal gear in an exasperated
search for just the right fly or spinner, no waiting for a hungry fish to cruise by.

Our gear was still piled helter-skelter on the beach, just
as it had come out of the Beaver, when I took my first cast
from the gravel bar beside the glass-clear creek spilling into
Happy Lake. The nymph did not sink more than a few centimetres before the first rainbow trout took with the typical
violence of a hard, bright fish raised in cold northern waters.
Each cast was immediately answered by a rainbow trout and
I quickly lost count of the number of casts and fish hooked.
My partner had rigged a spinning rod and was soon standing beside me, also hooking and releasing fish on almost
every cast. The fish were all about the same size, between

16 and 18 inches long, with small heads and deep bodies. Of course it was ridiculous, hooking fish after fish after fish, but we kept it up until a bone-chilling wind slammed down off the ice field high above us. The wind served as a sharp reminder that this was wilderness and we had best attend to chores; camp had yet to be rigged.

Happy Lake is part of the network of lakes and alpine tarns which form the headwaters of the Stikine River, but it is tucked away in a side valley of its own and thus is one step further removed. It was an easy day's travel by canoe—with one carry of less than two kilometres where the stream crashes out of the lake—from Happy Lake downstream to Tuaton Lake. It was wilderness travel at its civilized best. The stream flows through a vast alpine meadow covered in bunch grass, wildflowers and the shed antlers of Osborne caribou, largest of the North American caribou. No testing of a paddler's mettle was involved, no finely honed canoeing skills required. This small alpine stream is swift certainly, but its shallow, crystal waters seemed decidedly friendly. It was also loaded with fish; schools of them darted and flashed ahead of the canoe.

Tuaton Lake lies in the much larger valley of the Stikine itself, although at this point it was possible to jump across the mighty river. The setting remained typically alpine with wildflowers, low-lying willow and, much further up the hillsides leading to the vast Spatsizi Plateau, bands of small, stunted conifers. The air was so clear that the sky had no depth, no deep blues, and distances were almost impossible to judge accurately. What looked like two or three kilometres turned out to be 10 or 15 when calculated from the maps. This is the country Tommy Walker, guide-outfitter and the man most responsible for convincing a reluctant government to declare the Spatsizi a wilderness park, called the Stikine Prairie. A better example of the power and riveting beauty of the western landscape would be difficult to find.

Tuaton is actually like a widening of the river and more like two lakes than one. It has depth only where the river channel winds through along the northern shore, the rest being quite shallow, often too shallow even for a canoe. At one point the lake necks right down to river size and continues so for a short distance before spilling into what we called Lower Tuaton. The fishing at any of the inlets was almost too good to be real— every bit as good as what we had at Happy Lake, better, perhaps, because now there were large Dolly Varden char as well as rainbow trout. We spent several days fishing where Upper Tuaton drains into Lower Tuaton. One anecdote says it all.

I was knee-deep in the water, just to one side of the current and casting into quiet water. My partner remained just upstream, plying a spoon for Dollies. For some reason I happened to look down at my feet. A school of Dolly Varden were actually milling about right beside me, almost on my feet. I called for my friend to drift his spoon my way, but before it reached me an upstart rainbow grabbed hold. Suddenly his rod dipped into a deep bow and line peeled from the reel. A wild, erratic tussle followed, unlike anything either of us had ever seen before. When it finally ended there were two fish on the beach at the end of his rod, a rainbow and a fair-sized Dolly Varden. The Dolly, it turned out, was not even hooked. One loop of monofilament was neatly wrapped around its gills. Seems it saw the rainbow struggling with something in its mouth and moved in for a closer look. It was the first and only time I have ever seen an angler lasso his quarry.

The Stikine is still a small, grassy-banked stream where it flows from Lower Tuaton into Laslui Lake, the final lake in the headwaters chain. We fished Laslui only briefly, stopping at creek mouths only when they looked too good to bypass. We took fish everywhere we stopped. At the outlet of Laslui we carried our gear over a set of impassable rapids for about 2.5 kilometres to the pool at the end of the rapids.

Here the alpine gives way to open park land, bigger conifers set amid open fields, and the fishing changes from Dollies and rainbows to arctic grayling. We spent two days at that lovely pool, actually a wide bend in the now river-sized Stikine, taking grayling on the dry fly until our arms grew weary.

Picture it, two friends standing in pristine wilderness more than 300 kilometres from the nearest road, their hearts light and their fishing rods bent with the pressure of grayling sailing the currents. That is the vision I'd like to leave because that is where it started for us: as a carefully nurtured dream of a far and distant place.

Closeup: Babine Lake's Rainbow Alley

*A*t the northernmost tip of the province's second-largest natural lake lies a special place known to a handful of ardent north-country anglers as Rainbow Alley. Here Babine Lake's entire 50,247-hectare surface area quietly glides into a long journey to the Pacific via the Babine and Skeena rivers. Later, in the rapids and canyons of the Babine River, this same water will thunder and roar, but at Rainbow Alley it is as if the water itself were loath to leave, so gently does the seaward tug begin. After a scant few kilometres of lingering descent, the waters spread again, forming shallow, weed-edged Nilkitkwa Lake, where Babine natives yet maintain traditional smoke houses and cabins for the salmon season. Nilkitkwa grows ever narrower towards the north, splitting around a small maze of islands before the waters again form an even flow, only fractionally faster than the broad flow of Rainbow Alley. This is the start of the Babine River proper; the first rush of whitewater is less than four kilometres distant. The trout fisher will want to linger long in these upper reaches, for the rainbow trout which these waters foster are as spectacular as the setting in which they are found.

Rainbow Alley is flanked to east and west by the distant snow-capped peaks of the Frypan and Babine ranges. Through the long days of the northern summer, the angler's eye will be continually drawn to these cool, distant vistas, the high-floating dry fly left unattended in mid-drift. When the westering sun begins its descent behind the Babine Range (as late as 10 P.M. in midsummer) the whole of Rainbow Alley—the water, the trees, the sky, even the distant Frypan Range in the east—are suffused with coppery gold. Such sights are staggering in both their sweep and surreal coloration, but I recall one strange north-country evening when, in the midst of such a Rainbow Alley sunset, the full moon slowly rose over Babine Lake in the southeast, while off in the distant, amethyst-tinged east a violent thunderstorm hurled angry bolts of lightning into the wilderness between Babine and Takla lakes. And all the while, slashing in the golden, moon-reflecting, lightning-flashed waters, the rainbow trout of the Babine were rising steadily.

Such is the place known as Rainbow Alley. In strict geographical terms, Babine Lake straddles the middle of the province, about halfway between the U.S. and Yukon borders, but one need visit just once to know Babine belongs

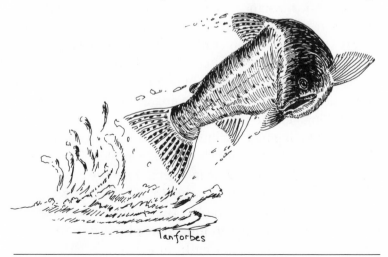

to the North. The rich colours and fantastic scenes are as if lifted from the canvas of a Ted Harrison painting and made real. Even when the wild rainbow trout are rising on all sides of the anchored boat, it can be difficult to focus hand and mind solely on the floating fly. I cannot begin to count the number of times I rediscovered my abandoned fly drowned somewhere in mid-river, pulled under and rejected by a rainbow trout I never saw. Rainbow Alley will do that to an angler, even the most serious of anglers, but its magic works the other way too. When the fishing is hot, as is so often the case, the angler's eyes will remain glued to the gently drifting fly. Inevitably, for the angler at least, the fish will steal the show.

Many if not most of the large lakes in the Skeena region harbour lake trout (char) and rainbow trout. The char grow large provided forage fish are available in sufficient numbers and anglers have not overharvested these slow-growing fish. The rainbow trout of such waters can also grow large, but the conditions required are far more exacting. Even so, assuming all chemical and biological factors are present for the rapid growth of rainbow trout, the angler is faced with a dilemma. Where in these large lakes does one fish? Babine Lake, for instance, is more than 180 kilometres long. Obvious fish-holding areas are not easily discovered in lakes of this size. Indeed, sometimes there are no holding areas at all. The fish constantly cruise the lake, forever on the move, seeking hapless wind-blown insects and schools of forage fish. On such waters the angler must seek the fish, and trolling, either flies or hardware, is often the only method of taking fish. Casting is possible, but usually only after a school of cruising fish has been located. These will-o-the-wisp fish are here one moment, gone the next, so the angler must expend considerable time and energy following. Those more accustomed to the pond-like lakes of the south will find this a frustrating game, but there are a few northern lakes where casting from a carefully chosen anchored position is not only possible, but even preferred. Babine is one of the finest examples of this type of north-country lake.

The explanation for this lies in the abundant run of sockeye salmon which uses the lake's tributary streams for spawning and the lake itself as a juvenile nursery. In the fall of the year many thousands of sockeye salmon arrive at Babine Lake via the Skeena and Babine rivers. Following an age-old ritual of death and renewal, the fish deposit their eggs in the gravel of small streams tributary to the lake and die, adding the nutrients of their bodies to the stream's own complex cycle. Through the long frozen months of winter the eggs remain buried and essentially unchanged, but as winter draws to a close the miraculous transformation begins. The eggs hatch in late winter or early spring, but remain under their protective shield of gravel for many weeks, taking sustenance from the yolk sacs to which they are still attached. Sometime between April and early June, most often mid-May for Babine sockeye, the fry move downstream and out into the lake, which will serve as their nursery for a period of about two years. It is at this point that the rainbow trout again enter the picture.

From scattered locations around the lake, the large native rainbows of Babine Lake react to a genetically imprinted message: the winter has broken and the time of plenty is at hand. The rainbow trout move to the creek mouths. The sockeye are like schools of herring in tidewater—easy prey with only the densely packed mass of their own bodies for protection. For the trout it is indeed a time of plenty, especially off the mouths of Pinkut Creek near Donald Landing and the Fulton River near Topley Landing, both far to the south of Rainbow Alley. The building of sockeye spawning channels under the Salmonid Enhancement Program has greatly increased the numbers of sockeye using these streams and, consequently, the numbers of Babine rainbows who mill there, waiting for descending fry.

None of this has gone unnoticed by anglers, and the May to June fishery off the mouths of these two creeks has reached the saturation point. Those who fish this "spring run," mostly anglers from Prince George, Terrace and the communities of the Bulkley Valley, describe it as "gunnel to gunnel fishing." Anglers who find themselves in the Burns Lake area at this time of year should by all means make the trek to one or the other of these locations, but those planning a fishing holiday to Babine would do better to wait for mid-June, when both the sockeye and the rainbow trout have moved up the lake to Rainbow Alley. Fishing conditions there are far less crowded and the angling itself is many times more complex and thus more rewarding too.

Almost at the same time as the year's newly hatched fry are descending to the lake, sockeye smolts which have already spent two years in the lake and are preparing for life at sea begin to make their way to the north end of the lake, towards Rainbow Alley and Nilkitkwa Lake. The rainbow trout will linger at the lake's creek mouths only while the fry migration is at its peak; soon after, they too disperse into the lake, but while their movements are erratic and individual, the general direction is always to the north, following the silvery seaward-bound sockeye.

And so we come full circle, from the arrival of the adult sockeye in the fall at Rainbow Alley, to the spring downstream migration of the smolts. The rainbow trout native to the open waters of the big lake now take up position in the gentle flow of this broad stream. The smaller rainbow trout resident to the stream are pushed aside to less favourable water within the flow: prime positions in the current are decided by size and aggressiveness and the stream-resident fish stand no chance against their larger lake-resident cousins. So things will remain through much of June, July and into August, although the feeding patterns and movements of the fish will change from one week to the next, sometimes from one day to the next or even from morning to afternoon of the same day.

Rainbow Alley consequently provides a vastly different fishery from the springtime savagery of the Fulton and Pinkut fishery. While it is the young sockeye which lure the large lake-resident trout to Rainbow Alley, concentrating a good percentage of the lake's population in a relatively small area, the sockeye are but one aspect of a complex, multilayered food chain. It is the hatches of aquatic insects and the opportunity to fish large dry flies in pristine waters which lures anglers to Rainbow Alley. Two varieties of stonefly, several different types of mayfly and at least one variety of caddisfly are among the major aquatic insect hatches. Later, starting sometime in July, the mayfly, dragonfly, damselfly and caddisfly go through their various cycles in Nilkitkwa Lake, adding yet another dimension to the fishery.

A novice to Rainbow Alley would be wise to drift through the entire length of the stream as far as the start of Nilkitkwa Lake before choosing one spot and setting the anchor. The flow is gentle enough to permit casting with only an occasional paddle stroke required to correct the angle of drift or to cover an exceptional fish not directly in line with the boat's path. There will be many exceptional fish. Even accomplished anglers have been known to fall apart at the sight of Rainbow Alley's large rainbows. It is not just the size of the fish—two-pounders are common fare—it is the sheer numbers in such a small area that is so impressive.

The drift starts upstream of the bridge which crosses Babine Lake where it necks down into Rainbow Alley. This recently built bridge crosses to the historic settlement of Fort Babine; the original Hudson's Bay trading post still stands amid the more modern houses of this semi-isolated village. While the current is not perceptible to the eye, the boat slowly begins to drift towards the bridge; anglers, suitably armed with high-floating dry flies and five or six-weight dry lines, should begin the game here. The fly is cast across and upstream—heroically long casts are not required, but the presentation must be dead drift, usually requiring no more than a single mend; later, in the somewhat faster water of Rainbow Alley proper, two or more mends of the line will be necessary to keep the fly floating at the speed of the current. The fishing here is normally slower than what awaits downstream, but many fine fish have been taken in this stretch of water, and the chance to hone casting skills before reaching the mayhem below should not be missed.

The first of the surface-feeding trout are normally visible at the bridge. Provided the angler remains in control—no easy feat in full view of large rainbow trout feeding with apparent abandon—the floating fly will disappear at the foot of the bridge in a neat swirl of water as the first fish takes hold. Immediately downstream of the bridge, with the Fort Babine coho and chinook salmon hatchery visible on the left bank, the water will be pock-marked everywhere with rising trout. This is due to the stonefly's preference for the faster current below the bridge, as opposed to the slower water upstream. The stonefly is by far the predominant aquatic insect of Rainbow Alley. Of the many members of this order of insects (Plecoptera) the small green stonefly (family Chloroperlidae) and the golden stonefly (family Perli-

Stonefly nymph

Stonefly adult

dae) call these northern waters home. While there is a fairly strong hatch of the golden stones at Rainbow Alley—a
hatch which always triggers the fish—this family generally
seeks faster water; the small green stonefly, on the other
hand, is entirely at home in this even flow and its hatches
can be legitimately termed super hatches.

With rising fish on all sides, the temptation will be to set
anchor and begin the game in earnest, but, unbelievably,
better fishing yet awaits downstream. The trick here is to
cast the fly in such a manner that its drift path will take it
to a specific fish. Remember that the fish feed in lanes (or
"alleys," hence Rainbow Alley) and that the best fish will
have taken position in the best water. It pays to stop casting
long enough to watch the water carefully, pick out the holding stations of the larger fish and then flick the line out upstream and in line with the fish's position. This is angling
at its best. There is the fish, a heavy leopard-spotted wild
rainbow trout consistently rising to the naturals which drift
by in parade. There are only seconds to react as the boat
itself is moving downstream with the current. False cast once,
twice and the line drops to the water, the leader fully un-
curled and the fly bobbing nicely, an imitation of either the
large golden or small green stonefly. One quick mend and
an angry swirl erupts below the fly, the hook is set and suddenly a four-pound trout clears the surface, silver shards
of water cascading from its sides. By the time the entire drift
is completed and the boat emerges at the smokehouses of
Nilkitkwa Lake, there will have been many such moments
and excitement will be running high, but now is the time
for calm, as a vital decision must be made.

The choice is either to run back up to the bridge—slowly
with as little disturbance to the water as possible, since a
large wake will disrupt everything and damage fragile aquatic
vegetation into the bargain—and repeat this fabulous drift
once again, or to run down the length of Nilkitkwa Lake
and on into the waters of the upper Babine River. In July

a third option makes the decision more difficult yet. By then Nilkitkwa Lake itself likely will be in full hatch and—take warning—the largest fish of the year are normally taken in this shallow, weed-edged lake, perhaps because the water is deeper than in the streams and the fish less cautious as a result. The flow of the upper Babine River is faster than at Rainbow Alley and the hatch of large golden stoneflies there is as prolific as the hatch of small green stones at Rainbow Alley. These larger insects make for exciting fishing since they are clumsy fliers and often rest on the water with madly beating wings. The fish respond to this with savagery, much in the manner of the Kamloops rainbow when presented with fluttering caddisflies. The size of the insects also adds an element of drama—both air and water appear thick with large, fluttering insects, adding an almost tropical element to the north-country settings.

As these hatches progress through their initial stages to full intensity, the fish become increasingly selective, as is the case everywhere. This is one of the few times when fishing Babine waters requires a high degree of technical ability, but even then there is an option available to those not yet comfortable with the intricacies of "matching the hatch" in its later stages. Almost never will the rainbow trout of the Babine refuse a salmon fry imitation presented dead drift. This may not be true of the smaller fish, but the largest fish, it seems, are always ready to attack a realistic imitation of their mainstay. It is well to remember that it is the salmon fry which account for the exceptional size and numbers of rainbow trout in this unique system. Even those who have difficulty presenting their fly in the required dead-drift manner will take fish with fry imitations. Although many of the Babine regulars will frown on this manner of "fly trolling," it is possible to anchor at the bow and strip out line behind the boat. Then, simply by lifting the rod high, the fly is brought back towards the boat and allowed to again drift down with the current. In this fashion even the novice fly fisher can cover a number of rising fish downstream of the boat.

Babine fish are large, often very large. Even hardened fisheries biologists concede the rainbow trout of Babine Lake fall into a special category. Many anglers think the fish they are catching are steelhead, but all scale samples show they are lake-resident rainbow trout. At times there are schools of between 200 and 300 of these fish visible in the waters of Rainbow Alley.

Babine is a daunting lake by virtue of its size alone; reaching an understanding of its fish, their feeding patterns and seasonal movements is the work of several lifetimes. Most of the information outlined here was gathered over several generations and preserved in family fishing traditions, passed from grandfather to grandson, father to son or daughter. Much of it was hard-won, gleaned by anglers who might have spent several days rowing to reach the fabled waters at the far northern end of a vast lake. This private store of angling lore was willingly shared with not just an outsider, but one who intended broadcasting their secrets in print. I am deeply indebted to those generous and open-hearted spirits who shared this private knowledge: master anglers Gordie Hetherington and Harry Cole of Smithers, Dave Hooper of Tukii Lodge at Smithers Landing, and Pierce Clegg of Norlakes Lodge for passing on 50 years of Babine fishing lore accumulated by Norlakes' many fine anglers.

Skeena Lakes

*T*he lakes of this region are divided into three groupings. The Lakes District heading takes in all waters north and south of Hwy 16 in the Burns Lake area. To make location easier, this area has been further divided into lakes lying north of Hwy 16, and those to the south of this highway. Coastal Skeena lakes are found under the Remote Coastal and Queen Charlotte Islands heading. Lakes of the far north are found under the Northern Skeena heading.

The Lakes District

Only a few short years ago it might have been easy to wax pessimistic over the various forms of despoliation inflicted on the lovely lake-splashed region north and south of Hwy 16 in the Burns Lake area. Logging and its attendant road-building have resulted in landscapes scarred by clear-cutting and the overfishing which appears an inevitable consequence of new access roads to formerly remote waters. To some extent this continues, but things have changed and I think the changes are with us for good. There is now room for optimism, if only of the cautious variety. Generally, logging plans are more sensitive than before. Landscape logging techniques, which include wildlife corridors and at least some acknowledgement of intangible wilderness values, have finally become part of the planning process. More important, plans are subject to public review and local resource committees have a real voice in how their forests are to be managed.

On the lake-angling front there is less room for optimism, at least over the long term. For now, there are still many fine angling lakes to discover and I think things are likely to remain that way for some time. This is more a result of the sheer number of lakes the region harbours than out of any conviction that management and angler concern will save the region's essentially fragile fishery. As elsewhere in the

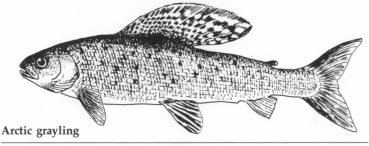

Arctic grayling

province, fisheries managers do an excellent job with the resources at their disposal. But one need only compare the size of the region with the number of biologists and technicians to arrive at an inescapable truth. Managers are thinly spread and such basic questions as angler harvest rates and their impact on fish stocks remain unknowns for most waters. With ever-increasing demands on already beleaguered tax dollars, a political decision to spend more on northern lake fisheries management seems unlikely at best and unrealistic given the problems which plague the region's river fisheries. Lakes, I'm afraid, are at the bottom of a long list and are likely to remain there for some time.

» HIGHWAY 16 SOUTH

» FRANCOIS LAKE—This lovely 120-kilometre-long lake with its many fishing lodges and heavy summer use remains a very special lake. Francois dominates virtually all approaches to the lakes district south of Hwy 16 and most visiting anglers will have to either cross the big lake on the free ferry or drive around it in order to explore the area. Despite reasonably heavy pressure, both Francois's rainbow trout and lake char populations appear to be holding up remarkably well. Be warned, however, that catching trophy-sized lake trout in Francois, or anywhere for that matter, requires intimate local knowledge. In Francois the big char move between a number of well-defined seasonal locations. The key is to ask other anglers and lodge owners for details and to get out on the water early enough to see where the regular char fishers are concentrated. Rainbow trout tend to be small, but appear incredibly numerous and are suckers for a trolled willow leaf and worm combination. Fly fishers will despair of these fish except on the rare occasions when a school of surface-feeding trout are located. Late June through July are best for rainbow trout. A paved road south from Burns Lake (Hwy 35) provides the best access.

» TAKYSIE LAKE—One of very few lakes in the area which offer consistent action for fly fishers, likely because it holds scuds (see chapter five) and does not have the mixed stocks of most other lakes. Kamloops-style patterns, I'm told by anglers met at Francois, do very well at Takysie, and while its rainbow trout are not as large as those found in southern lakes, they are wild fish with the breed's typical special vigour. Even quite small Takysie rainbows will strip reels well into the backing. To get there, take the Francois Lake ferry to Southbank, the Southbank road to Grassy Plains, then head south on the Ootsa Lake road as far as the east-turning Takysie access road.

» UNCHA AND BINTA LAKES—These two smaller (by Lakes District standards) lakes hold reasonable numbers of very large lake trout, fish to 30 pounds and better. Local information is required to ferret out the best char locations, but this should be no more difficult than chatting to local anglers or stopping by the resort. Wire lines or downriggers will be required and the usual assortment of large plugs or spoons. Early morning seems the favourite time, although I have caught large char at midday as well. Best seasons are from ice-off (late April to mid-May) through to the end of July. August fishing is slower, then picks up again in the fall months. Both are good lakes for those interested in trophy-sized char. Rainbow trout reportedly run to three pounds, but the average size is closer to one pound or less. To get there, cross Francois Lake on the ferry to Southbank, then go left (east) on the Uncha Lake road. Binta lies just to the south of Uncha; there is one section of rough road.

» PARROT LAKES—Centred in the area of the devastating 1983 forest fire which has now greened over, this chain of four small, intimate lakes offers fast fishing for small, wild rainbow trout and good chances for wildlife viewing. These lakes appeal to canoeists, who should be able to travel between all four lakes. Small dry flies can provide hours of delightful angling. There is a Forest Service campsite, but canoeists will find good remote camping spots and excellent fly fishing. West of Houston, turn south on the Buck Creek road (note: not the Morice River road); after about 35 kilometres, branch south to the lakes.

» NADINA LAKE—This rainbow trout and kokanee lake is located far enough to the west for the Coast Mountains to be visible, but not close enough to impinge on the lake's north-country woods flavour. There are no char, which often means larger rainbow trout, and that's the case at Nadina, which yields lovely wild northern rainbow trout to four pounds and better with some regularity, although there is considerable variation from year to year. Generally, Nadina can be counted on to provide good but slow trolling for larger rainbow trout. Fishing is slower than on other lakes in the area, but pressure is consequently lighter. Fly fishers will want a good supply of streamer patterns. New roads will soon provide access to nearby Newcombe Lake and its population of large native rainbows. To get there continue west on the Francois Lake road, then southwest on the Nadina River road to the lake. Alternately, take the Morice River road south from Houston to the Francois Lake/Nadina River junction.

» EUTSUK LAKE—This huge, take-your-breath-away lake in Tweedsmuir Park's Coast Mountains offers exceptional angling for wild, coho-sized rainbow trout. The lake is part of a 325-kilometre loop boat trip which includes Nechako Reservoir waters (formerly Ootsa, Tahtsa and Whitesail lakes), although Eutsuk is unaffected by the flooding. Guides are needed to make this trip, as flooding from the Kinney Dam, with drowned forest, floating debris, and difficult shore access, makes for treacherous boating. A hand-operated railway portage provides access from the reservoir to Eutsuk for boats up to 7.5 metres long. Guides for the boat trip or air access to Eutsuk are available in Burns Lake (as well as arrangements for cabins and guide service). Nechako Reservoir waters can be reached on a number of roads (south from Southbank at Francois Lake and past Takysie Lake is the most scenic drive) but boaters should not venture far on these dangerous waters. Take warning: intimate local knowledge is required. The reservoir offers good fishing for scattered rainbow trout in the five- to eight-pound range, with some chances of still larger fish.

» TWINKLE AND SWEENY LAKES—These two smaller, secluded lakes offer very fast fishing for generally small rainbow trout, although hard-fighting fish to about two pounds can be expected. Both are excellent fly fishing lakes which provide good angling through the hot-weather months. Twinkle is easier to reach than Sweeny, which will likely require four-wheel drive for its rough access road. To get to Twinkle, continue past Nadina Lake (see above) for about 15 kilometres to the Twinkle turnoff. Twinkle is part of a chain of five lakes (also a number of ponds). Continue south on the same road for another 15 kilometres to reach Sweeny. This road continues to a Forest Service campsite on Ootsa Lake's Tahtsa Reach (Nechako Reservoir waters; see the Eutsuk entry for restrictions), with much larger rainbow trout.

» **HIGHWAY 16 NORTH**

» BABINE LAKE—This is the second-largest natural lake in the province. It offers good fishing for both large rainbow trout and lake char, but local knowledge is required for the best fishing. (See the story on Rainbow Alley in this chapter for details.) Rainbows gather near Donald Landing in the spring to take advantage of descending sockeye fry, but conditions are often crowded. Later, try the far north end near Fort Babine. Nearby Nilkitkwa Lake (boat access from north end of Babine) offers fantastic fly fishing for large rainbow trout starting in mid-July and continuing through August. Kamloops-style patterns should do well. Char waters can be reached from Granisle/Topley Landing. The Smithers Landing area offers excellent char fishing and conditions are often better than farther south, as the lake narrows considerably at about this point, offering less exposed fishing. Trolling just off weed beds in the Smithers Landing area provides slow fishing for large rainbow trout. There are various access roads north off Hwy 16 to all areas mentioned.

» TALTAPIN LAKE—This is another good char lake with some larger rainbow trout, to three pounds and better, although averages will be considerably smaller. Lake trout (char) regularly run to 20 pounds, with some chances for larger fish, although as is true everywhere except in remote lakes, trophy-size char are becoming increasingly rare. Once harvested, the large char are unlikely to reappear without long-term closure of the fishery. New char management plans, expected to be in effect for the 1992 season, will likely see reduced limits, fall closures to protect spawning fish, and closure of some waters to char fishing. This lake provides good fishing through the summer. Take Decker Creek road north off Hwy 16 at Burns Lake, branching east after Division Lake, then east again on a branch road right after crossing Pinkut Creek.

» CO-OP AND HELENE LAKES—Both these lakes are managed (stocked), Co-op with brook trout, Helene with rainbow trout, and both offer angling for similar-sized fish. Locally, Co-op has a reputation for producing small brook trout, but fly fishers will quickly discover otherwise. We spent two days at Co-op in late June and saw several dragonfly patterns battered beyond recognition. We took fish on virtually every cast, good brookies to about two pounds. Willow leaf and worm trollers took small fish. There is limited camping, but it is a pleasant lake to fish, with extensive weed growth and few deep spots. It gets heavy pressure in winter. Helene Lake is said to offer similar fishing for rainbow trout. To get to Co-op, take the Augier Lake road off Hwy 16 east of Burns Lake (flashing amber light, heavy logging traffic); about five kilometres in, take a troublesome branch road east to the lake. For Helene, continue on Augier Lake road for another two kilometres, then go east on the Hannay Lake road for about 25 kilometres to the Helene access road.

» RICHMOND, LACROIX AND ROSS LAKES—All three are managed lakes atypical of the area and are lumped together here for their proximity to Hwy 16 and larger-than-average rainbow trout. All are good fly lakes and provide handy waters for those travelling through. Richmond is the most easterly, about 30 kilometres east of Burns Lake, and reached over the Priestly road with a rough final approach. Rainbow trout run to five pounds and better. Fly fishers should do well. Lacroix, locally known as Round Lake, is another small, fertile lake which grows rainbow trout to about five pounds and cutthroat to about two pounds. It is located on the north side of Hwy 16 about 10 kilometres east of Telkwa. Ross Lake is part of 307-hectare Ross lake provincial park (day-use only). It is difficult to give credence to the stories one hears about the size of this small lake's rainbow trout, but it is a rich lake and should produce trout to five pounds, if not the rumoured 10-pound giants. The park lies about 10 kilometres east of New Hazelton.

Remote Coastal and Queen Charlotte Islands Lakes

Good coast lakes holding large native cutthroat are quickly disappearing in areas where roads provide access. Populations of larger, older cutthroat are quickly harvested and slow growth rates coupled with ever-increasing angling pressure means these fish are unlikely to be replaced. Some of the best road-accessible cutthroat trout lakes are discussed in chapters one and two; fans of these wonderful fish will want to read the section on cutthroat trout in chapter one. Remote Skeena cutthroat lakes are a different proposition altogether. These lakes are not managed, the fish are wild—the genuine article— and access is difficult. Experienced boaters can reach many remote coastal lakes from Prince Rupert, although substantial hikes through dense coastal forests may be required from tidewater and logistics can be formidable. Inexperienced saltwater boaters should under no circumstances attempt these waters. Flying in is the sensible alternative, but be warned that coastal cutthroat lakes, even though they may well hold 10-pound-plus fish, are notoriously moody waters. It is possible to fly in and never see a large trout, although chances are the fishing will be good, notably in spring and fall. Fly fishing can be good, even exceptional, but I wouldn't fly without a spinning rod and lures tucked away in the pack. Prime candidates for such trips would be any of the lakes lying off Grenville Channel south of Prince Rupert, notably the four Lowe Inlet lakes, Lowe, Simpson, Weare and multiarmed Gamble. Closer to Rupert, both Khtada and Leverson lakes have reputations for large cutthroat.

The Queen Charlotte Islands are, of course, a salmon-fishing mecca. Little outside interest is focussed on freshwater lakes, but I must at least mention Yakoun Lake. This clear-water gem is not easy to reach and even more difficult if a canoe is to be portaged over the trail. Access is off the road to Rennell Sound from Queen Charlotte City (inquire locally for specific directions). A trail leads to the lake from the back end of a logged area, which, it is hoped, will not be extended any further. The walk itself is worth the trip; it passes through old-growth stands of Sitka spruce with open glades beneath the towering trees. The lake is set amid similar trees with mountains off the west end. It is rarely fished and is said to hold good numbers of cutthroat trout with some larger fish. It is well worth the effort by anyone visiting the Charlottes, even if the fishing poles are left behind.

Northern Skeena Lakes

The lakes of the northern Skeena region are among my all-time favourite angling waters, so expect the prejudice to show. Excellent fishing can often be found in waters lying alongside Hwy 37 from Stewart to Cassiar, a function of the area's remoteness from the high population densities of the south. This remoteness is something of a double-edged sword. On the one hand, it means reduced pressure on wild fish stocks; on the other, anglers must drive long distances and have considerable free time to sample these waters. There is no question as to where I stand on this issue. Take the time to make a northern fishing trip and, if at all possible, budget for the costs of charter air service. Most road-side lakes are wonderful in their own right, but not to be compared with fishing the wilderness lakes reached by float-plane. These lakes are the stuff of dreams; fishing will often take a back seat to the vistas which ring the remote lakes.

Large rainbow trout are an exception rather than the rule, but this hardly matters given the settings. Arctic grayling, a fly fisher's fish if there ever was one, are scarce in any waters with road access, but abundant in the remote lakes which hold them. By all means keep enough for a pan-fry, but pinch back barbs and release as many fish as possible. Grayling caught in road-accessible waters should be released without exception; they are becoming all too rare in such waters.

» MEZIADEN LAKE—This strange lake is at the jumping-off point to the Cassiar, with Hwy 37 continuing north from the lake and Hwy 37A branching west to Stewart. The drive to Stewart winds through spectacularly rugged country, with the roadside Bear Glacier an obvious and awe-inspiring attraction. Most services, including fishing information, are available at the junction of the two roads. Meziaden is a large, north-country-style lake, but I recall being surprised at the lake's extensive shallows and weed areas. This, coupled with a good sockeye salmon run (Nass River fish), had us hoping for rather large rainbow trout and Dolly Varden char, as the lake is known to hold both species. In early August the tributary streams were choked with spawning sockeye and we fished where these streams spill into the lake. This is a wonderful natural spectacle, but it attracts many bears; caution is required. The rainbows proved willing takers, notably on egg patterns, but the size was uniformly small, fish of 14 to 16 inches. Dolly Vardens are said to grow much larger. The extensive shoals allow fishing with waders, but bring a boat if for no other reason than to explore the spawning creeks.

» ISKUT LAKES—This chain of five lakes forms the headwaters of the Iskut River, a major tributary to the Stikine River, and lies alongside Hwy 37. Fishing is exceptional even in the most easily reached locations, such as the provincial park at the south end of Kinaskan Lake. The resort at Tatogga, with lakeshore cabins built by Tommy Walker, the man most responsible for having the Spatsizi declared a wilderness park, was closed at time of writing, but will likely soon find new owners. The best fishing lake of the group, in terms of sizes if not numbers, is tiny Natadesleen, last and most southerly of the chain. There is trail access only to this lake and a boat will be wanted; an inflatable or canoe is possible. Concentrate on the inlet stream from Kinaskan which should provide nonstop angling for rainbow trout to two pounds, with averages between one and 1.5 pounds. The outlet stream at Kinaskan, just minutes from the park, provides similar fishing for slightly smaller fish; a boat is required, but use caution as the outlet flows can be strong. The larger fish are most often taken on the wet line; try wooly worms and like patterns. Dry fly fishing is good for smaller rainbows. Spin fishing is also productive, but the fly will account for most fish. Give due consideration to catch-and-release fishing.

» EALUE LAKE—A road east from Hwy 37 in the Totogga Lake area provides access to this fine rainbow trout lake with campground and boat rentals. One of the few off-highway lakes which can be reached by road, it holds mostly the smaller rainbow trout typical of the region, with some larger fish.

» SPATSIZI PARK LAKES—Reached by air, either from Dease Lake or the floatplane based at Eddontenajon Lake lodge, these are true wilderness waters with awe-inspiring scenery and incredibly fast fishing. Cold Fish Lake, site of Tommy Walker's base camp for many years (a parks cabin is available on a first-come first-served basis), offers exceptional angling for large rainbow trout and Dolly Varden char. This is the traditional heart of the park and good trails provide access to the wildlife-rich plateau. Buckinghorse Lake is a fly fisher's dream come true: wilderness waters holding exceptional rainbow trout amid typical spellbinding Spatsizi settings. See the introduction to this chapter for details on Stikine headwater lakes. There is good arctic grayling fishing in Stikine River pools below Laslui Lake, reached over a good portage trail (around dangerous rapids at the Laslui Lake outfall). A Smithers-based outfitter has remote cabins at a number of locations and offers packhorse fishing trips or fly-in fishing. Outside the park, try air-access Tumeka and Klahawya lakes for large rainbow trout (mandatory release; see regulations).

» HWY 37 LAKES NORTH OF DEASE LAKE—Road conditions vary greatly with the season and amount of industrial traffic, but there is generally reliable gravel through the summer months. A number of small lakes lie alongside the road between Dease Lake and the Yukon border. They offer good-to-excellent fishing for Dolly Varden char and arctic grayling, although the latter species, due to its willingness to take most small lures and especially flies, is becoming increasingly rare where easily available. Pike, generally small for this species, are also accessible in some lakes. Try Joe Irwin Lake for Dollies and grayling; Pinetree and Cotton for char, Dollies and some grayling; Good Hope Lake for char and grayling in a fabulous mountain setting; and Boya Lake for the incredible colour of its water and the chance to fish for char and grayling while camped in the 4,600-hectare provincial park (34-site campground and 10 walk-in sites). Pike Lake, just north of the Blue River bridge, lives up to its name, offering fair-sized weed-bank pike and some arctic grayling.

» TESLIN LAKE—This huge lake straddles the B.C./Yukon border; the Alaska Highway follows its northern half from near Teslin to Johnsons Crossing. The lake holds some very large northern pike and lake trout, as well as arctic grayling, mostly at creek and river inlets and in the streams themselves. Best bet for up-to-the-minute fishing reports is to inquire at any one of a number of resorts. Fly fishing for pike is possible with large streamer patterns. The fly will take more and better grayling than any other method. This is a good lake for those unfamiliar with the sporting qualities of large pike from cold waters, a vastly different fish from the warm-water pikes.

» ATLIN LAKE—There is good lake char fishing in this, the largest lake of them all. Local knowledge is required for safety and best fishing. Air access is available from Atlin to any number of northern pike, grayling and char lakes, as well as river fishing for salmon. Adventuresome anglers with good boating and remote-camping skills can access Taku wilderness waters via the Atlin River, which leads to Tagish Lake, as well as a number of smaller waters.

Exceptional wilderness settings and angling. Some of the best grayling fishing in the province is found in remote Atlin-area waters. Cancel the trip to Hawaii and head north to Atlin for unmatched wilderness.

For more information contact:

Fisheries Branch
Bag 5000, 3726 Alfred Street
Smithers, B.C.
V0J 2N0

North By Northwest Tourist Association
Box 103, 3940 Alfred Street
Smithers, B.C.
V0J 2N0

CHAPTER NINE

Omineca-Peace

*U*nique waters blend in this sprawling northern region to provide angling quite unlike anything found elsewhere in the province. It is home to the only river in North America to breach the Rocky Mountains, the mighty Peace. This natural aquatic bridge has allowed prairie species such as perch, walleye and goldeye to invade the northeast portion of the Omineca-Peace. Arctic waters, which include the Peace River system, add a further dimension to the fishery: ancient lake chars, survivors of Pleistocene glaciation, arctic grayling, northern pike, bull trout and exotic inconnu are arctic residents of the Omineca-Peace. B.C. anglers tend to ignore most of these species, concentrating instead on fish most often associated with Pacific drainages, such as kokanee, rainbow trout, and mountain whitefish. To this already abundant mix man has added two further species, that durable transplant, the brook trout, and the Yellowstone cutthroat.

Only in the northeast do all these species come together, which is just as well. Were predatory pike to establish themselves in the rainbow trout waters of the region's Pacific drainages, a fine fishery would be irreparably damaged. There is, in fact, a standing watch for pike on the Arctic/Pacific divide. The Fisheries Branch has long asked anglers to report any northern pike encountered in Summit Lake, just north of Prince George, the Crooked River, and Williston Reservoir and its tributaries. Such an invasion is not nearly as unlikely as it may at first appear. Fish are great colonizers of new waters. In the neighbouring Skeena region, arctic grayling are found in a Pacific river, the Stikine. Grayling have no business swimming the swift-flowing Stikine. No one knows how they got there, but the best guess is that a bird dropped fertilized eggs into the river. Other examples of fish colonization abound: black crappies in the Lower Mainland and Okanagan regions; perch, carp and a long list of other species, including the salmonids, which regularly show up in the most unlikely places.

Aside from the northeast's wonderful if confusing diversity, fish distribution breaks down along lines which will be familiar to most B.C. anglers. Summit Lake at Prince George and Stuart Lake at Fort St. James are at or near the divide between Arctic and Pacific waters. From Summit Lake the Crooked River, once a highway of the voyageurs, flows to the Peace and, eventually, the Beaufort Sea. Stuart Lake's waters empty into the Pacific via the Fraser, while the nearby Nation Lakes flow to the north. So we find the familiar northern mix of rainbow trout and char in the more southerly waters, and rainbow trout, char and grayling to the north.

Fishing techniques are not as familiar. In much of the province the rainbow is recognized as a fly fisher's fish, often demanding refined match-the-hatch skills. This does not hold in the north, at least not as regularly as it does in more southerly waters. The northern rainbow's lot is harsh, an aquatic version of northern tooth and fang realities. At least two distinct strains have evolved to deal with those realities: one prowling the depths for forage fish, the other roaming the surface zones for insects. Trolling is therefore the most popular and normally most successful method for these fish. This does not apply in the small, shallow eutrophic lakes; the fish of these waters will respond in ways familiar to southern anglers. Nor does it apply at all times. There are occasions when even the largest predatory rainbows will take aquatic insects. Spring and fall are typical times, but there are also wonderful exceptions through the summer.

The best advice for fly fishers bent on hunting large northern rainbows is to persevere with quick-sinking lines and large minnow patterns, trolled or cast, although trolling is really the way to go on the large lakes.

Lake char are a fish of the depths, as any northern char fisher will attest. They prefer colder waters and occupy lake zones little-used by other species, thereby avoiding competition. This tactic has allowed them to survive when others have faltered—until man entered the picture with wire lines and downriggers to penetrate the preserve of the big chars. Most anglers are aware that char are in serious trouble from overfishing and that the Fisheries Branch's renewed emphasis on wild-stock management will focus on species like the lake char. Regulations will be further adjusted to preserve remaining stocks. Many long-time char fishers agree such measures are needed and seem braced for further restrictions. Most have favourite waters where populations of older fish, the 20-, 30-and even 50-year-old char, have been seriously eroded. Not even air-access waters have escaped unscathed, as witness the far-flung Tuchodi Lakes west of Fort Nelson, high in the Muskwa River drainage.

These are remote lakes even by Omineca-Peace standards, yet anglers report the two lakes' once-great char fishing is now a thing of the past. There are still char to be caught, even some very large fish, but the days of easy fishing for large fish are quickly disappearing. Clearly a change in attitude is required if these fish are to survive. Changing the way we fish for char would, I think, be a good first step. Wire-line and downrigger trolling with large plugs and depth sounders is an effective way to fish for char, but is hardly sporting. Quite aside from any consideration of sporting ethics, I have yet to catch a char in this manner that proved a good game fish.

Pulling char up from the depths is normally merely a matter of cranking the line in. Once on the surface, these handsome fish will roll and splash about a great deal, but they generally come to the net rather meekly for large, strong fish. Shallow-water char are an altogether different proposition. Char do move to shallow water with some regularity and I think these are the times to concentrate on them. Spawning char use shallow water, but angling for them at this time is both difficult (spawning fish rarely feed) and unsporting. The expected new regulations will in any case see most char waters closed during the mid-September to mid-November spawning season, but there are other times when char move to shallower water.

In the spring of the year, especially during the magic time following ice-off, char will be found in shallow water. At this time the stratification of lake waters breaks down and water temperatures will be consistent throughout the lake. Char can then be found anywhere in the lake, but they regularly hunt the shallows. In the clear-water lakes of the north, this makes casting to visible fish, even with the fly, an alternative to deep-water trolling. In shallow water, and very likely in deep water as well, char have a strikingly peculiar way of attacking their prey, one which makes for exciting angling.

Pike are often described as engulfing their prey, but these fish use their long, toothy jaws; the lake char uses its entire body to ensnare the prey fish, an incredible sight to witness. The big char literally encircle their prey, then clamp down on the trapped fish by turning their heads in to the circle formed by their bodies. The first time it happened, early one windless morning, my dozing partner was so startled by the thrashing splash and suddenly screaming reel that he almost upset the boat. The fish was off as suddenly as it had struck—a not unusual occurrence with this style of char fishing. Anglers lucky enough to hook char in shallow water had best hang on to their rods. In my experience, char taken in shallow water live up to the largely eastern-held view of the char as a legendary game fish.

Surface or near-surface fishing for char is not limited to ice-off. Char can be found in shallow water during any of the spring months and even into early summer. Early and late in the day are good times to try. Contrary to popular belief, char do not remain in deep water through the summer. All char roam, changing location to a timetable uniquely their own, but the largest fish regularly hunt the lake's shallow water through the year and the canny anglers will be there to find them.

The arctic grayling, the mysterious *poisson bleu* of the voyagers, also suffers from overharvesting. Virtually all waters with road access have severely reduced numbers of grayling, and large fish have vanished from all such waters. This is a function of the grayling's readiness to take any offering pitched its way, providing only that they are of a size to match the grayling's small mouth. Grayling evolved this trait over time as an effective survival tool, but it makes them extremely vulnerable to anglers.

Lake-resident grayling are something of a rarity, but there are good grayling lakes, and the Omineca-Peace is the place to find them. Only a very few drive-to lakes hold grayling, so fishing for them is really adventure angling of the finest kind. It is the country we go to in quest of grayling—often the most remote, wildlife-rich corners of the province—which makes them so special. They are the fish of wilderness waters and really ought to be treated as rare treasures. Curb the urge to take the largest and best fish; in any case, a pan-fry of small grayling makes a better meal.

There are a number of wonderful arctic grayling lakes reached by floatplane from either Fort Nelson or Fort St. John. Trimble, Redfern and far-flung Netson, best reached from Muncho Lake, offer outstanding wilderness settings and unmatched angling for larger lake-resident grayling. The best grayling fishing often comes as a surprise. A Fort St. John hunter told me about a remote unnamed alpine tarn holding 20-inch grayling which, in the rare moments when the mountain winds stilled, provided spectacular dry-fly fishing. Regional Fisheries Branch offices will provide tip-offs to such waters and are always worth visiting, but in the far north it is best to avoid hunting season as floatplanes will be busy ferrying hunters; most outfitters with remote cabins will give off-season anglers a break on rates.

Rainbow-trout fishing in these remote locations can also be the stuff of dreams: a number of exceptional lakes hold very large fish. The lakes of Tatlatui Park are as spectacular as neighbouring Spatsizi Park lakes (see chapter eight), and hold larger fish. Then there's Kwadacha Park's Fern Lake, Wolverine and Rainbow lakes in the Turnagain River drainage, the small pond near the Ithaca Glacier which was stocked by air-drop and where rainbow trout have taken off . . . but there is no end to wilderness Omineca-Peace lakes. By all means consider fishing in wilderness waters. These places must be used if they are to be protected; the "use it or lose it" philosophy gains more credence with each passing year.

Closeup: Fish of the Forgotten Goldfields

*O*n the charts there are two small settlements in the Omineca Mountains north of the Nation Lakes: Manson Creek and Germansen Landing. From the south, a thin red line starting at Fort St. James indicates a gravel road snaking north to the two communities. South of Germansen Landing, the only settlement on the Omineca River, lies Germansen Lake, a fairly large lake lying in an east-west mountain trough. East and south of Manson Creek lies a small chain of interconnected lakes called Manson Lakes. For those who stare at maps and dream, the lakes, the road and the two isolated communities are like snares set to capture the imagination. Who knows what strange adventures might have unfolded in the far-flung Omineca or what angling adventures might linger yet in the little-known fishing waters of Germansen Landing and Manson Creek?

Even today, many long and eventful years since the two communities were founded, Germansen and Manson Creek are not known as fishing destinations by the ever-growing number of anglers who roam the province. On any given day the three Forest Service campsites on Germansen Lake might see one or two campers. More likely the lake will be entirely deserted, as it was during a visit in June's prime-time fishing weeks. Yet each spring the population of tiny Manson Creek swells and every tumble-down shack and cabin is occupied. It is the promise of gold which lures people to the Omineca every spring in a migration as certain as the return of the geese from their wintering grounds. Queries about fishing are met with blank stares. Who has the time or inclination to fish when there is gold to be found, perhaps a fortune to be made? No one fishes or camps for sheer pleasure. There is a fever in the air, gold fever, for over the years many a fortune has been made and lost. And there are men, dozens of them, who are certain there are fortunes yet to be made in the much-worked ground, if only one could find the right spot, perhaps some unworked pocket overlooked by the iron-hard men who first put pick and shovel to work in the creeks of the Manson-Germansen area 120 years ago.

The year was 1870 and word had just reached the outside of a rich gold discovery in the Omineca near Manson Creek, at that time still truly wild country, although not entirely unknown. The same crazed hordes who had poured into the Cariboo for that gold rush now turned north to slash their way into the wilderness of the vast Omineca. Fort St. James, the one-time seat of government for the whole of New Caledonia, was already well established, having been founded in 1806. Most of the newcomers struck north from the Fort, creating a trail which would serve as the main road in until 1939. That year a new road was built to circumvent Baldy Mountain, 1,782 metres high and the scene of many disasters, accounting for the deaths of countless horses and, judging by the graves later discovered, not a few men.

Few written accounts remain of that first gold rush, for these miners were men of action and few words, at least few written words. We would have had to be content with the pictures our imaginations paint were it not for William Francis Butler, a soldier, traveller, adventurer, man of the world and, most important to us, a man of letters. Butler, seemingly for the pure joy of adventure and discovery, made two major trips into the hinterlands of the Canadian west, one in 1870 and the other in 1872. He wrote two books, both classics, describing his Canadian wanderings, *The Great Lone Land* and *The Wild North Land*. In the spring of 1873, having come by dog sled and canoe up the Peace, the Finlay and finally the Omineca rivers, Butler and his loyal dog Cerf-Vola the Untiring reached Germansen and Manson Creek. Here, in his own words, is what Butler found.

Late on the evening of the 20th of May I reached the mining camp of Germansen, three miles south of the Omineca River. A queer place was this mining camp of Germansen, the most northern and remote of all the mines on the American continent.

Deep in the bottom of a valley, from whose steep sides the forest had been cleared or burned off, stood some dozen or twenty well-built wooden houses; a few figures moved in the dreary valley, ditches and drains ran along the hill-sides, and here and there men were at work with pick and shovel in the varied toil of gold-mining. . . .

Twelve miles from Germansen Creek stood the other mining camp of Manson. More ditches, more drains, more miners, more drinking; two or three larger saloons; more sixes and sevens of diamonds and debilitated looking kings and queens of spades littering the dusty street; . . . and Manson lay the same miserable-looking place that its older rival had already appeared to me. Yet every person was kind and obliging.

A spine-chilling tale Butler later recounts makes one wonder about the "kind and obliging" nature of those early miners. At the end of the 1871 season it seems the digging was too good to leave and many men waited too long before hitting the long trail south to the civilized comforts of Quesnel. "Suddenly, on their return march, the winter broke; horses and mules perished miserably along the forest trail. At length the Fraser was reached, a few canoes were obtained, but the ice was fast filling the river. The men crowded into the canoes till they were filled to the edge; three wretched miners could find no room; they were left on shore to their fate; their comrades pushed away. Two or three days later the three castaways were found frozen stiff on the inhospitable shore."

By the end of the 1873 season all the gold men could reach with pick and shovel had petered out, or so it seemed. All would be quiet in that part of the Omineca for more than 50 years, until April 1935, when the north-woods silence was again shattered, this time with the roar of machinery, hydraulics, steam shovels and large-scale water diversion projects the miners of 1870 would have thought impossible.

Again the cycle of boom and bust, triumph and tragedy, gold dust poker and home-made liquor, was repeated in the wilds of the Omineca. The old trail over Baldy Mountain was still the main route in, but now cat trains and aircraft helped move in the heavy equipment and tons of supplies. By 1936 the Hudson's Bay Company had established a store at Manson and for the first time men coming in were certain of having enough food for the return to the Fort. The old trading post still stands today, although no longer run by the Bay. By the start of the war the second gold rush was over, but mountains of gold had been recovered, as witness this account from Ralph Hall's book, *Goldseekers.* "The amount of gold taken in less than one month (from a single pit of one operation) was hardly credible. What the total number of ounces was, I do not know. . . . I helped pack the concentrates and larger nuggets to a pickup truck. There were more than 200 nuggets which weighed over half an ounce each, and the largest was better than five ounces." It wasn't until July 27, 1936, that the first-ever gasoline-driven vehicle arrived in Manson Creek, still coming by way of Baldy.

Today a circle tour is possible by way of logging roads. Our own route in was by way of Highway 97 to Windy Point north of McLeod Lake, then the logging road following the western shores of Williston Reservoir, around Mount Bison by way of Blackwater Creek and finally the Manson River to Manson Creek. On the way out we took the Nation Lakes-Fort St. James road which now bypasses Baldy Mountain, but can still have its share of hair-raising moments (sleet, snow and gumbo on the hills above Gaffney Creek). This great circle tour, which crosses the Arctic/Pacific divide (at Summit Lake on the way north and at Stuart Lake on the way south), touches on the routes taken by the first Europeans to roam the country drained by the north branch of the Peace River, the now much reduced Finlay River.

The route followed by Butler and others before him, notably Samuel Black, who in 1824 became the first and only man ever to travel the full length of the Finlay by boat from mouth to headwaters and back again, is now lost forever, drowned under the Williston Reservoir. The stories of these early explorers, adventurers and gold seekers are vividly told by R. M. Patterson in his book *Finlay's River*. Patterson interweaves the historical tales with an account of his own 1949 canoe travels on the Finlay. One of his adventures bears repeating since it echoes the hair-raising adventure which befell my partner and me in the Omineca.

Although Patterson was never an angler first and foremost, he was known to stop and fish when the bottom of the grub box appeared near. And so it was when Patterson, travelling alone, found himself drifting in an eddy of the Finlay. "I got one nice fish and was intent on getting a second which I could plainly see down through the very clear water

...[when] I half noticed...a black thing that had got into the eddy with me. That dimly registered, and I found myself automatically thinking: charred log—forest fire up river? ...Then some odd movement from the black thing made me look—and it was a bear and it seemed quite anxious to come aboard. The fish was forgotten: the rod hit the tarp alongside the pole and the paddle swung over my head and into the water at my right hand....Then I got out of that eddy, racing downstream faster than a bear could swim....a grayling couldn't have moved quicker."

My partner James and I arrived at Germansen Lake late in the afternoon of the day we had left Highway 97, covering, in a few hours driving time, the distance it took the men of poles and paddles weeks of hard toil to traverse. We floated our sleek fibreglass canoe in the crystal waters of the lake, failed to catch any fish and returned to the camper for a late dinner. Idly glancing out through the camper window I saw a large, glossy-coated black bear strolling through the otherwise deserted campsite. We thought nothing of it for a time, but when the bear was still about after dinner had been cleared, circling ever closer, we employed the usual strategies—banging pots and pans and so forth. Instead of turning tail for the high slopes which ring the lake, the bear made directly for us.

The fun was over now. Obviously the bear was a well-educated garbage bear and knew the scenario very well. We slammed the door and remained under siege until darkness fell, which is quite late in June that far north. Assuming the bear had lost interest and had gone his way, we gingerly opened the door, both of us standing side-by-side on the tailgate. There was Bruin, just beyond the tailgate, down on all fours, stamping his feet and shaking his big head from side to side. James was first to bolt for the open door and I was right on his heels, but I had to turn and reach out to pull the door shut. I slammed it as hard as I've ever slammed any door. Unfortunately, my thumb was still in the metal door jamb! By two in the morning it was at least twice its normal size and throbbing painfully, an uncomfortable reminder of the bear, which by now had wandered off.

So much for adventure in the Omineca. The fishing went badly; the sore thumb was distracting, to say the least, and made working the fly rod awkward. But we did see fish, rainbow trout working the edges where the lake necks down and the road crosses just before the third campsite. Some of them were quite large, but not as large as the Dolly Varden char we saw finning quietly in the deep pool where the road crosses the lake at the narrows. July is a better time to fish the Dollies unless equipped with a boat large enough to travel the often wind-swept lake. The spring run of Dolly Vardens occurs in June when the Dollies congregate at creek mouths to take advantage of spawning rainbow trout. Most of the larger creek inlets are on the far side of the lake and getting to them in a canoe involves a long trip, but even tin boaters should use caution. Whether these fish are in fact Dolly Varden char or their close cousin the bull trout is a moot point for most anglers. Until 1978 bull trout and Dolly Varden were classified as a single species. Now the bull trout is *Salvelinus confluentus*, the char of the river confluence, a separate species from *Salvelinus malma*, the Dolly Varden, which takes its colourful name from a character in Charles Dickens' *Barnaby Rudge*. Distinguishing between the two is impossible outside the laboratory, so anglers can take their pick, although I continue to call lake-resident fish Dolly Varden and the river fish bull trout.

As to fish size in Germansen Lake, fisheries biologists figure the rainbow trout average about two pounds and the Dollies about four pounds. Fishing pressure is light, so there should be good numbers of larger fish, usually the first to go in heavily fished waters. Dry flies should prove effective for the rainbows, but spinning or trolling with spoons and plugs is better for the big Dolly Varden. We were unable to unearth any fishing lore concerning Germansen or the Manson Lakes—gold was the overriding topic of conversation. To get some idea of the

size of the char in the region, we must go back to the Finlay
River country and a tale recounted by Patterson in *Finlay's River*
concerning Paul Leland Haworth, an American history profes-
sor who travelled the Finlay with considerable difficulty in
1916—constantly short of food, forever taking wrong turns and
always overburdened.

At the foot of the portage over Deserter's Canyon (named
by Black after two of his crew deserted), Haworth and his
French-Canadian guide Joe Lavoie stopped to camp. Lavoie
had cleaned some grayling at the river's edge for their dinner. When Haworth later went down to the canoe for something, he was startled by the big Dollies which had moved
in for the grayling leftovers. Haworth ran for his .32 and stood
there quietly. When the big dark shape again drifted into the
shallows, he fired and hit the fish hard. Just as he was reaching for his prize, it sprang to life and dashed for deep water.
After that he did manage to land an eight-pound Dolly on
rod and reel, but the next morning he tied into a really big
fish which tested his tackle to the limits. They finally beached
the fish and would have lost it at the last moment had not
Lavoie grabbed it just as the line broke. This, a much larger
fish than the eight-pounder, proved to be the one he had shot
the night before. The four-inch bullet wound had not even
slowed the big Dolly.

The goldfields in the Germansen-Manson area may be all
but played out, but the gold that anglers seek still waits to
be discovered, for there can be little doubt that monster Dollies like the one shot by Paul Haworth still prowl the depths
of Germansen Lake and the small chain which makes up the
Manson Lakes—fish of the forgotten goldfields.

Omineca-Peace Lakes

*T*he lakes of this region are grouped under
four headings. Rainbow trout and lake char
waters lying west of Prince George are found under the Fort
St. James North and Vanderhoof South headings. Lakes best

reached off Hwy 97 to the north and south of Prince George are found under the Prince George Area Lakes heading. Far northern waters and the lakes of the northeast are found under the Peace Country and Far Northern Waters heading.

Fort St. James North

Lakes under this heading take in waters north of Vanderhoof, except the small handful best reached from Hwy 97 north of Prince George—these are listed under Prince George Area Lakes. Waters north of the Omineca River (Germansen Lake area) are listed under the Peace Country and Far Northern Waters heading. Babine Lake provides the western boundary for lakes found under this heading.

These are essentially rainbow trout and lake trout (char) waters and in many ways represent a northern extension of the type of angling found in the Burns Lake area, both north and south of Hwy 16. The major difference lies in degrees of remoteness. Many of the best lakes require charter aircraft, with Fort St. James the base of operations. Roads are constantly changing and conditions vary greatly with the time of year and amount of industrial traffic. Both Fisheries Branch and Forest Service offices, either in Prince George or locally, should be contacted by those contemplating drives to remote waters. Air access should be given serious consideration; much time and trouble can be saved, especially if the last few kilometres of a long drive prove impassable. The best road network maps are available from the Forest Service. These maps are essential for those attempting to drive to remoter parts of the area.

» STUART, TREMBLEUR AND TAKLA LAKES—Most large, deep lakes in the area hold large lake trout, but populations of old fish—the 20-, 30- and even 50-year-old giants—are much reduced. New management strategies have been developed (see the introduction to this chapter) and are expected to be in place for the 1992 season, but, once harvested, it is unlikely we will ever see similar fish again. Still, all is not doom and gloom. There are still huge lake trout to be had and these three massive lakes are among the better waters to try. It is possible to travel between these lakes by boat, but such mega-voyages should not be attempted without local guides. The connecting rivers are dangerous, as are the lakes themselves. Guided angling is in any case the best bet for anglers with limited time, as a lifetime may not be enough to learn the secrets of these inland-sea-style lakes. Concerned anglers should consider catch-and-release for lake trout, especially the large, older fish. All three lakes hold scattered rainbow trout in the three- to five-pound range with occasional much larger fish. It is possible to catch rainbow trout weighing more than 10 pounds, but they are rare. Fort St. James sits on the southern shore of Stuart Lake and the Leo Creek road provides rough access to Sakeniche Crossing on Takla Lake, where there is a boat launch and camping. Inquire locally about fly-in char and rainbow trout waters.

» CAMSELL, OGSTON, GRASSHAM AND CUNNINGHAM LAKES—All are reported as good to excellent rainbow trout lakes, with Cunningham also holding large lake trout. Two-pound rainbows can be expected in the interconnected Camsell group, with chances of very much larger fish, rainbow trout to five-pounds-plus. Cunningham offers similar-sized rainbow trout. Fly fishing is best on Ogston and Grassham. The Cunningham Forest road provides access, reached south of Fort St. James from Parrens Beach Park; the lakes lie about 60 kilometres to the west. The access road to Grassham can be very rough and is certain trouble in wet conditions. Cunningham is an air-access lake, but may possibly be reached by four-wheel drive; inquire first.

» McKELVEY LAKE—A remote lake requiring air transport from Fort St. James, although new roads beyond Tachie on Stuart Lake may provide rough access; inquire at Fort St. James. This lake has a reputation for good numbers of large rainbow trout and is a good bet for adventuresome fly fishers. Nearby Tarnezell Lake has rough road access and would be worth a look by anyone already in the area.

» KLOCH AND KAZCHEK LAKES—Recent road access may mean these previously air-access-only lakes no longer hold good numbers of the large rainbow trout and lake char which made them famous among dedicated anglers. Still, fishing should be at least fair for larger rainbow trout and char. To get there, follow the north shore of Stuart Lake to the Leo Creek road, which branches north shortly before Tachie. Kazchek is reached shortly after crossing Inzana Creek; watch for a roadside parking area with trail access to the lake (a canoe or inflatable is required). Kloch, which lies farther on, has a small campsite and rough boat launch. Air access should be considered.

» NATION LAKES—These are among the finest canoeing/fishing waters in the province and high on my list of personal favourites. Jet boats travel the entire chain and this should also be possible in tin boats, although the connecting rivers are shallow, with some rapids that will require lining. Canoes can make the trip either way, up or down. Road access to the remotest lake, Tsayta, is possible but questionable. Air or jet-boat access (arrange for jet boats through Chuchi Lake resorts, aircraft at Fort St. James) is better. Bigger lake char run to 20 pounds—although that's rare now—and rainbow trout can easily go better than five pounds, with much smaller averages. Still, there is very good rainbow trout fishing, notably at inlet and outlet streams and where Nation river exits Chuchi. Road access to Chuchi is good; take the Germansen Landing road north from Fort St. James for about 100 kilometres.

» GERMANSEN, MANSON AND WOLVERINE LAKES—All are remote, lightly fished waters offering small rainbow trout and large Dolly Varden char. Germansen reportedly holds large lake char, but those who fish the lake concentrate on the Dollies. This lake may also hold some large rainbow trout; try the narrows early and late in the day, notably with spinners and dry flies. Launching is difficult at the two Manson Lakes (canoes and small boats are possible), but there are good numbers of small rainbow trout and larger Dolly Varden char. Arctic grayling are found in the inlet stream and may be found in the lakes as well. The Wolverine Lakes have limited access (they are on reserve land), but offer good fly fishing for small, northern rainbows. Most direct access is north from Fort St. James on the Germansen Landing road for about 160 kilometres to Manson Creek. Road conditions are generally good.

Vanderhoof South

Lakes under this heading take in all waters south of Hwy 16, with Hwy 97 south of Prince George providing the eastern boundary. The Nechako River provides the western boundary, while Pelican Lake near the Euchiniko River represents the area's most southerly edge. Generally these are richer waters than those found north of Hwy 16, and consequently are more popular with local anglers. Roads also tend to be better than those found farther north.

» NULKI LAKE—Anglers who have yet to discover the northern version of the rainbow and do not have time to roam should try this easily reached lake. Northern anglers are convinced, and say so in no uncertain terms, that "their" rainbow trout are better fish than the "fat and lazy Kamloops." I'll not debate their relative merits, but will acknowledge that the northern strains of rainbow trout are a breed apart. Aching wrists and long struggles are to be expected from even fairly small fish, and Nulki offers good chances of testing wits and mettle against quite large specimens, although not so large as in the remoter lakes. Expect fish better than two pounds, with four- and five-pounders not rare. There is good fly fishing in spring and fall; try bloodworm patterns (see chapter three) fished deep. To get there take the Kenney Dam road south from Vanderhoof for about 20 kilometres.

» TACHICK LAKE—Just north of Nulki Lake and reached on the same road, this larger lake offers similar fishing with some reports of larger fish than those found in Nulki, rainbow trout to six pounds and better. Average sizes will be considerably smaller, but Tachick has a reputation as a good fly lake and is easily reached.

» HALLETT LAKE—Long considered a fly-in lake, Hallett has a longstanding reputation for large rainbow trout. Road access is possible, but four-wheel drive is likely required. Inquire locally at Fort Fraser on Hwy 16. By road, take the Holy Cross Forest road south from Fort Fraser, branch east to tiny Lily Lake, then south for about 25 kilometres.

» GRAVEYARD, LITTLE BOBTAIL, BOBTAIL AND GRIZZLY LAKES—All are popular lakes for Prince George area anglers and are regularly stocked with rainbow trout which can grow to respectable sizes. Grizzly is known as a good fly lake, but all provide good fly fishing at times, notably spring and fall. Fish size varies from two to six-pounds-plus. Graveyard has the smallest fish, with Little Bobtail and Grizzly vying for the big-fish honours. Bobtail was known for fish in the five-pound-plus bracket, but maximum size is now probably closer to three pounds. Final access for both Graveyard and Little Bobtail is rough. To reach these lakes take the Bobtail Forest road south off Hwy 16 about 55 kilometres west of Prince George. Graveyard (named for an ancient Indian burial ground) comes first, about 50 kilometres in; Little Bobtail is reached from the Forest Service campsite at the north end of Graveyard, about 10 kilometres farther on. Bobtail, a pretty lake which also holds kokanee and lake trout, is a short distance south on this road, part of the Telegraph Trail. Grizzly is reached from the Forest Service campsite on Graveyard's west shore, with the final access road branching west off the Bobtail road after about kilometre 60.

» LINTZ, TAGAI AND PELICAN LAKES—These are popular, small good-fishing lakes with numbers of rainbow trout in the two-pound class and some larger, notably in Pelican. Fly fishing can be very good, especially in early summer and fall. The lakes are reached over the Blackwater road, which heads south off Hwy 16 about 10 kilometres west of Prince George. Continue south on this road for about 20 kilometres, passing West Lake Park on the way, then branch west on the Clearlake Sawmill road for about 60 kilometres. Access to Tagai is rough when wet. All have Forest Service campsites: large at Lintz and Tagai, smaller at more remote Pelican, which lies about 20 kilometres south of Tagai.

Prince George Area Lakes

More than 1,600 lakes within a 150-kilometre radius of Prince George hold rainbow trout; many of these have been enhanced. As always, a number of small eutrophic lakes (see the section on reading lakes in chapter four) produce exceptional angling. But conditions change from year to year, sometimes from season to season, and it's tough to give information that will withstand the test of time. The best bet for anglers is to stop in at the Fisheries Branch regional headquarters in Prince George. Biologists will not only have information on current hot spots, but will explain the reasons behind regulations. Informed anglers are not only better fishers, they're also better conservationists.

» NESS, VIVIAN AND VERDANT LAKES—Vivian and Verdant rank among the better brook trout waters in the province; fish to five pounds can be expected. Both are good fly waters.

Ness also holds brookies, but is known chiefly for its large, tough-to-catch rainbow trout, fish to five-pounds-plus. Ness is also a good fly lake, though temperamental, with a convoluted shoreline providing interesting angling. To get there, head north of Prince George on Hwy 97 for about 10 kilometres, then go west on the Chief Lake road for another 20 kilometres to Ness Lake Regional Park. Vivian is about five kilometres farther down the road and is reached over a branch road north; there is trail access to Verdant.

» CRYSTAL AND EMERALD LAKES—These two small, exceptionally clear lakes in cottage country north of Prince George offer large but difficult rainbow trout. Both lakes contain scuds (see chapter five), iron-blue in colour, which account for the sizes of their trout, fish to five-pounds-plus. Crystal was originally stocked by mistake in the 1950s, when an air-drop was made into the wrong lake. The largest fish taken there was an 18-pound giant. About 10 kilometres past Summit Lake north of Prince George on Hwy 97, look for a turnoff to the east and continue past the gravel pit to the lake. Smaller Emerald lies just to the north.

» WICHEEDA LAKE—This little-known lake holds some very nice rainbow trout. Access may be difficult and a walk is likely required; inquire first. To get there, take the Chuchinka Forest road east off Hwy 97 in the vicinity of the Davie Lake south campsite, which is about 70 kilometres north of Prince George. The Chuchinka road also provides access to the Parsnip River (as does the Anzac Forest road, reached farther north by way of Tacheeda Lakes) and, for those with jet boats, river access to Arctic Lake, and trail access to Portage and Pacific lakes from Arctic. These are lovely, remote rainbow and Dolly Varden waters (inquire in Prince George for charter-air/guide services).

» FIRTH AND JUNKERS LAKES—Rainbow trout in the three- to six-pound range are the draws to these two difficult-to-reach lakes. Smaller Junkers, which reportedly holds the larger fish, is commonly reached by trail from Firth, although it does have a rough access road found south of the Hwy 97 turnoff to Firth. Reaching Firth is difficult due to steep final access; consider walking in. The access road is found 116 kilometres north of Prince George, east off Hwy 97 on a B.C. Telephone service road.

» CARP LAKE—One of the richest lakes in the area, Carp continues to offer good rainbow trout fishing despite its summer popularity. Located within 19,350-hectare Carp Lake Provincial Park, the lake has a convoluted shoreline and many islands, making it an interesting and highly scenic fishing lake. Best camping for anglers is on the islands, away from the crowds and beaches. Two-pound fish can be expected, with five-pounders not rare. To get there, turn west off Hwy 97 at McLeod Lake; Carp lies about 30 kilometres in on this road.

» SOUTHEAST AREA LAKES—There are a number of fine angling lakes in the mountainous country southeast of Prince George bounded by Hwy 97 in the west and Hwy 16 to the north. Logging road networks provide access from a number of points along both these highways. Grizzly Lake is reached off the Willow Forest road and offers larger rainbow trout. Pinkerton Lake is reached by branching south off Hwy 16 on Bowron River road, then on the Tumuch Lake access road, and provides good angling for rainbow trout. Chubb Lake holds good rainbow trout and is reached over the Plett and Quesnel-Hixon roads; these roads are found by branching east off Hwy 97, about 75 kilometres south of Prince George. For details on these and other lakes in the area, inquire at the Prince George Fisheries Branch office.

Peace Country and Far Northern Waters

Due to the diversity of species available, these waters are listed by species rather than the usual lake-by-lake listing. Broadly speaking, Peace country lakes are oligotrophic, poor in the essential building blocks required for richer waters. When such lakes are off the beaten track, angling can be rewarding. Even relatively poor waters produce numbers of larger fish, though they will not withstand pressure. However, low angler numbers do not necessarily equate with lightly harvested waters. A handful of knowledgeable anglers can soon harvest the larger, older fish, so dreams of big fish in wilderness waters must be tempered by biological realities. Small, rich (eutrophic) lakes do exist in the Peace country, generally in the lovely aspen parkland country typical of the Chetwynd/Dawson Creek areas. The following listing concentrates on these waters, with a few pointers now and again to the so-called pristine lakes.

» RAINBOW TROUT LAKE—Virtually all of the lakes listed here provide atypical north-country rainbow trout angling: larger, generally fussy, fish. Heart Lake lies just off the south side of Hwy 97, 70 kilometres west of Chetwynd. One Island Lake is reached by turning west off Hwy 2 at Swan Lake Park on the Alberta/B.C. border, and continuing on this road for about 30 kilometres. Sundance Lake lies on the south side of Hwy 97 between Chetwynd and East Pine. Moose Lake lies just south of Gwillim Lake Park and is reached by taking Hwy 26 south from Chetwynd for about 70 kilometres. Chinaman Lake lies 25 kilometres northwest of Hudson Hope, with a rough access road. Dinosaur Lake lies southwest of Hudson Hope between the Bennett and Peace Canyon dams. Inga Lake lies just northwest of Fort St. John.

» BROOK TROUT LAKES—These stocked fish reach the five-pound-plus range and have gained quick popularity from local anglers. They often occur in mixed populations with rainbow trout. Lakes to look for include: One Island, Heart, and Inga lakes (see rainbow trout lakes for location), and Gantahaz Lake, three kilometres north of McKenzie.

» ARCTIC GRAYLING LAKES—Grayling tend to be river fish, so finding them in a lake is a special experience. Treat both the lakes and fish as the treasures they are. Try the fly-in lakes for adventure angling. Netson Lake lies west of Fort Nelson and offers very large grayling, as do Trimble, Fairy and Redfern lakes, all south and west of Fort Nelson. Redfern holds huge grayling, fish to 20 inches. For drive-to grayling, try the beautiful limestone waters of Muncho Lake in the park of the same name, located at kilometre 741 on the Alaska Highway.

» PIKE AND WALLEYE LAKES—Generally, Peace country pike and walleye are not large fish, but there are exceptions. For larger pike try Moberly Lake, about 20 kilometres north of Chetwynd on Hwy 29; Maxhamish Lake, located north of Fort Nelson, for large fly-in pike and walleye; and Charlie Lake, located beside Hwy 97 just north of Fort St. John, for large pike, walleye and yellow perch. Charlie Lake yellow perch reach large sizes, to two pounds. Swan Lake, about 30 kilometres south of Dawson Creek on the east side of Hwy 2, also holds good perch, as well as pike to about 10 pounds.

» LAKE TROUT LAKES—The best lake trout fishing in the region is found farther south, in the lakes lying north and south

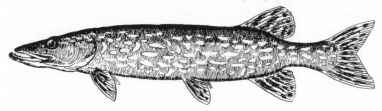

Northern pike

of Hwy 16 in the Vanderhoof area. Exceptions include Moberly and Muncho lakes, both of which hold some larger fish. Gwillim Lake, located about 70 kilometres south of Chetwynd on Hwy 26 in a park named for the lake, also has a reputation for large char. Maxhamish Lake, as well as larger pike and walleye, also holds large lake char and the flying distance from Fort Nelson is not great. Farther afield, try Tuchodi Lakes, reached by air from Fort Nelson, or Kluachesi Lake, 120 kilometres southwest of Fort Nelson by charter air.

For more information contact:

Fisheries Branch
Plaza 400, 1011 Fourth Avenue
Prince George, B.C.
V2L 3H9

Fisheries Branch
10142-101 Avenue
Fort St. John, B.C.
V1J 2B3

Peace River Alaska Highway Tourist Association
Box 6580
Fort St. John, B.C.
V1J 4J3

Metric Conversion Chart

*T*his book conforms to the metric system, with the exception references to size and weight of fish, explained in the introduction to the book. The following chart is designed to provide simple multiplication factors for conversion of metric to imperial equivalents.

FAHRENHEIT/
CELSIUS
SCALE

TO CHANGE	TO	MULTIPLY BY
centimetres	inches	.4
metres	feet	3.3
kilometres	miles	.63
square metres	square yards	1.25
square kilometres	square miles	.4
hectares	acres	2.5
kilograms	pounds	2.2
inches	centimetres	2.5
feet	metres	.3
miles	kilometres	1.6
square yards	square metres	.8
square miles	square kilometres	2.6
acres	hectares	.4
pounds	kilograms	.45

°F   °C

90
    30
80

70
    20
60

50   10

40

30   0

20

    – 10
10

0
    – 20
– 10

Bibliography

Belhumeur, Art, Ed. *B.C. Fishing Directory & Atlas*. Port Co-quitlam: Art Belhumeur Ent. Ltd., 1991.

Bennett, Tiny. *The Art of Angling*. Scarborough: Prentice-Hall Canada Inc., 1970.

Butler, William Francis. *The Great Lone Land*. Edmonton: M. G. Hurtig Ltd., 1968.

Cordes, Ron and Randall Kaufmann. *Lake Fishing With A Fly*. Portland: Frank Amato Publications, 1984.

Davy, Alfred G., Ed. *The Gilly*. Kelowna: Alf Davy, 1985.

Griffith, Bob and Alison Griffith. *Guide to Freshwater Fishing: Okanagan*. Duncan: Pacific Rim Publications.

Griffith, Bob and Alison Griffith. *Guide to Freshwater Fishing: Thompson-Nicola*. Duncan: Pacific Rim Publications.

Griffith, Bob and Alison Griffith. *Guide to Freshwater Fishing: Upper and Lower Mainland*. Duncan: Pacific Rim Publications.

Griffith, Bob and Alison Griffith. *Guide to Freshwater Fishing: Vancouver Island*. Duncan: Pacific Rim Publications.

Hafele, Rick and Dave Hughes. *The Complete Book of Western Hatches*. Portland: Frank Amato Publications, 1982.

Ministry of Environment. *British Columbia Recreational Atlas*. Victoria: B.C. Ministry of Environment and Infomap, 1990.

Raymond, Steve. Kamloops: *An Angler's Study of the Kamloops Trout*. Portland: Frank Amato Publications, 1980.

Russell-Hunter, W. D. *Aquatic Productivity*. Toronto: Collier-MacMillan Canada Ltd., 1970.

Stewart, Dave. *Fishing Guide to Fresh Water in British Columbia*. Vancouver: Special Interest Publications Division, MacLean Hunter Limited, 1985.

Wright, Richard and Rochelle Wright. *Canoe Routes British Columbia*. Vancouver: Douglas & McIntyre, 1980.

Wright, Richard Thomas. *The Bowron Lakes: A Year-Round Guide*. Vancouver: Special Interest Publications Division, MacLean Hunter Limited, 1985.

INDEX OF LAKES BY REGION

Thompson-Nicola Lakes

GENERAL INDEX